The Fiction of
RUTH RENDELL

Ancient Tragedy
and The
Modern Family

BARBARA FASS LEAVY

ISBN: 1-4392-7014-7
ISBN-13: 9781439270141

This book is dedicated to my mother,
Marion Widom
1918–2005

THE FICTION OF RUTH RENDELL:
ANCIENT TRAGEDY AND THE MODERN FAMILY

TABLE OF CONTENTS

CHAPTER I

Introduction

In one of the earliest books in Ruth Rendell's popular Inspector Wexford series, *A Guilty Thing Surprised,* Wexford identifies a murderer after reading a work of literary criticism, gaining that elusive insight fictional detectives count on for solving crimes. The brother of the victim had published a scholarly study of the English romantic poet, William Wordsworth, and to the inspector's surprise, he is drawn into a history of disturbed family relations, of secrets hidden behind a respectable façade. There are suspicions of brother-sister incest and definite evidence of psychological incest, of the inability of two siblings to extricate themselves from emotionally damaging attachments. Although the subject of the book Wexford was reading had lived two centuries earlier, Wexford encountered similarly blighted family landscapes every time he investigated a new case. They are the domestic battlefields that Ruth Rendell has repopulated with different families in the fifty-eight novels and large body of shorter fiction that she has written. (With more likely to come.)

Not finding the author of the Wordsworth study sympathetic, Wexford had expected to find his book tiresome, and he was surprised at how compelling the story was that gripped him. The reading itself was not unusual, for Wexford frequently read literary biographies and critical studies of authors. His wife Dora would often ask why he read what someone else said about a book instead of just reading the

1

book itself. The inspector would find himself at a loss to describe a pleasure perhaps only comprehensible to someone who already shared it. But he would patiently explain that literary criticism was a form of education and, as was true of all education, its purpose was "to turn the soul's eyes toward the light." When Ruth Rendell used Wexford's reading to articulate this defense of the art of criticism, did she hope that someday she would be the subject of such a study? Could she be such a subject so long as she was praised as the "best mystery writer anywhere in the English-speaking world," and crime fiction was thought of essentially as the construction of ingeniously wrought puzzles? As a literary critic who has published on writers acknowledged to be worthy of critical analysis, I have taken Ruth Rendell's celebration of criticism as a starting point to study her as I have other authors, as a literary artist who deserves critical attention.

A Guilty Thing Surprised is the fifth of the twenty-two books that, at this writing, comprise the Wexford series, also known by the fictional rural town in which the inspector lives and works, the Kingsmarkham series. The first one was published in 1964, the most recent in 2009, the series having endeared itself to Rendell readers for forty-five years. During that time, there have appeared numerous books not part of the series, several of the most compelling written under the pseudonym Barbara Vine. Ten of the thirteen novels written by Rendell as Vine will be discussed at length in this study: to identify them, see the list of books at the end. For to avoid confusion, I will only use the name Ruth Rendell. There are also collections of short stories, and works of non-fiction. That Rendell is a prolific author is obvious, and every time I think I have finished this book, another novel appears to require further consideration or elaboration of an idea or theme about which I thought I had nothing more to say.

One example reveals very clearly that neither Rendell's fictional world nor her characters are static creations, and that her writing reflects changes in a world she has always observed with her keen eye and analytical mind. In *Live*

Flesh (1986), Rendell constructs a coherent and unified case study of a serial rapist in which all the psychological pieces seem to neatly explain the criminal. Later, in *The Rottweiler* (2003), a serial killer will desperately try to create his own case study in the hope that if he achieves self-understanding, he may be able to resist the impulse to attack women. What he discovers is a trigger that initiates such assaults, but *triggers* and *causes* are clearly not the same. Self-sufficient enlightenment eludes the criminal, the reader, and perhaps even the author, who has come to understand that the more that is known about human behavior, the more elusive seem attempts to fully account for it. The coherent case history may be a thing of the past, may in fact falsify reality. *Causes* of human action may remain mysteries, and unlike the solutions to specific crimes, they may not be susceptible to final resolutions. Rendell says as much in *The Blood Doctor,* noting that even psychologists and psychiatrists cannot provide self-sufficient explanations for why people act as they do.

In that novel and in *Anna's Book,* a missing notebook or missing pages of a diary hinder the search for the truth that adheres to a mystery not yet solved. These lost pages can perhaps be read as metaphors for the uncertainty that attaches to any attempt to fully understand people. That some of Rendell's later novels may therefore appear less "neat" in their construction than her former books is not a sign of exhausted talents and too much prolixity, but is rather a sign of how her work reflects the changing times. Today, there are more, not fewer, controversies concerning human behavior. The nature vs. nurture argument, for instance, a subject that has drawn Rendell's interest throughout her writing career, seems more problematic than ever. For what are called the hard sciences, along with evolutionary psychology, have in their attempts at explanation reversed the direction of the pendulum that began centuries ago to move away from ideas of original sin and innate depravity to the effects of the environment in which people are raised and live out their lives. Today, the mystery writer who takes on the challenges of these new explorations into the mind and brain (if they can be differentiated) will be indistinguishable from serious novelists for whom the uncertainties of human existence supply perennial subjects. Ruth Rendell should be read not specifically as a writer of mysteries but rather as a novelist who rightfully enjoys her fine reputation among other acclaimed authors, such as Toni Morrison and Joyce Carol Oates, who have read and praised her fiction. But despite a growing body of scholarly work on the crime fiction genre and some of its notable practitioners, the mystery novel as a form of popular entertainment has yet to relinquish its defensiveness when it claims the status of serious literature. It is one of the purposes of this study of Rendell to challenge the assumptions that cling to the genre.

The gap between mysteries as mere entertainment and crime fiction as significant art is the subject of a book with the intriguing title *The Mystery to a Solution: Poe, Borges, and the Analytic Detective Story*. John T. Irwin poses what he calls a simple-minded question: "How does one write analytic detective fiction as high art when the genre's central narrative mechanism seems to discourage the unlimited rereading associated with serious writing?" If the point of crime fiction is the "deductive solution of a mystery," how does the writer create a "work that can be reread by people other than those with poor memories?" Irwin creates a metaphor out of Edgar Allan Poe's short story, "The Purloined Letter." Poe's renowned detective, August Dupin, an ancestor of Reginald Wexford as he is of countless other fictional investigators, has been asked to recover a letter highly incriminating of an important person. Although the police have vainly torn apart the dwelling where the letter should have been found, Dupin easily finds it "hidden" in full view, turned inside out with a false address and addressee written on it. In Irwin's study, the letter becomes emblematic of his subject. For just as the letter can be turned inside-out and outside-in, so too can some mysteries be read and reread, each reading yielding some new pleasure or insight. The solution to the crime, the plot, and the revelation of *whodunit* become less important as characterization, psychology, and complex themes command readers' interest.

Rendell's novels are, nonetheless, traditional mysteries insofar as crimes are committed and criminals sought and apprehended. But if that were all, she would fail the test that Irwin applies to distinguish mysteries that are high art from crime writing that essentially works through a puzzle, however entertaining and absorbing that puzzle may be. Some of Rendell's most compelling mysteries, moreover, deviate from familiar narrative patterns. In *The House of Stairs,* it is the identity of the victim and not that of the criminal that is withheld until the story's end. In *A Fatal Inversion,* both victim and murderer are unknown until the book's conclusion. The suspense in an early work, *The Face of Trespass,* and in the later, much acclaimed *The Bridesmaid,* builds over whether a besotted young man will acquiesce to his lover's demands that he prove his devotion by killing someone. In the earlier novel, an inconvenient husband has to be gotten out of the way, a common enough motive for murder. By the later book, Rendell's forays into human psychology resemble those of Dostoevsky and Camus, who wrote about motiveless crimes, or at least ones in which the ostensible motive hardly begins to explain the killing. In *The Bridesmaid,* the most randomly chosen victim will satisfy the psychotic woman whose deluded lover can hardly believe she wishes him to kill someone, and for no reason. But because he is so enthralled by his femme fatale, readers will be caught up in the uncertainty of whether he will deliver this proof of his love.

Not that the conventional mystery necessarily lacks psychological or philosophical depth. Writers of crime fiction will inevitably come to their craft with ideas or beliefs about evil and its origins, about fate and its vagaries, and therefore about the reasons why crimes are committed. Even implicitly, their books will raise questions concerning what it means to speak of human nature, or conversely, why it is said when a particularly gruesome crime has been committed that the perpetrator is an *animal*. But those mystery writers who meet Irwin's standards for the mystery novel as art will more actively engage their reader in a deeper exploration of these subjects than the puzzle requires. Increasingly in her novels Ruth Rendell moves into the realms of the social and even hard sciences. In *The House of Stairs*, she takes up the genetic uncertainties associated with Huntington's disease (at the time in which the novel is set), but also asks whether there might be a gene that corresponds to the so-called bad seed, and writes a book that constantly questions how much free will humans can claim to possess. Later, in *The Blood Doctor*, Rendell will add to these considerations the consequences of human freedom that has perhaps breached the limits beyond which people probably ought not venture. Rendell understands very well that ambiguities lie not in the answers to questions posed about human behavior, but in the questions themselves.

This study of Ruth Rendell will emphasize how she roots her novels in the biological and social units known as the family. In particular, it will show how she has explored in depth the tensions within families that lead to murder. For in most of Ruth Rendell's novels, and certainly in the best of them, speculations concerning human motivation emerge from her brilliant portrayals of highly *dysfunctional* families. The adjective is apparently not one that Rendell favors. The word *dysfunctional* is used ironically in *Babes in the Woods* where a woman protests that her daughter, her son-in-law, and grandchildren are not a dysfunctional family, when in fact they constitute an extremely disturbed family unit. In *Thirteen Steps Down*, published soon after, the word appears in the musings of an unsympathetic character, an upwardly mobile young man who will not commit himself to a woman until he is satisfied that, as his wife, she will fit into the neat scheme he has devised for his life. And this scheme excludes troubled family relations. In *End in Tears*, Jenny Burden uses the word as a convenient designation of a large group of people she deals with as a teacher.

Just how sensitive Rendell is to language and how carefully she assigns words to her characters are made clear in another recent book, *The Minotaur.* Her first-person narrator is Kerstin, a young Swedish woman who accepts employment in an extremely disturbed English family, writing years later about the strange events she had been witness to and to which she had perhaps contributed. Although fluent in English, Kerstin considers the language with the interest but also detachment of a non-native speaker, and will sometimes remark on how a word that could define a situation (for example, *sexist*) had not been current when the incident it could describe actually occurred.

Ruth Rendell can therefore acknowledge the usefulness of a word while disapproving of popular jargon, which reduces the power of language and—in the case of *dysfunctional*—converts complex problems into mere pop-psychology. Still, Rendell is a genius at portraying disturbed families. From her earliest books, motives for murder have been rooted in the intrapersonal dynamics of mismatched husbands and wives who have come to loathe each other; in overtly destructive or—just as damaging—indifferent parents and sometimes their equally repellent children; and in siblings who perpetuate with each other and within their own families the pathology that in one Wexford novel the inspector traces to the first family, Adam and Eve, and therefore implicitly to the first murderer and victim, Cain and Abel. It is commonplace to point out that people are more likely to be hurt or killed by members of their own family than by strangers on the street. Something deeply embedded in family dynamics creates a potential for violence.

Today, as the *whodunit* gives way to the popularity of the *whydunit,* many crime writers draw on the hidden family secret that explodes in a horrible crime, the secret itself often supplying the story's final revelation (that the victim was the object or perpetrator of sexual abuse has become so common a plot element that it has ceased to deliver an effective surprise). But no writer in the mystery genre takes readers on as complex a journey into the variety of troubled family relations as does Rendell (a renowned writer, Ross Macdonald, tends to play variations on a more narrow, Freudian-based family paradigm).

In her fiction, Rendell can inspire in her readers the kind of pity and terror traditionally associated with ancient tragedy, which as Aristotle pointed out in his *Poetics*, consistently takes for its subject families who have perpetuated terrible acts or who have suffered from them. A similar claim is made in Rendell's *The Brimstone Wedding*, in which one of the two main characters, Genevieve, says of the community that surrounds her that they are "a family, but you have to remember families are where most of the trouble starts in this world." And in *No Night is Too Long*, a book supplies the means by which two lovers are brought together. Its title is *The Golovlyov Family*, and the family it portrays makes the Karamazovs seem by comparison to consist of benign and loving relations. What Wexford thinks when he has to deal with the Hathall family in *Shake Hands Forever*, that he had "never come across a family so nourished on hatred," could apply as well to other families he meets with in the course of his investigations. Aristotle's description of the place of family in tragedy suggests his strong influence on Rendell novels.

Rendell has acknowledged her deep interest in the classics. She has been quoted as saying that, after she stopped working at a job to raise her son, she studied on her own two subjects that she would have pursued had she gone to a university. One of these was ancient Greek. In Greek literature, two families—The House of Atreus and The House of Laius—supplied material for the Homeric epics and more than half of the Greek plays that have survived from ancient times. Greek myths and narratives created for centuries a literary treasure trove for authors who drew on them for their own plots and characters. Ancient writers possessed such keen insight into family dynamics that even authors who did not borrow directly from the classics can be studied within traditions traceable to them. This study of Ruth Rendell will argue that, not only did she make the family her central and recurring motif, but also that the ancient writers, particularly Homer and the playwrights Aeschylus, Sophocles, and Euripides, as well as the psychological theories derived from their understanding of family dynamics, were sources from which Rendell consistently borrowed (see Chapter 3).

Although this study of Ruth Rendell is not primarily a source study, it will claim that insight into her fiction can be attained by studying how the two major dynastic families portrayed in Greek myth, epic, and, especially, tragedy, make themselves felt in her writing. The House of Atreus involves the events leading to and following the Trojan War, and to the murder of Clytemnestra committed by Orestes with the aid of Electra, who are avenging the murder of their father Agamemnon. The story of the House of Laius tells how Oedipus unknowingly slays his father Laius, marries his mother Jocasta, and embroils his own children in the consequences of his patricide (see Chapter 2 for a detailed summary of these family sagas). Both of these dynastic stories eventually gave a name to a psychological theory—the Oedipus and Electra complexes of, respectively, Sigmund Freud and Carl Jung—and Ruth Rendell's novels demonstrate that she is as familiar with competing psychological paradigms as she is with the ancient narratives that supplied their names.

The next chapter of this book will outline the classical narratives, reminders to those who may have forgotten some of the details or introductions to those who never knew them well. Similarly, Rendell's readings of Freud and Jung and her awareness of the theoretical differences that eventually alienated these giants of psychological theory help frame her own stories. Chapter 3 will discuss how the Oedipus complex of Freud and the Electra complex of Jung make their way into Rendell's fiction. She frequently refers to Oedipus but, if my numerous readings of her books have not failed me, there are no direct references to Electra, although Electra's mother, Clytemnestra, is named in the novels. Electra's devotion to her father and, perhaps more to the point, her hatred of Clytemnestra, create a pattern defining many Rendell plots. For there is perhaps no other author who portrays mother-daughter conflict as starkly as Rendell does. She also treats in her novels a theme that emerges from the three Electra plays of the Greek tragedians (one each by Aeschylus, Sophocles, and Euripides—see Chapters 8 and 9), the problematic daddy's girl, not pampered pet but rather the obsessed victim of a male-dominated society. A seemingly only moderate feminist, who in her later Wexford books slyly satirizes the excesses of the woman's movement, Rendell seems usually to avoid the word *patriarchy* as she does *dysfunctional*. Still, the concepts associated with patriarchy can be found throughout her books.

This study of Ruth Rendell will, in short, place her writing in a complex cultural framework. *Culture*, however, is a word whose definition confounds even the anthropologists who have made of it a discipline that has become increasingly important in the social sciences. It would therefore be useful to discuss briefly how any study of Rendell inevitably becomes a study in culture. First, that Rendell draws on the ancient Greek tragedians is itself a cultural phenomenon in the sense that in studying the crime fiction genre, one might distinguish between a so-called high culture (Dostoevsky) and a lower one (Agatha Christie). This meaning of *culture* is not ordinarily the one anthropologists and sociologists are concerned with, although of course the art of a people is important to describing and individuating it. Second, to read through Rendell's novels chronologically is to recognize how she has described the changes in English society as a homogeneous urban population in the early Kingsmarkham novels gives way to what is now popularly designated as ethnic diversity.

In a late Wexford book, *Not in the Flesh*, Rendell also takes up the subject of cultural relativism. The Somali immigrants who have come to England practice female genital mutilation (clitorodectomies), what is sometimes called female circumcision. Although this practice was denounced by many Africans who came to England to spare their daughters this ordeal, and although the procedure was illegal in England, there remained families determined that their daughters undergo it. Not because they did not love their children, but because they did. From their perspective, they were ensuring their daughters would eventually find suitable husbands. One little girl in the novel speaks to the tragic results when a people are forced to give up their customs before they themselves are ready to do so. In the next Wexford novel, *The Monster in the Box*, the inspector thinks about how "experience had taught him what deep waters one struggles to swim in when plunging into the traditions of another culture." The most politically correct member of his team, Hannah Goldsmith, finds herself confounded by the tension between her radical feminism and her determination to be sensitive to the practices of other cultures and thereby to avoid racism. At issue are forced arranged marriages practiced by some Moslem families, although, like clitorodectomies, such marriages are illegal in England.

Later chapters in this study will discuss how Kingsmarkham changes over the course of years, acquiring the social problems that were formerly associated only with the big cities. In the earlier Wexford books, the inspector finds in the beauty and peace of his country dwelling refuge from the ills that infect such places as London. By the more recent books in the series, the urban problems have spread to the suburban areas. In *The Monster in the Box*, contrasts between Kingsmarkham when Wexford was young and a new policeman, and the present, when he persistently ruminates on these changes, supply reiterated motifs in the novel. Similarly, although class distinctions were always present in Rendell's fiction, as they would almost inevitably be in any fiction written by an English author, the later books emphasize the connections between class and the criminal justice system. Wexford, for example, finds it increasingly difficult to do his job as restrictions in investigative procedures reflect a culturally based institution undergoing change. In *Not in the Flesh,* however, it is not only the underclass that is altering Kingsmarkham for the worse, nor only the developers who have transformed the beautiful landscape into housing units, but also a youthful population whose cafés and upscale boutiques have irrevocably altered the face of the town.

Finally, by making the nuclear and sometimes extended family the focus of her writing, Rendell effectively enters into one of the most problematic areas of cultural studies, in which the family itself becomes a highly controversial unit of study, complicated by how its members are defined by gender. Social scientists do not agree about whether the nuclear family or something closely resembling it is universal and, in that sense, is somehow essential to human survival. More important, perhaps, is the role of so-called family values in distinguishing lines to be drawn between socially and politically conservative or radical ideas. Among the questions Rendell's books raise, therefore, is whether the threatened breakdown of the traditional family is to be deplored or, if not celebrated, at least approved. As anthropologist Adam Kuper has succinctly described it,

> In the mid-twentieth century, mainstream sociologists and psychoanalysts tended to represent the family as a crucial source of social stability, but critics, less content with the outcome, were less respectful of the family itself. The modern nuclear family was quite commonly represented as the source of grave, perhaps terminal, social problems. It was too authoritarian, too claustrophobic, riven by irresolvable emotional strains. The family restricted the opportunities of women, fomented emotional crises that it could not resolve, protected perpetrators of violence and child abuse.

Kuper adds that in 1967, the anthropologist Edmund Leach shocked the British public in his BBC lectures "with the claim 'that far from being the basis of the good society, the family, with its narrow privacy and tawdry secrets, is the source of all our discontents.'" Only three years earlier, Ruth Rendell published her first mystery novel, *From Doon with Death*, whose subject might indeed be described as portraying the narrow privacy and tawdry secrets of a family.

In one of her most recent novels, *End in Tears*, however, Rendell appears reluctant to mark the demise of the family, represented by the Wexfords, even though the body of her work supplies example after example for those eager to attack the institution. In this late book in the Wexford series (2005), the inspector's family is brought to the brink of collapse, but then Rendell draws back from the final catastrophe. When Wexford's daughter Sylvia decides to become a surrogate mother and bear a child for her ex-husband and his new partner, who are experiencing a fertility problem, the Wexford family is perhaps brought to the end point of a process that had begun several novels back. For some time, the Wexfords had held together despite experiencing an erosion of what their family represented, and now it confronts the threatened loss of a family member and therefore the family itself. In the end, however, some order is restored, but it is an uneasy order that might imminently disintegrate in a later novel.

End in Tears is not, however, the first book in which Rendell takes up questions of bioethics and the many new ways that families can be created. In *The Blood Doctor*, Rendell acerbically, if also ambiguously, treats the idea of "designer babies." In this book, the ancient theme of the family curse that wends its way through ancient tragedies is expressed not only through genetically-based diseases, but also through the biological and ethical implications of the technology surrounding human reproduction.

The interaction of culture (with its various meanings), family and technology is particularly marked in *The*

Minotaur. In this novel—once again about a highly disturbed family—beautiful objects, a geode and a Roman vase, are defiantly appropriated by family members to demonstrate each one's power and importance in relation to the others. They virtually steal the objects from each other. A geode is a rock that, when split, reveals a beautiful interior formed of minerals, such as amethyst, and that takes ages to develop (although just how long geologists do not know). Once the interior design is revealed, it proves unique, different from any other geode. The geode is thus both ancient and also highly individualized, and can easily serve as a model of human biology. One's DNA results from ages of continuous genetic inheritance and creates a biological identity that differs from anyone else's (except an identical twin's). The Cosway family in *The Minotaur* has taken countless generations to reach its present psychological configuration, both typical of disturbed families but also unique in how it is expressed in their intra-familial strife. The beautiful interior of the geode may symbolize the unfulfilled gifts possessed by the only Cosway son, John, who, born with some seemingly genetic disorder, has unfairly become what some psychologists call the family's "designated victim" (or scapegoat), the one upon whom all family tensions descend. The geode can also be a metaphor for human potential: the rough exterior stone is the disturbed family, but the beautiful crystal formation inside is the possibility of a joy none of the Cosways realize, although some of them pursue it avidly. The geode may also symbolize the very novel Rendell has written, the work of art created from a subject that focuses on biological and psychological diseased states of being.

Readers of *The Minotaur* receive a more explicit invitation to consider the origins of the Roman vase that inspires in the narrator an "urge to possess it." Again, the vase speaks to time passing as generations succeed generations. The narrator muses that an "ancestor" of the Cosways had found the vase "miraculously intact," and thinks about how householders "tend to throw away their rubbish on the same site as that used by the generation immediately before them, while that previous generation favors the site used by his forebears and so on back for centuries." So to dig down through layers of garbage may result in the discovery of a treasure. Given Rendell's wide reading, her specific interest in and knowledge of the transmission of inherited diseases (see, especially, *The Blood Doctor*), it is likely that she is familiar with the concept of junk DNA, those long stretches of genetic code inscribed on human chromosomes that so far remain unexplained in terms of function or biological significance. Yet the accumulated "junk" remains part of an individual's inheritance, its meaning perhaps on the verge of discovery. To extend this idea to a cultural inheritance is far from saying that Ruth Rendell would view as junk the inherited reading that reaches back from her work to the ancient classics, but only that she has made the Roman vase into a possible figure of her own literary creation as she draws on the great tradition of ancient literature, too often relegated in modern times to the junk heap of neglected classics. Just as the Roman vase in *The Minotaur* survives as a reminder of ancient glories, so too could Rendell keep alive in her own work the classics threatened with extinction, with burial under the detritus of modern tastes. The very title of her novel, of course, draws on Greek mythology, on the multi-layered story about a family whose members turn on each other—as do those in the novel. *The Minotaur* can be read as a summing up, of the bringing together in sharp relief those themes that had commanded Rendell's attention from the beginning of her writing career. As she continued to write, these themes had been transformed by the rapidly changing world in which Rendell lives and which she has always observed, often with keen irony, down to the smallest details.

Although it was stated above that "whodunit" is less important in a Rendell novel than "whydunit," readers of this study might not appreciate being provided with the solution to a mystery in a book they have not yet read. In his biographical work on Agatha Christie, Charles Osborne assures his readers that they may proceed without fear that he will ever reveal the identity of an Agatha Christie murderer. I cannot make such a wholesale promise, but nonetheless will usually refrain from disclosing secrets Rendell did not intend to give away until a book's conclusion. That I usually can so refrain despite detailed analyses of the novels is itself evidence that Rendell has done far more than create the kinds of intricate puzzles that characterize mystery novels, and that she usually fulfills the criterion for crime fiction that can claim the status of serious literature, capable of rereading for character analysis, layers of psychological meaning, and treatment of social concerns. Sometimes, as in the analysis of *No Night is Too Long*, the discussion will require a secret be revealed, but it is one that Rendell discloses about two-thirds of the way through this fascinating novel, and one that will not surprise the discerning readers who have paid close attention to subtle clues provided earlier. Occasionally, I may tease my own readers with partially disclosed information, but this will hopefully inspire a reading or rereading of the work under discussion.

Once again, this book is not primarily a study in sources. Sources, however, are very important in discussions of Rendell's fiction, because she is both a voracious reader and also an extremely allusive writer. As she says of the connection between books she has read and those she has written, "I store these things and they come out." The literature that has fed Ruth Rendell's imagination is so vast that an encyclopedia of influences and allusions could be constructed. No attempt will be made to point out all of those I have recognized, even when an interpretation could benefit from following the path of a source through a Rendell novel. And I know I have not picked up all of her allusions. Sometimes, however, one of these will be so meaningful that it will be discussed in some detail. Occasionally, Rendell herself will make a source explicit, as she does when the plot of Henry James's *The Wings of the Dove* is integrated into the plot of her own *The House of Stairs*, or when the references to *Tess of the d'Urbervilles* heighten the suspense in *The Water's Lovely*. At other times, Rendell seems to invite well-read readers into a more private literary world that they can share with her and that the majority of Rendell fans are unlikely to enter. Again, Henry James's novel is central to *The House of Stairs* but a less obvious allusion in the same novel, to Coleridge's "Christabel," can be appreciated only by those familiar with the narrative poem that gives the murderess Bell her name (see Chapter 8). An even more esoteric source is Herman Melville's failed, notorious, and little read novel *Pierre: or the Ambiguities*, on whose theme of sibling incest Rendell appears to have drawn for one of her strangest but also most brilliant novels, *No Night is Too Long*.

Often, Rendell will take a source and invert the narrative elements in it, as she does in *Harm Done*, one of the later Inspector Wexford books. The novel provides a paradigm for how Rendell uses sources and how they supply additional levels of complexity to her writing. In *Harm Done*, domestic abuse is a major theme, the inspector's daughter Sylvia having signed on as a volunteer in a shelter for endangered women. The shelter's director is named Griselda Cooper. Any Rendell readers unfamiliar with the story of Patient Griselda will be able to proceed through the novel without experiencing any loss of meaning. But readers familiar with how the medieval authors Geoffrey Chaucer and Giovanni Boccaccio told Griselda's story in their monumental works, *The Canterbury Tales* and *The Decameron*, will immediately recognize the irony involved in giving to the director of a woman's shelter the name of one of Western literature's most abused women. Moreover, Rendell's plot will emerge in sharper focus, because its sources in the early works will become obvious. In both Rendell's novel, on one side, and Chaucer's and Boccaccio's works, on the other, the inherent tensions in a husband-wife relationship lead to the abduction of children. Again, this thematic complexity is enhanced by Rendell's choice of a name, Griselda, but recognition is not required to follow her story.

To survey, however briefly, these sources for Ruth Rendell's writing, may seem to blur the focus of this study on the ancient narratives that cluster around the Houses of Atreus and Laius. But these ancient narratives themselves have been the fountainhead of Western literature, and the themes that will be treated in the following chapters will be those that are essential to reading and understanding these classical masterpieces. Literary descendents of such characters as Clytemnestra fill the annals of dangerous women found in centuries of writing. Griselda's husband, who tested his wife's obedience by taking away her children, may not be directly descended from Agamemnon, who sacrificed his daughter and expected Clytemnestra to bear the loss, but these husbands are similar and Rendell would recognize them as such. In short, other literary works beside those written in ancient Greece have strongly influenced Ruth Rendell, but these later works carry the themes already present in classical literature, on which this study of her writing will focus.

Ancient literature has, moreover, not only given me a way into the complex world of Rendell's novels, but a way of describing my method in writing about them. One of the major characters in the Trojan War tales is Penelope, who, while her husband Odysseus spent ten years at war and another ten meandering years returning to his kingdom and family, staved off suitors by agreeing she would take one of them as her husband when she finished weaving a garment that occupied her time. By day Penelope wove, and by night she undid her work, delaying the moment when she must choose a new spouse. In one of Rendell's short stories, "A Needle for the Devil," a minor character who writes crime fiction would "weave plots out of all kinds of common household incidents." The themes associated with family relations are similarly woven through Rendell novels.

In the following chapters, these novels will be unwoven and rewoven to accommodate the organization of this study, which isolates familial relationships and analyzes how

Rendell has treated them. This isolation will, despite its organizational benefits, create some problems. For example, the Oedipus complex involves a triadic relationship in which a young man is caught between his father and mother. But in later chapters, father-son and mother-son dyads have been separated from each other, involving, again, the unweaving of what is in Rendell's fiction a tightly woven narrative cloth. Similarly, the daughter who prefers her father to her mother is also part of a triangular relationship. Yet it will become clear that while never losing sight of the triads, Rendell thematically emphasizes the dyads. This need to separate and integrate will also extend to the other family relationships around which this book is organized.

Some words about the following chapters may help describe how the two dynastic families that dominated classical literature have influenced the organization of this book. The next chapter will, as already stated, acquaint or reacquaint my readers with details from the ancient narratives. Chapter 3 will relate how the psychologist Carl Jung used the Electra story to challenge Sigmund Freud's emphasis on the Oedipus complex. References to Rendell novels will, again, demonstrate she is very familiar with the theories that divided Jung and Freud. Chapter 4 will follow four themes that appear throughout classical literature and throughout Rendell's fiction. Short stories as well as her novels reveal the influence of ancient writing on her work.

Until the concluding chapter, Chapters 5 through 10 will be divided according to whether, thematically, they can be most readily attached to the stories of Oedipus or of Electra. One of the relatively neglected motifs in the Oedipus tale is his search for his identity as an adopted child looking for his origins. Self-realization through self-discovery is a reiterated narrative idea in Rendell's fiction and, in *Anna's Book,* the connection to the Oedipus story emerges very clearly. Then, as already indicated, triadic relationships will be divided into dyadic ones, the father-son relationship treated separately from mother and son. Because brothers and sisters (and less frequently brother and brother) are in Rendell's fiction sometimes substitutes for these parent-child pairings, they too will be treated under the Oedipus heading.

Chapters 8, 9, and 10 will be organized according to the Electra story. Although, as noted above, Rendell does not directly refer to Agamemnon's vengeful daughter, there are characters to be found throughout her writing who bear an uncanny resemblance to the three Electras of Greek tragedy. In one novel, Rendell describes such a character as a *fey girl*, and I have given this designation to the type in Chapter 8. The Agamemnon-Electra-Clytemnestra triad is—again—divided into the chapters on fathers and daughters (which will treat the Wexford books as a group) and mothers and daughters. The tension between the latter is also reflected in antagonism between female siblings. There are usually two sisters in conflict, but in *The Minotaur*, the family strife is divided among four sisters (not all easily distinguished) and a brother—almost as if Rendell was reacting against the emphasis she had usually placed on dyadic relationships.

The conclusion of this book will pull together themes Rendell weaves throughout her fiction, all of them possessing implications for family relationships. Whether she is taking up the question of genetics as a modern rendering of the theme of the family curse, the significance of gender within the family, the amount of free will any person can claim to possess, questions surrounding nature and nurture, the need to know oneself, the feasibility of a perfect or utopian existence, or the working out of justice in human society, her characters are specific actors within the troubled family whose conflicts result in aggressive acts, often crimes, committed against each other.

CHAPTER 2

THE ANCIENT STORIES

The ancient stories alluded to throughout this study of Rendell are related in Homer's epics, *The Iliad* and *The Odyssey*, and in twenty of the thirty-three surviving tragedies written by Aeschylus, Sophocles, and Euripides. Each playwright dramatized episodes and drew characters from the history of two dynasties, which will be referred to below as the houses of Laius and Atreus.

Atreus's descendents are major figures in the Trojan War tales. Paris of Troy kidnaps Helen, wife of Menelaus, and the Greeks, led by Menelaus's brother Agamemnon, go to war to recover her and to avenge this outrage. Aeschylus's trilogy, the *Oresteia,* begins when Agamemnon returns home from the ten-year war and is slain by his wife Clytemnestra and her lover Aegisthus. The other dynastic story tells how the King of Thebes, Laius, and his wife Jocasta are warned by the Delphic oracle not to have children, because any son born to Laius would kill his father. Oedipus is nonetheless conceived and, without knowing the identity of his victim, eventually slays his father. Subsequently, he marries his mother. From that incestuous union are born two sons who would eventually fight to the death over Thebes, and two daughters, one of whom, Antigone, would martyr herself so that her brother Polyneices received ritual burial.

When the two dynastic narratives with their central episodes, pre-histories, and epilogues are summarized, they depict virtually every imaginable crime a mystery writer might imagine: cannibalism, kidnapping, incest, homosexual rape, adultery and the murder of a spouse, infanticide, fratricide, patricide, matricide. To these can be added the crimes of sacrilege and human sacrifice. The lust for power, greed, and obsession are common to both sets of stories. In each, sisters confront each other, disagreeing over their appropriate roles within the family. And in each, the antagonism between brothers leads to enmity and death. No wonder that for centuries after the Greeks recorded these stories, authors have found in them a treasure trove of characters, motives, incidents, and themes. The Greeks may not only have had all the plots, but also may have imagined every possible variation of disturbed family relationships.

Hardly the stuff of comedy. And yet one of Ruth Rendell's specific allusions to the House of Atreus proves very funny because of the enormous gap between Wexford's domestic situation and the domestic situation dramatized in the ancient literature. In *The Best Man to Die,* Inspector Wexford finds himself not for the first nor last time bedeviled by his favorite daughter, Sheila. This time she has brought him a dog to care for while she and its owner, her current lover, enjoy a vacation. That Wexford dislikes dogs is not the only ironic aspect of his reluctant acquiescence to Sheila's demand. The yapping, unprepossessing canine is called Clytemnestra, the name of one of the most notorious murderers in literature, an accomplice in the slaying of her husband Agamemnon when he returns from the Trojan War. What may ameliorate this portrait of an evil woman is that she was also the victim of her husband, who had tricked her into handing over their daughter Iphigenia as a sacrifice to Artemis so that the winds carrying Greek ships to Troy would blow. And what makes her a far more complex and developed character than her renowned but passive sister, Helen, is that Clytemnestra would become the victim of matricide, a revenge crime perpetrated by her own children, Electra and Orestes. Matricide evokes more horror than any other intra-familial crime except infanticide.

22

In Book Eleven of *The Odyssey,* the ghost of Agamemnon congratulates Odysseus for his wiser choice of a spouse, the clever and faithful Penelope, whose weaving is emblematic of her domestic role, and who keeps the hearth warm and secure for twenty years while her husband Odysseus fights the Trojan War and then makes his meandering way home. If a Penelope-like character could be identified in Rendell's fiction, it is Wexford's wife Dora. It is therefore very amusing that she should find herself hosting Clytemnestra— even if in a canine incarnation. In an early novel, *The Lake of Darkness,* Rendell juxtaposes the images of the faithless Clytemnestra and the faithful Penelope. The protagonist's mother is said to resemble Lord Frederick Leighton's painting of Clytemnestra. But in an ironic twist typical of Rendell's allusions (see Chapter 1), this mother's chief occupation is her needlework, as she does quilting and appliqué work to help her through the stresses of menopause. There is nothing wrong with her occupying herself in this way, but unlike Penelope's weaving, her needlework is done for her own benefit. Homer's Penelope and Rendell's Dora occupy themselves in similar ways for the benefit of their families.

To appreciate the extent to which the worlds of Ruth Rendell's novels are illuminated by the families depicted in classical literature, and to follow the details from ancient works in subsequent chapters of this book, a more extensive summary of the stories will be useful. Such a summary, moreover, reveals a fascinating narrative element not usually pointed out when these ancient families are studied. For when traced back to their very early episodes, the seemingly separate stories concerning the houses of Laius and Atreus converge. Three brothers—a singleton and a pair of twins— stand at the place where these story groups meet. Their common grandfather, Tantalus, commits a gruesome crime that sets in motion generations of intra-familial atrocities.

Hosting the Olympian gods at a dinner, Tantalus, in an act of extreme pride, decides to test divine omniscience. He butchers his son Pelops and serves him cooked in a stew.

But Tantalus does not fool the Olympians except, briefly, the goddess Demeter, who is grieving over the kidnapping of her daughter Persephone. The young girl had been abducted by Hades, ruler of the underworld. Distracted by her grief, Demeter swallows some of Tantalus's dish. Because eating disorders and grotesque feasts supply narrative motifs found throughout Rendell's novels, it is interesting to note here that had Persephone not also eaten what she should not have (six seeds of a pomegranate fruit), she would have been permanently reunited with her mother. As it is, she must return to Hades for half of each year during which Demeter leaves the earth fallow and nothing grows. That Demeter absently consumes part of Pelops and that her daughter eats the seeds that would bind her to Hades involve a thematic continuity that, again, suggests the ways in which families express recurrent pathologies.

The gods, in any event, resurrect Pelops, but because he is missing that part of his shoulder eaten by Demeter, it is necessary to fashion for him an ivory prosthesis. Subsequently, he leads a rather uneventful life, but his sons set in motion a series of horrible events. The least well known of these children in the numerous retellings of these ancient stories is a beautiful young boy named Chrysippus, who becomes a significant character in the Oedipus story, although one who has yet fully to emerge from the obscurity to which he has been consigned by skittish writers of mythological dictionaries and handbooks. For, claim some, it is because of a crime against Pelops's beloved Chryssipus that Laius is doomed to be murdered by his own son. But this offense on Laius's part occurred prior to the familiar episodes in the Laius/Oedipus story depicted in the tragedies.

Those well-known episodes begin with Laius's marriage to Jocasta and the couple's failure to heed a divine warning against giving birth to the son who would kill his father. Originally, Laius and Jocasta agree to evade their fate by refraining from sexual intercourse, but either because of one night's drunkenness and the lust it releases, or because their desire to found a dynasty is irresistible (or both), Oedipus is conceived. In a second attempt to thwart fate, Laius and Jocasta arrange to have the infant taken from Thebes and exposed to the elements, presumably until he dies. The exposure motif in myth and literature also leaves open the possibility that the child may be found by another who would care for him (the story of Moses readily comes to mind). In the Oedipus story, the person charged with abandoning Oedipus in the wild arranges to have the baby sheltered by a family. Oedipus therefore survives and is raised by King Peleus and Queen Merope, whom Oedipus takes to be his biological parents. But eventually, Oedipus must confront two unwelcome pieces of information: that Peleus and Merope are not his parents (which they deny), and that he is destined to kill his father. Rather than harm Peleus, Oedipus flees his home only to encounter and slay Laius. The words written at the Delphic oracle, "Know Thyself," thus become an important part of Oedipus's story as he both strives to learn and later also evades learning the truth about himself.

Oedipus's story can be said to resemble that of adopted children who today demand access to their birth records and with great eagerness or trepidation seek out their birth parents. In Ruth Rendell's *Anna's Book,* one of the characters is similarly informed that she is mistaken about her birth and family origins and becomes obsessed with discovering who her parents are. As was true of Oedipus, she is denied full disclosure by her adoptive parent. The solution to the mystery of her birth is also the solution to a murder (see Chapter 5).

After killing Laius, Oedipus encounters the Sphinx, who demands of all travelers that they either solve the riddle she poses to them or die. What, the contestants are asked, goes on four legs in the morning, on two legs at noon, and on three legs in the evening? A "game as ordeal" is a common motif in ancient narratives, and in most stories spun around it, the hero who survives will win a princess as his wife. In *The Chimney Sweeper's Boy,* Rendell creates a variant on this motif, and it helps extend her use of the Oedipus story in the novel (see Chapter 5). In the Oedipus story, Laius's son correctly answers that it is man who crawls on all fours as a baby, walks upright throughout most of his life, and toward the end of it must employ a cane to sustain mobility. His prize is Jocasta and the throne of Thebes, but he does not know that she is his mother or that rule of the kingdom had always been rightfully his.

Eventually, a plague that decimates Thebes leads Oedipus to consult the Delphic oracle, setting in motion the series of revelations that expose the crimes of which Oedipus has been unwittingly guilty, patricide and incest. Jocasta hangs herself in shame. Oedipus blinds himself, making literal what had been symbolic, and goes into exile. The rule of Thebes is to be divided between his sons Polyneices and Eteocles, who kill each other because they are not willing to share their legacy. Thebes is now ruled by Jocasta's brother, Creon, who denies one of Oedipus's sons his traditional funeral rites. Deeming Creon's action a sacrilege, Antigone defies him, for which she is executed. Her death brings to a conclusion the family curse that overwhelmed Laius's family.

It is the question of why Laius was doomed that arouses puzzlement in those who may wonder why he and his family incurred the enmity of Apollo (who presided over the Oracle at Delphi). Because of Sophocles' renowned play *Oedipus the King*, now the best-known source for this story, and because Freud later drew on Sophocles to formulate his equally famous Oedipus complex, what happens to Laius and his son constitutes a familiar tale. But unless the capriciousness of the gods is invoked, sustaining the argument of Shakespeare and Thomas Hardy that they torture human beings for sport (see Chapter 11 for Rendell's possible use of this idea in *The Water is Lovely*), Oedipus's fate seems undeserved. In the conflict between fate and free will, which permeates his story, pieces seem missing.

To answer why Laius and his descendents were doomed (according to the ancient stories) requires more knowledge of Greek mythology than, again, writers of mythological handbooks were in the past willing to impart. In Aeschylus's *Seven Against Thebes,* Eteocles, realizing he is going to die in the battle with his brother, cries out that his family was one hated by Apollo. But in Greek myth, the gods have reasons, if often trivial ones, for having it in for mortals. Apollo's enmity toward Laius therefore requires some explanation, and a generally neglected element of the story has been brought forward to supply it.

After Laius's father Labdacus dies, conspiracies against Laius jeopardize his life and his right to rule Thebes. Laius flees and takes refuge with Pelops, the man resurrected by the gods after his father Tantalus butchered him. While a protected guest in Pelops's home, Laius is overcome with passion for Pelops's beautiful young son Chryssipus, whom he kidnaps and rapes. In shame, Chryssipus kills himself, and Pelops is deprived of his favorite child. Retaliating, Pelops curses Laius: just as Laius had caused Pelops to lose a son, so, antithetically, would Laius be doomed to be killed by his own son. Apollo probably comes into the story because it is one of his roles in Greek mythology to be guardian and protector of young men, just as it is his twin sister Artemis's role to protect young maidens. Apollo, moreover, had remained sorrowful and guilt-ridden over the death of his own young male lover, Hyacinthus, whom he had inadvertently slain, and he was probably particularly sensitive to Chrysippus's plight. In *The Chimney Sweeper's Boy,* a statue of Apollo is used as a weapon by a homosexual man to bludgeon to death his unfaithful lover. Much has been written about homosexual love in ancient Greece but only two points need be made here. For a highborn young man such as Chryssipus, homosexual relations required mutual consent. Laius, however, had abducted Chryssipus. The host-guest relationship was, moreover, almost sacred, the basis of social trust. In kidnapping Chryssipus, Laius betrayed Pelops, who had provided Laius with shelter from his enemies.

The Laius/Chryssipus story is being detailed here in some length because it may help explain the conjunction of the Oedipus story and the subject of homosexuality in two of Ruth Rendell's most brilliant novels: *No Night is Too Long* and *The Chimney Sweeper's Boy* (see Chapters 5 and 7). The Laius/Chryssipus story has also become something of a controversy in Freud studies (see Chapter 3). By the nineteenth century, the relatively little discussed episode had acquired some currency. Its content, however, the homosexual rape of Chryssipus followed by his suicide, apparently made writers of mythological handbooks uncomfortable; or perhaps conventions that once dominated the publishing of books restrained them. They would note that Laius loved Chrysippus and ran away with him, but they would also avoid making explicit just what that would mean. Acknowledging this early stage in Oedipus's family history would, moreover, significantly alter the way the father-son relationship could be perceived. Briefly, instead of being his son's victim, claim some, Laius effectively destroyed Oedipus by invoking a curse upon their family. Marianne Krüll has written in very strong terms about the Chryssipus episode, "According to the legend, Laius was thus a 'perverse' person, an active homosexual with sadistic traits, the type of father who . . . had to be considered the cause of his own children's neuroses. Oedipus, by contrast, was an innocent victim, who had to atone for the sins of his father."

When the story of Oedipus is pushed back to that of his ancestor, Tantalus, the succeeding generations that presided over Thebes involve a complicated series of dynastic rulers among whom there is no uninterrupted linear descent from father to son until Oedipus succeeds Laius. Fortunately, it is not necessary to begin Oedipus's story at his family's beginning, although it is worth noting that previous incidents of incest and infanticide (not summarized here) are part of Oedipus's inheritance. But where it comes to the House of Atreus, and the rivalry and hatred that existed between Chryssipus' twin half-brothers, Atreus and Thyestes, narrative development involves clearly-defined parallels as well as intersecting episodes.

Again, it will be useful to begin with relatively familiar episodes and work backwards. When Agamemnon joins his brother Menelaus to wage war on Troy after Paris abducts Helen, he is thwarted by the lack of sufficient wind to move his ships away from Argos. Consulting an oracle, Agamemnon is commanded to sacrifice his daughter Iphigenia to the goddess Artemis. Later, when Clytemnestra tries to justify killing her husband after he returned from war, she invokes a mother's grief over the loss of the child slain by Agamemnon. Her surviving daughter Electra, however, dismisses this plea as a rationalization to cover the fact that while Agamemnon was fighting a war, Clytemnestra took his cousin Aegisthus as her lover. Together they planned to rule Argos.

Because the contemporary feminist movement—what Rendell in *An Unkindness of Ravens* calls the woman's movement—provides several themes in her fiction, eventually an important one for distinguishing between Wexford's two daughters (see Chapter 9), it is worth a brief digression here to note that for centuries Electra's view of her mother prevailed. Clytemnestra was excoriated and despised. But today, feminists, led by the influential writing of Kate Millett, have taken up Clytemnestra's cause (see Sources). For them, the murder of Clytemnestra signals the end of matriarchy in Greece, the triumph of patriarchy, and this historical sequence is to be deplored. It may have been the case that Clytemnestra hoped that Aegisthus would be more willing to share power with his queen than Agamemnon would have been. In the Greek plays, so-called masculine traits attributed to Clytemnestra are part of the criticism leveled against her: she is not properly womanly, that is, suitably subservient to her husband. As noted above, in *The Odyssey,* Homer explicitly contrasts Clytemnestra with Penelope, who—again— had spent the war years keeping the home fires burning until her husband's return. In Book Eleven, Odysseus descends to the underworld, encounters the ghost of Agamemnon, and hears how Clytemnestra and Aegisthus murdered him. This is the only mention of Clytemnestra in *The Odyssey*, but she is a major as well as complex character in the Greek tragedies that recount the stories of the Trojan War, its beginnings and its aftermath.

The persistent rivalry between Clytemnestra's two husbands, the cousins Agamemnon and Aegisthus, is both political and personal. It can be traced to the blatantly political rivalry of their fathers Atreus and Thyestes for the rule of Greece. Originally, most of the gods favored Thyestes, but as is often the case in ancient Greek mythology, the quarrels among mortals mirror conflicts among their deities. Zeus does not look kindly on Thyestes and, to show his displeasure, he causes the sun to reverse its customary course from east to west. Frightened, Thyestes abdicates his rule and goes into exile, leaving Atreus to occupy the throne. Not content to let matters stand, however, Atreus, in feigned brotherly sympathy, calls Thyestes back from his self-banishment. At a feast to mark their reunion, Atreus serves Thyestes his own sons for dinner—this second episode of cannibalism echoing his grandfather Tantalus' cooking his son (Atreus's father) Pelops to serve to the Olympic gods.

Thyestes, now deprived of children, for his were not resurrected as Pelops had been, incestuously impregnates his own daughter. Aegisthus is thus the fruit of a heinous act that foreshadows his eventually destructive role in the family saga. Meanwhile, the ruling brother Atreus, worried about repercussions, instructs his own sons to kill Thyestes. Why Agamemnon and Menelaus do not forthrightly kill their uncle and their cousin Aegisthus remains puzzling. Instead, they unsuccessfully try to coerce Aegisthus into killing his own father. Left alive, Aegisthus murders his uncle Atreus and later conspires with Clytemnestra to kill Atreus's son Agamemnon. In short, the cousins Aegisthus and Agamemnon inherit the family feud that can be traced to their fathers, Thyestes and Atreus. When Orestes plans his mother's, Clytemnestra's, death, he is only too aware of descending from a family in which in-group murder has paved the way for his own murderous act.

If these narrative threads appear tangled, all that is necessary to bear in mind is that Atreus and Thyestes were the twins who fought over the rule of Greece, and that their sons, Agamemnon and Aegisthus, would continue their feud. And in the event that Agamemnon, a renowned hero of the Trojan War, appears more sympathetic than his cousin, it is important to remember that it was Agamemnon's father, Atreus, who was guilty of the heinous act of murdering his nephews and serving them as food to their father. Laius may have inadvertently doomed his descendents by his actions, but Atreus's crimes were consciously directed against members of his own family and he unquestionably doomed his descendants.

Eventually, the family feud descends on Agamemnon's children, Orestes and Electra, who murder their mother Clytemnestra. But justice no longer rests on an ancient code of vengeance. Orestes stands trial for his crime and is acquitted, much to the displeasure of the Furies, whom Rendell would powerfully invoke in *A Dark Adapted Eye* (see Chapter 11 for a discussion of justice in Rendell's fiction).

After Clytemnestra and Aegisthus succeed in killing Agamemnon, the latter's two children pose a serious threat (Sophocles would add a third child, a daughter Chrysothemis, to the story). What happens at this point will vary according to the Greek tragedian who took up the story and explained why Orestes was left alive to return to Argos and exact the revenge that custom required of him. Aeschylus, Sophocles, and Euripides agree that, while still a child, Orestes had been sent abroad to get him out of harm's way, and that without the presence and aid of her brother, an obsessed Electra was helpless to avenge Agamemnon's death. But then subtle distinctions differentiate the playwrights. Whether Orestes had been spirited away by his sister Electra, who, helpless on her own to act against her mother and stepfather, awaits her brother's return; or whether he was sent abroad by the teacher who had helped raise him; or, finally, whether he was saved by some maternal affection on the part of his mother Clytemnestra, will depend on which play is being considered. The choices made about Orestes' survival by Aeschylus, Sophocles, or Euripides would determine whether his play focused on the brother/sister or mother/son relationship.

In Aeschylus, an obsessed but powerless Electra awaits her brother's return to avenge their father's murder. For on her own, a woman without power, demoted in status in her own land and family, she cannot act. Even when Orestes returns, Electra is relegated to the background. For the major confrontation takes place between mother and son as Clytemnestra understands that Orestes means to kill her. Her appeal to the mother-son bond could add pathos to the story unless the audience concludes that once again Clytemnestra employs rationalization of her behavior to manipulate circumstances, in this instance trying to save her own life. In Sophocles, the major confrontation takes place between Electra and Clytemnestra, the daughter implacable in her condemnation of her mother. But it is in Euripides' play that Electra plays the most active role in the actual murder of Clytemnestra. She lures Clytemnestra to her death by lying about having given birth and needing a mother's care, a chilling piece of duplicity. She later describes how she symbolically laid her own her hand on the sword Orestes plunged into their mother, thereby acknowledging her complicity in the crime. Then, to comfort Orestes, she appears to share his guilt and remorse. In short, in each of the ancient plays, Electra's part in the murder of Clytemnestra is presented differently. (See Chapter 8.) What is consistent among the tragedies is that Electra is, to use contemporary jargon, a decidedly daddy's girl whose life is characterized, however, less by her love for Agamemnon than her hatred for Clytemnestra. The number of young women who similarly despise their mothers in Rendell's fiction is noteworthy, and this subject will be discussed in detail in later chapters.

The murder of Clytemnestra will of course be shocking to anyone who takes the mother-child bond for granted—which Rendell's fiction never does. Even the Athenian jury that must assess Orestes' guilt and, if necessary, fix his punishment, is forced to deal with matricide as in itself a repellent, unnatural act. In *The Eumenides,* the last play of Aeschylus's *Oresteia* and what some have designated the first courtroom drama in Western literature, the jury has to decide whether it is more blameworthy to kill a mother or to fail to avenge a father's death. Their deliberations end in their being split six to six in their decision. The goddess Athena, who serves as judge in the case, is called upon to break the tie. But it is important to remember that Athena is the goddess without a mother, the daughter of Zeus who sprang fully grown and fully armored from her father's head. No intrinsic sympathy for mothers would sway her. The goddess would have no difficulty accepting the defense's argument that a child's true parent is its father, the mother a mere vessel in which the male parent's seed develops until birth takes place. As a result of Athena's decision, Orestes is acquitted. In general, this last play in Aeschylus's trilogy, with its trial by jury, is celebrated to this day as bringing to an end the blood feuds that characterized the House of Atreus as well as initiating in Greece a more enlightened system of justice. But among thoughtful fiction writers, here is where questions of justice just begin.

In considering what was available to Ruth Rendell from ancient literature and stories derived from the two dynastic families, it would be an error to think only in terms of composite portraits. Any writer who drew inspiration from the Greek tragedians would benefit from being sensitive to differences in their treatments of the same characters and incidents. Again, Aeschylus wrote the *Oresteia,* three plays about the aftermath of the Trojan War, the only trilogy that has come down to us from ancient Greek drama. He had also written a trilogy about Oedipus and his family, but only one play, *Seven Against Thebes,* has survived. It teasingly hints at how Aeschylus's portrait of Oedipus might have differed from Sophocles' and how such differences, had they survived, might have changed the history of Western psychology. From Sophocles, in contrast, we have three plays about Oedipus (a trio of dramas but not an integrated trilogy) and his children, but only one drama employing the Trojan material, *Electra*. From Euripides comes the largest group of surviving Greek tragedies, nineteen plays. Some of the best-known plays, such as *Medea,* are unrelated to either the Trojan or Theban stories. In four plays, the Trojan War provides background but is not central to the drama.

One play, *The Phoenician Women*, supplies another view of Oedipus and his family from the one provided by Sophocles. In Euripides, Jocasta herself relates the story of her ill-fated union with her son/husband. In light of Rendell's novel, *The Chimney Sweeper's Boy,* a discussion of which will draw on the Oedipus story, it is possible to realize that whereas the Oedipus drama is as much about Jocasta as about Laius, rarely does the queen appear as subject and not merely object in her own story. At least one feminist writer has noted this neglect of Jocasta. Even if briefly, Euripides gives her a voice (see Chapter 5). Noteworthy among Euripides' Trojan dramas are two plays about Iphigenia, the daughter Agamemnon sacrificed at the directive of the Delphic oracle so that the winds would blow and the Greek ships could set sail for Troy. Here it is worth pausing to reiterate that many contemporary feminists would dissent from the view that the *Oresteia* ends on a positive note with the replacement of personal revenge and family feuds by a criminal justice system involving advocates for the defendant, for the state, as well as judges and juries. Again, they interpret the matricide and Orestes' acquittal as the final triumph of Greek patriarchy over a more archaic matriarchy whose remnants can be perceived in the character of Clytemnestra. For them, Iphigenia is the symbolic victim of patriarchy. Her sister Electra is, on the other side, the ultimate apostate from an ancient matriarchy, a traitor to her sex who employs male strength (Orestes) against

34

her female parent (Clytemnestra) as retaliation for the murder of her male parent (Agamemnon). In *Iphigenia in Aulis,* moreover, Euripides portrays a very different Clytemnestra from the one found in Aeschylus and Sophocles. In Chapter 4, it will be argued that Rendell probably drew on Euripides' play in her novel *Gallowglass,* in which the Trojan War story is told by one of the characters to another. But, again, it is in *The Chimney Sweeper's Boy* that a father virtually sweeps away his wife's importance to their two daughters. He claims them as purely his own, much as it could be argued—and Cytemnestra does argue as she tries to justify her murder of her husband—that Agamemnon had claimed Iphigenia as his own, to do with as he willed without concern for his wife, the child's mother. This sacrifice theme is implicit in *The Chimney Sweeper's Boy.* It is, however, the House of Laius rather than the House of Atreus that influenced this absorbing novel, in which Rendell has given her Jocasta-figure a voice.

It would have been possible in this chapter, with its survey of the two dynastic stories treated so extensively by ancient writers, to reinforce the argument for their influence on Rendell's novels with more allusions to her work. To do so, however, would have necessitated too much repetition of discussion to come. One more chapter will be useful before this study of Rendell begins a detailed analysis of how she drew on these stories. It will cover another area with which she is obviously conversant, the renowned theories of Sigmund Freud and the lesser-known tenets of his favorite but ultimately renegade disciple, Carl Jung. It will be seen how Jung, Freud, and their eventual and perhaps inevitable split can be described in terms of an opposition between the Oedipus and Electra complexes, and that these, in turn, are deeply implicated in how family dynamics may be understood. The conflicts between these two giants supply another entry into an understanding of Rendell's treatment of the family in her novels.

CHAPTER 3

FREUD, JUNG, AND THEIR COMPLEXES

R uth Rendell's *An Unkindness of Ravens* begins with a search for the missing Rodney Williams, who proves to be a bigamist. One wife is a superficial, doll-like woman with whom he has a daughter Veronica. The other wife is a slattern who dotes on her son and seems to loathe her daughter Sara. The beautiful half-sisters are close in age, and so similar in looks that inevitably they discover each other and their relatedness. But they are quite different in personality. Veronica is timid and passive, Sara aggressive and ambitious. Almost in defiance of the family hopes pinned on her brother, Sara studies very hard and realistically expects to be admitted to medical school.

When Wexford interviews Sara, he finds books in her room consisting of works on sexual pathology, incest, and the lives of psychologists, including Freud. Wexford subsequently discovers that Sara had told her mother that Rodney had sexually abused her, incurring her mother's rage at being confronted with this information. Mrs. Williams retaliates with the charge that it was rather an over-sexed Sara who had seduced her father. Wexford later concludes that Sara has fabricated the incest, asking Dr. Crocker, Kingsmarkham's medical examiner, to explain Freud's seduction theory to his investigative partner, Mike Burden. With great erudition, to the point of recalling the date of Freud's controversial paper, Crocker supplies a thumbnail history. Freud believed the origin of neuroses could be traced to the childhood sexual abuse of his patients by a parent or other close family relative. Later, he decided that most accounts of incest reflected fantasy, not reality, his retraction laying the groundwork for his formulation of the Oedipus complex.

According to Wexford, who is explaining the crimes involving the Williams family, Sara's accusation suggested an attachment to her father much stronger than his to her. Following Freud, Wexford theorizes that her contempt for Rodney probably masked an unresolved erotic attraction to him. More than fifteen years later, Rendell's *Babes in the Wood* portrayed another teenager, Sophie, who unequivocally hates her father. Her dislike as well as sexual knowledge beyond what would be expected of a thirteen-year-old leads Wexford to speculate that her father had sexually abused Sophie. Her paternal grandmother is of the same opinion because she had been abused as a child. But although incest and pedophilia are important themes in this novel, both Wexford and the grandmother are mistaken, and the inspector has to rethink his assumptions. In both *An Unkindness of Ravens* and *Babes in the Wood*, Wexford has effectively followed in Freud's footsteps, first hypothesizing that parent-child incest has taken place, only to arrive later at a different theory. Like Freud, Wexford is seeking the origins of obsessions and neuroses; unlike Freud, he requires this knowledge to discover the motive for a crime and the identity of a murderer.

A mother's admission of sexual desire for her son and, this time, Freudian method rather than just theory, supply important themes in *The Veiled One*, a book whose subtitle might be, "Freud confronts Jung." Clifford Sanders suffers from a psychosis at least in part traceable to one of the most disturbed mother-son relationships in Rendell's fiction. He is undergoing Jungian therapy and he refers to his mother as his shadow, a Jungian term for the negative side of the personality most people take pains to hide from others, or the primitive side of the self that is infantile or socially unacceptable and is therefore usually repressed. When, in the course of investigating a murder, Burden learns that

Clifford discovered the body, he becomes convinced that Clifford is the murderer. Despite Clifford's denials, Burden is confident he can break him down through intensive interrogation. The unhappy young man is unexpectedly only too willing to attend the questioning sessions because he is given free reign to talk about himself, and Burden seems only too willing to listen.

Clifford and Burden embark on what psychology has called the talking cure, although, of course, no cure takes place. Their interaction is especially ironic because Burden disdains Clifford's accounts of himself and his behavior and is, in general, skeptical of psychological explanations for criminal actions. At the same time, Clifford's Jungian therapist, noting that Clifford appears to be experiencing what Freudians call a transference, an emotional attachment to Burden, wonders if his patient had not needed Freudian psychotherapy all along. It is when Burden runs out of patience, abandoning his hopes of eliciting a confession from Clifford and putting an end to their meetings, that a catastrophe occurs.

These are not the only books in which Rendell reveals her knowledge and understanding of psychological theory. These three, however, show the extent to which she has read in psychology, with Sara Williams' library only a miniature of what must be Rendell's own. Freud's early theories eventually led him to what he insisted was the cornerstone of human psychology, the Oedipus complex. Less well known is Jung's counter-formulation of an Electra complex. Or rather, even when known, the Electra complex is frequently and mistakenly attributed to Freud as the term he uses to describe female psychological development. Freud, in fact, rejected Jung's Electra complex, insisting that the father-daughter relationship could be adequately understood within the context of the Oedipus complex.

There are several reasons for exploring the split between Freud and Jung in this study of Rendell's fiction—aside from the fact that their differences interested her. The Electra complex and its place in Jung's psychology supply a significant context for analyzing Rendell's novels and their roots in disturbed family relationships. For, whereas Freud rejected the Electra complex as a piece of theoretical redundancy, Jung invoked the ancient story as a corrective to Freud. Jung argued that family life involved a myriad of relationships that could go wrong and thereby harm the individual unable to break away. This study of Rendell is therefore organized according to Jungian principles insofar as it breaks down the various family constellations she explores as supplying motives for murder. Most individual chapters have been grouped according to whether the themes or family relationships highlighted in a Rendell novel are more readily traceable to the Oedipus or to the Electra stories. But neither tale nor the theory derived from it will be held to be self-sufficient, independent of the other.

It would be going too far to argue that the difference between Oedipus and Electra is the essential paradigm for the split that occurred between Freud and Jung, Freud having discovered that his favorite disciple was more of an apostate than a follower. It is, however, noteworthy that Jung introduced the Electra complex in 1912, the year that the schism between Freud and Jung became obvious and apparently irremediable. Jung had delivered a lecture on the Oedipus complex, one of a series of talks at Fordham University in New York, whose purpose was to educate Americans about Freud's psychoanalytic theories. Instead, Jung conveyed disagreement with his master on important ideas and effectively announced publicly that he was no longer willing to have a master.

The Oedipus complex involves a rather complicated web of relationships, involving as it does the differences between a child's and an adult's fantasies; the need to repress forbidden desires and the difficulty of later accessing the contents of the unconscious, where these wishes continue to have their effects; stages of childhood development; and fixations that impede movement from one stage to another, standing in the way of normal adulthood. Simply put, as Jung put it when he tried to explain the Oedipus complex to his American audience, the male child wants to be rid of his father so that he can have his mother to himself. The very simplicity of Jung's formulation may have in itself been a backhanded swipe at Freud. Still, a summary of Freud's argument as presented by Jung is as follows. The attachment of a boy to his mother is an erotic one that he must eventually relinquish, and the rivalry with the father leads to murderous impulses directed toward the male parent.

For Freud, Sophocles' play *Oedipus the King* portrays a universal fantasy from which no individual is free, the desire to murder his father and sleep with his mother. Whether the Oedipus complex can also encompass female development is part of the disagreement between Freud and Jung. The latter's growing interest in spiritualism eventually led to his emphasis on matriarchy, on the archetyhpe of the Great Mother, whereas Freud's emphasis was on patriarchy, which he equated with rational thought. For the most part, even followers of Freud will often admit that his explanation of female psychological development leaves much unexplained, particularly how it is that young girls initially turn away from their mothers to their fathers. In the context of the House of Atreus and its legacy, it is possible to ask, why *did* Electra so hate Clytemnestra, and why was her attachment to Agamemnon so obsessive? In Chapters 7 and 10, on Rendell's treatment of Mothers and Sons and Mothers and Daughters, Freud's essay on "Femininity," quoted in two of her novels, but reflected in several of them, will be discussed. It is in this essay that Freud tries to account for a girl's repudiation of her mother in favor of her father.

For now, it can be noted that the triangular relationship of mother, father, and son involves the young man in two family relationships that can go wrong. Ideally, his erotic attraction to the mother is resolved when the young man in the normal course of events transfers his sexual desires to other women, one of whom will be his wife. But the mother is in at least two ways capable of interfering with this process. Perhaps she is unfulfilled in her own marriage, for as literature from Greek myth to contemporary fiction demonstrates, marriage can be a very dreary matter, particularly disappointing for a woman whose role is defined by her place in the home. Then her son will become the most important man in her life, and she may refuse to let him separate from her. This will be so even when she seems to encourage him to succeed in his endeavors, for it is not his satisfaction she seeks but rather her own, vicariously experienced through him. Again, it is interesting that in the psychological literature, very little is said about what fantasies led Jocasta to marry her son. She is almost always rendered an object in Oedipus's story, rarely a subject with her own needs and conflicts. Her suicide is treated as a simple act of shame rather than the sad conclusion to a life that has taken a turn she is emotionally unable to cope with as, for the most part, the men in her life shape her destiny.

Another way that the mother can interfere with her son's emotional development is to vent on him the rage she feels toward his father in the disappointing marriage. So she may belittle her son or frustrate his ability to make his way in the world by telling him he is incapable of doing so and would be better off remaining with her and not taking on what he cannot handle. When a mother so behaves, her son's animosity, originally directed at the rival father, may be directed instead against her, even if he represses its outward show. Virtually all of these obstacles to a boy's working through his Oedipus complex are portrayed in the title story of Ruth Rendell's collection of short fiction, *From Piranha to Scurfy*, which portrays several of Rendell's pathological mothers and sons. It is noteworthy that a piranha is an aggressively flesh-eating—that is, symbolically, castrating—fish, and that scurfy is a skin disease associated with scurvy, a condition resulting from the lack of adequate nourishment.

The threat of castration in Freudian theory comes from the father, and it is his son's awareness that his father can punish him that leads in the first place to the son's repression of forbidden Oedipal impulses. Resolving the father-son conflict may be, however, more difficult even in theory than resolving conflict with the mother. For the ramifications of the father-son relationship extend more decisively into the world in which the young man is expected to make his way. For one thing, the father remains a representative of society's laws, and fear of punishment for breaking one of them will almost inevitably invoke the earlier fear of or anger toward the father. Moreover, the essential conflict between the individual and society generated by the need for law and order will turn the father-son relationship into a metaphor for something extending outside the familial bond.

Finally, the father remains a potentially emasculating influence if he does not help his son achieve his own goals, or if the son feels that he cannot compete with the successful older man. Oedipus must slay Laius to rule Thebes. At the same time, Oedipus is doomed by his father's own transgressions and weaknesses. A boy may also resent his father if the older man, far from being a success, is a failure or in some other way does not provide a model his son can admire. Rendell treats all of these developmental problems in her fiction, and they are central to *Master of the Moor, Live Flesh,* and *A Fatal Inversion.*

There were several changes that took place in Freud's theory when he replaced childhood sexual abuse with the Oedipus complex as the etiology of neurosis. For one, so long as the neurotic patient was seen to be suffering an injury inflicted on him by an abusive parent, then in a sense were the sins of the father visited upon the child (*Sins of the Fathers* is the American title of the second book in the Wexford series). But the Oedipus complex reverses the blame—for want of a better word—for the patient's suffering. No longer is the child afflicted by an injury immediately traceable to the parent or parents; rather, he is caught in the web of conflicts that came into being when he did. In that sense, the child becomes the author of his own misery, his plight comparable to that of one born already tainted by original sin, blameless for the flaw, but at the same time bearing responsibility for controlling destructive instincts. For some commentators on the Oedipus complex, however, this shift of responsibility from parent to child is unacceptable for two surprisingly antithetical reasons.

On one side, it rather lets the parents off the theoretical hook as contributors to the child's sufferings (it would surely be difficult, however, to find a responsible psychoanalyst who discounted parental influences). According to anthropologist and psychologist George Devereux, this aspect of the Oedipus complex would have its appeal because of "the adult's deep-seated need to place all responsibility for the Oedipus complex upon the child." On the other side, as Devereux writes, "regardless of how loving and humane the father may be, the infant will nonetheless view him primarily as a monster, because of instinctually determined and phylogenetically anchored fantasies of its own."

In her writing, Ruth Rendell manages dramatically to render all of these possibilities. Her novels supply a portrait gallery of some of the worst parents to be found in literature, mothers and fathers who are justifiably the object of their children's strongly negative conscious and unconscious emotions, and parents who, through overtly brutal acts or withdrawal of love or just plain indifference, significantly damage their offspring. At the same time, Rendell creates another group of characters, unlikable and even vicious children, many of whom could strain the good will of even the best-intentioned parents, potentially turning them into the monsters their children thought they were to begin with. The interplay of nature, nurture, and individual will comprises Rendell's most consistent themes.

Another important feature of Freud's shift from the seduction theory to the Oedipus complex cannot be attributed to Freud alone, for his ideas reflect a significant change in Western thought. Objective views of the world and the individual's relationship to it gave way to an increasing emphasis on subjective "reality." When Coleridge, a poet frequently alluded to by Rendell, wrote in his "Dejection: An Ode" that "we receive but what we give / And in our lives alone does nature live," he was expressing the nineteenth-century romantic premise that the human mind shapes the external world and does not merely mirror it. For therapeutic ends, the patient's fantasies of seduction may be as significant as actual seduction, the narratives that comprise the patient's account of the past thereby treated as if it were actual history. The inaccuracies of conscious memory will, under the direction of the trained psychoanalyst, yield truths buried in the unconscious.

Putting aside questions about whether there is in fact an unconscious and whether its so-called buried truths could be unearthed and unequivocally demonstrated to be true (at this writing, Rendell has not taken up the subject of the so-called memory wars), it remains the case that in the genre of crime fiction, the *whydunit* takes for granted the possibility of understanding human behavior, of constructing a coherent case history. Or at least it has up to recent times. At a point at which mystery writers might admit that human behavior is at best only partially explainable, the reasons for crime might once again have to revert to the most one-dimensional motives for murder: greed, adultery, uncontrolled rage, irresistible impulse caused by some trigger in the brain or an extra chromosome in the genes. That, moreover, the human mind creates its own reality and that this reality can never be fully grasped by another, is most frighteningly suggested in Rendell's novel *The House of Stairs*. Bell, a convicted murderer considered a psychopath by the court, muses on the charge, claiming that she sees the world the same way others do. But then she pauses to ask herself if in fact that is the case. In *The Bridesmaid* Senta is also a psychopath, one who arbitrarily demands a murder be committed as proof of love for her. Her mother and stepfather appear as spectral images in the book, unconnected to her, and so emotional abandonment may account for her behavior. But clearly this is not the whole story, and as a character, Senta remains the novel's central, unsolved mystery.

In the real world, particularly if murder is involved, whether the suspect or victim was really sexually abused by a relative or authority figure or spiritual advisor, or was only fantasizing, is going to matter a great deal. In recent years, courts have had to rule on cases that rest on recovered memories, and conflicting expert witnesses have complicated the processes by which they have had to arrive at rulings. Rendell does not, however, write courtroom dramas—at least she has not so far, although in *Anna's Book*, there is the recounting of a trial that has taken place before the main action of the novel. Again, in real time, when the alleged abuser faces prosecution, the reality of the accusation is very important. When Sara accuses Rodney Williams of incest and flings this accusation at the mother she loathes, she may be acting out an Electra-like thwarted attachment to her father, but she also knows she is lying.

A lot of ink has been spilled about why Freud rejected the seduction theory in favor of the Oedipus complex. In recent years, the primacy of this developmental pattern has been challenged. Mother-daughter novels have been written to join traditional father-son fiction (*The Crocodile Bird* is Rendell's brilliant contribution to this body of writing). And politically correct psychoanalytic writers have tried to describe the Oedipus complex in gender-neutral terms: the *child's* erotic attachment to the *opposite sex parent* results in rivalry with the *same sex parent*. But since even this latter phenomenon is tied to Freud's paradigm, its weaknesses continue to draw attention. Freud himself described the two-fold difficulty faced by girls as they matured, for they faced two instances (their brothers only one) in which they had to shift their main affections from one person to another: first from mother to father; then from father to husband.

Since for both boy and girl child the first pleasurable bond is usually with the mother or some other female caregiver (today the number of househusbands as primary caregivers is growing and will inevitably change the face of psychology), why the girl child develops a primary attachment to her father requires explanation. The reason becomes especially problematic because her male parent will ordinarily spend most of his daughter's waking time outside the house to earn the family's living. In *An Unkindness of Ravens,* the conventional pattern of daily life in which the man works and his wife stays home explains how Rodney Williams is able to hide his bigamy for so long. How either Veronica or Sara could even theoretically become a daddy's girl becomes particularly mystifying. In his essay on "Femininity," again, an essay that is reflected in Rendell's fiction, Freud attempts an account of why the female child transfers her love from her mother to her father, and subsequently to her husband.

Most of Freud's critics concur that it is here that Freud falters, and not only because his explanation results in one of his most criticized theories, one perhaps most susceptible to parody, that women turn away from their mothers because their female parent lacks a penis. For the daughter comes to understand that she too lacks this sign of male status and power and comes to resent her anatomical connection with her mother. In any event, female psychological development is often cited as a weak point in Freud's theories, even by many of his followers. The psychologist had admitted himself that women had remained a puzzle for him, because he never could answer the question of what it was they really wanted. And perhaps his basic approach to the female Oedipus complex—that women who remained fixated on their fathers were not really in such great trouble since they need only transfer their affection from father to the husband who would perpetuate the father's authority—prevented him from pursuing the subject. Electra's obsessions would not have worried Freud so long as Euripides' solution prevailed. His Electra, unhappily married to a farmer, finds at the end of his play a more suitable husband, her brother's friend (only one step removed from a father-surrogate).

But Freud—significantly—did not interest himself in the *Oresteia*. His only written comment on the murder of Clytemnestra in *Moses and Monotheism* has to do with his view of its intrinsic symbolism, the defeat of a feminine and hence irrational principle by patriarchy and hence reason. That Jung, Freud's favorite disciple, might be regressing to embrace this feminine principle as the supposed source of a more profound wisdom than reason yielded, was for Freud a cause for increasing dismay. His concern was added to the other disagreements that were dividing the two. There has been a great deal written about the Freud-Jung relationship, about how Freud hoped that the younger Jung would ensure the survival of psychoanalysis beyond Freud's lifetime. Their collaboration lasted only six years, because Jung was ready to spurn the psychoanalytic throne if it meant concurring with Freud in areas he, Jung, disagreed with. Theirs was indeed an Oedipal struggle, the father unwilling to yield to the son his say on the theoretical differences between them, the son frustrated by the father's unwillingness to grant him autonomy.

The letters exchanged between Freud and Jung in 1912 involve different but related areas of discourse. There are personal remonstrations about the frequency of letter writing, as well as protestations of allegiance and charges of withdrawal of affection. Freud accuses Jung of neglecting the Psychoanalytic Association's journal and of a failure to move forward in planning another Congress. Jung responds rather testily about "drowning in platitudinous case material" and about his preference for working on book-length projects rather than short essays.

Perhaps it was to goad his "father" as Jung's relationship with Freud drifted into troubled waters, or perhaps it was only because he, Jung, was already moving toward the esoteric studies and spiritualism that has to this day weakened his reputation, but in their troubled last days of collaboration, Jung proclaims his commitment to a symbolic matriarchy. In response to Freud's charge that Jung is sojourning in a "religious-libidinal cloud," Jung responds that to the contrary, he is conducting his own inquiries into mother-incest, which requires a descent "to the realm of the Mothers." The Great Mother is among his archetypes. In any event, these exchanges took place in 1912, when Fordham University in New York invited Freud to give a series of lectures. Freud was at that time too ill to travel to the United States and Jung went in his place—again, ostensibly to explain Freud's theories to Americans. His sixth lecture was on the Oedipus complex, and in claiming to elucidate Freud's theories, Jung reveals how much he differed with some of Freud's most essential ideas. It is also in this lecture that Jung introduces his idea of an Electra complex.

From the outset, Jung refers his audience to his own work rather than Freud's for understanding ideas that could not be fit into the allotted time of the lecture. He also distances himself from Freud in such phrases as "according to him," signaling his own reservations about how Freud deals with the problem of incest. For what is perhaps most important in this lecture, Jung challenges Freud's ideas about infant sexuality, rejecting Freud's claim that the young boy's earliest bond to his mother is erotic. As an apostate, Jung would have thus revealed the most sensitive area of his defection. Finally, Jung opens the door to Freud's weakness in applying the Oedipus complex to the development of the female child. Jung admits that with regard to childhood fantasy, it is not surprising that girls experience the Oedipus complex too. But he adds that "regardless of sex," the "first love of a child . . . belongs to its mother." While not explicitly asking how it is that the attachment to her father comes about, Jung notes that an early (but not infantile) "budding eroticism" acquires strength as the years go by, leading to the classical Oedipus complex. He goes on, the "conflict takes on a more masculine and therefore more typical form in a son, whereas a daughter develops a specific liking for the father, with a correspondingly jealous attitude toward the mother. We could call this the Electra complex. As everyone knows, Electra took vengeance on her mother Clytemnestra for murdering her husband Agamemnon and thus robbing her—Electra—of her beloved father."

There is something uncertain about this formulation, as if Jung himself had not completely thought through the relation of the Electra to the Oedipus complex. He certainly does not ask how Agamemnon, absent as was customary from the household in which Electra grew up, and ready, in any event, to sacrifice another daughter so that a war might be fought, became Electra's beloved father. But the father-daughter relationship is not Jung's main concern. To the contrary, what he argues for is a general need to broaden the range of intra-familial conflict beyond the triadic paradigm that so crucially informs the Oedipus complex. Therefore, to juxtapose the Electra complex against the Oedipus complex, Jung against Freud, is not just to add an independent mother-daughter-father construct to the more familiar mother-son-father relationship. Rather, Jung insists that all family relationships create the tensions and conflicts that would significantly impact on an individual's life.

From anthropology, Jung borrows a term that defines the psychological task that confronts every person: exogamy. What Jung sees as the struggle of youth is to separate from the family into which the young person is born in order to start a new family. What this means is to become free of the conflicts that involve both parents and also siblings. "We all start life as helpless children," proclaims Jung. "We all have to emancipate ourselves from parents and other adults and face life and its challenges independently."

For Jung, therefore, incest and Freud's Oedipal drama were not to be understood as literally as Freud was supposed to have understood them. Rarely would a boy want to sleep with his mother or a girl with her father, and even the fantasies of doing so had to be understood as symbolizing psychological needs rather than sexual desire. To extrapolate from Jung's writing, the real problem then was psychological incest, the inability to separate from the parent, particularly acute in the case of a boy because he had to distance himself more radically than his sister had to from his originally nurturing mother. His sister would not face the same kind of rupture unless marriage involved a complete separation from her family— emotional or spatial—in order that she live among her husband's people. Ordinarily, however, the daughter's tie to her mother could be sustained without necessarily damaging the newly married couple. Rendell's *The Best Man to Die* describes an upcoming wedding and an easy and warm familiarity between mother and daughter, one not threatened by the impending marriage, which never takes place because the groom is murdered.

That the father-daughter relationship is unique and requires a paradigm other than the Oedipus complex is an idea Freud never accepted. It could not be said that Jung fared better, because he is rarely credited with the Electra complex, even though his theories would find favor among many feminists. His very formulation of an Electra complex gives women psychological status and argues for the need to consider the uniqueness of female development. Moreover, his interest in the archetype of the Great Mother allies him with those who claim that the world was originally organized according to matriarchal principles and that history can be written according to how and why patriarchy succeeded in replacing the Great Mother. Again, Freud agreed that the *Oresteia* traces such an historical development, but he approved of the substitution of patriarchy for a reigning feminine principle, which, again, he understood as emblematic of the triumph of reason over irrationality.

Most theories of the father-daughter bond will ultimately be traced back to the role of women in society, the father in one way or another coming to stand for the autonomy and achievement to a greater or lesser extent denied his daughter. Freud's idea of penis envy in his essay on "Femininity" seems less startling if understood not literally but as symbolic of a young girl's growing sense of inferiority and helplessness. This is a theme in *An Unkindness of Ravens,* but more about that in Chapter 9. When reading the ancient Electra plays, it is difficult not to recognize an inherent connection between Electra's helplessness to avenge her father's murder until Orestes returns from abroad and her obsessive attachment to her father to begin with.

It was not until 1920, eight years after Jung's lecture on the Oedipus complex that Freud responded directly in print to the idea of a complementary Electra complex. In "A Case of Homosexuality in a Woman," Freud relates that the early development of the girl in question had been uneventful and that she had passed through the early stages of the "female Oedipus complex." In a footnote, not his text, he writes that he sees no advantage to the use of the term Electra complex, dismissing it not as wrong so much as unnecessary. Eleven years later, in his 1931 essay on "Female Sexuality," Freud moved the idea of an Electra complex from note to text, but only to reject it once again. His argument is rather startling, claiming as he does that the intensity of the feelings of erotic attachment to the opposite-sex parent and rivalry with the same-sex parent apply "with complete strictness to the male child only." He continues, "It is only in the male child that we find the fateful combination of love for the one parent and simultaneous hatred for the other as a rival." Clearly the Electra story was no part of his theoretical formulations and had made little, if any, impact on his imagination.

Freud nonetheless seemed unable to shake off the impulse to respond to Jung's challenge. In 1938, in his *Outline of Psycho-Analysis*, Freud admits in effect that the Electra complex could supply a short-hand description of the father-daughter relationship. But, he concludes, this would be a minor gain, hardly necessary for either theoretical or practical reasons. "It does little harm to a woman if she remains in her feminine Oedipus attitude," writes Freud, adding that "the term 'Electra complex' has been proposed for it." That he once again fails to acknowledge Jung by name has led many of his followers and critics to misattribute the idea of an Electra complex to Freud himself. He, however, had insisted that the Oedipus complex was sufficient for analyzing women. Moreover, if a woman remained stuck in the Oedipus complex, it would merely be required that she "in that case choose her husband for his paternal characteristics and be ready to recognize his authority." Jung, however, may in effect have forced Freud to think about the House of Atreus. It was in the same year that his defense of the matricide, his symbolic reading of Clytemnestra's murder, appeared.

Almost twenty-five years after his break with Freud, Jung summarized his position with regard to the Oedipus complex and what he took to be its weaknesses, its narrow range for explaining instinctual behavior, and its limitations concerning which family relations affect psychological development.

> If the Oedipus complex represents a universal type of instinctive behavior independent of time, place, and individual conditioning, it follows inevitably that it cannot be the only one. Although the incest complex is undoubtedly one of the most fundamental and best-known complexes, it must obviously have its feminine counterpart that will express itself in corresponding forms. (At [one] time I proposed calling it the Electra complex.) But incest, after all, is not the only complication in human life, though this sometimes seems to be the case according to Freudian psychology. There are also other typical patterns [that] regulate the relation of father to son, mother to daughter, parents to children, brothers and sisters to each other, and so on.

In her fiction, Ruth Rendell frequently makes reference to the Oedipus complex and in two books she quotes Freud's view, expressed in the essay on "Femininity," that the most perfect parent-child relationship is that of mother and son (only to demonstrate how far from perfect it is). She does not, however, specifically name the Electra complex, even though her novels implicitly argue for the importance of a theory that is unique to female psychological development, and even though the Clytemnestra-Electra conflict is re-enacted over and over in the pages of her books. Where Ruth Rendell best exemplifies Jungian principles is in the fact that her books explore every possible combination of intra-familial stress that drives people to criminal acts or allows them to be victimized by criminals: mother and son, father and son, mother and daughter, father and daughter, sister and sister, brother and brother, and brother and sister.

It is not the argument of this study that Rendell is a Jungian, although it is clear that she knows Jung's work and how his theories differ from Freud's. Her novels, when understood as a working through of every different family combination, can nonetheless serve to illustrate the validity of Jung's conviction that it is necessary to expand beyond the range of the Oedipus story to reach an understanding of family tensions from which individuals must free themselves. To repeat a point already stressed, the Oedipus complex diminishes the importance of family relationships outside the triad of mother-son-father, excluding the Electra complex as theoretically redundant and minimizing the conflicts experienced by women in their development. In contrast, Jung used the Electra complex to argue for a more inclusive theory, one extending to all members of a family. Ruth Rendell's fiction demonstrates how valid this extension is.

CHAPTER 4

SELECTED ANCIENT MOTIFS IN
RUTH RENDELL'S FICTION

By examining four narrative motifs that Ruth Rendell's fiction and ancient Greek literature have in common, this chapter will strengthen the argument that in the classics, Rendell found models for the characters, incidents, and themes that inform her own work. Here, however, a qualification about literary influence may be called for. The classics exerted an influence on centuries of writers. Rendell, an avid reader, was familiar not only with this fountain of literary inspiration, but also with the many writers who drank from it. It might be the case, for instance, that a seeming borrowing from Aeschylus's *Oresteia* was actually influenced by another work, perhaps Eugene O'Neill's *Mourning Becomes Electra,* which draws on both the Oedipus and the Electra complexes. But even if it were possible to trace the sequence of Rendell's reading, the result would thwart any coherent study of her work. The ancient literary works will therefore be my consistent point of reference in this and following chapters.

Four narrative motifs will be discussed in this chapter. The first is the adulterous relationship between Clytemnestra and Aegisthus as a motive for killing Agamemnon. Countless mysteries can claim membership in any group defined by this theme, but Rendell's variations are often highly original. The second theme involves the sacrifice of Iphigenia as a paradigm for the conflicting demands of child and parent. Such conflicts are found throughout Rendell's fiction, particularly striking when a parent is almost indifferently ready to sacrifice a child to his or her own pleasures. Third will be the echoes in Rendell's fiction of the mistakenly reported death of Orestes, who uses this ruse to catch his mother and stepfather off guard so that he can kill them. The frequency with which missing characters in a Rendell book are thought to be dead but prove alive will become obvious. Finally, the fourth theme will focus on what one classicist, who has analyzed the cannibalistic feasts of Tantalus and Atreus, has with ironic understatement called "inappropriate eating." Eating disorders and unpleasant dining experiences are staples in Rendell's novels. The gruesome massacre at a family dinner early in *Kissing the Gunner's Daughter* virtually duplicates Agamemnon's description in Book Eleven of *The Odyssey* of how Clytemnestra and Aegisthus disarmed him with a welcoming home dinner and proceeded to murder him and his followers at the table.

Adultery and homicide, committed out of lust and greed, constitute the plot of so many stories as to be cliched. Clytemnestra insists that her relationship with Aegisthus was not the reason she killed her husband, but rather that Agamemnon died as her revenge for his sacrificing Iphigenia. She argues that she lost her daughter not for the good of their people but rather because of Helen and also because of Agamemnon's need to find glory as a warrior. Agamemnon had, moreover, brought a concubine, Cassandra, back from the Trojan War. Why was his adultery acceptable? But Electra is deaf to what she interprets as her mother's mere excuses, and in her defense of her father, Clytemnestra's acts are reduced to the simple terms of sex and power.

For the most part, Rendell avoids adultery and greed, either separately or in combination, as the basis for the plots of her novels. *In Sickness and in Health,* one of her earliest books, is constructed around a mistaken presumption of marital infidelity, and who is or is not sleeping with whom proves to be the basis of the mystery. Not that there is any shortage of adulterous spouses in Rendell's fiction, but it is rare for infidelity to be the plot's focus. Even in *The Secret House of Death,* in which adultery and the pain it causes the deceived spouse are central to the story, it is the tedium of marriage between mismatched people that seems the more compelling theme. Rendell has, moreover, supplied an interesting twist to the commonplace situation: the spouses whose supposed infidelity appears to be the motive for murder prove to have been faithful. The actually adulterous pair is not revealed until the novel's end.

An even more original treatment of adultery appears in *The Brimstone Wedding.* In this novel, a young healthcare worker, Genevieve, is in love with a married man. She cares for an older woman, Stella, dying of cancer. As the two become close, Genevieve gradually learns about Stella's past and the adulterous relationship that resulted in the death of her lover's wife. But Stella's history actually serves as a cautionary tale, and Genevieve comes to view her own love affair in a different light. Although Stella's spun out narrative lends the book most of its suspense, it is the developing closeness between the older and younger woman and not the adulteries themselves that inform the novel's themes. Theirs is an idealized if pseudo-mother-daughter relationship at odds with the usual destructive pairing found in Rendell's fiction. Genevieve actually has a caring mother, but it would be difficult for even the closest of mothers and daughters to share the complexities and intimate details of their sexual history.

This point is made explicit in *The Chimney Sweeper's Boy,* in which Ursula contemplates the possibility that if her daughters understood how she had been sexually cheated in her marriage, she might win some sympathy or at least understanding from them, but she cannot join that minority of women she knows who are willing to share such details with their daughters. In *The Brimstone Wedding,* it is Genevieve who seeks a more understanding confidant than she can find in her mother. In these novels, Rendell has not only avoided all the commonplaces that ordinarily attach themselves to the subjects of adultery and death, but also has added an additional dimension to her treatment of mothers and daughters (see Chapter 10).

It is in Rendell's short stories rather than in her novels that adultery supplies her plot. But even in the short fiction, what will impress itself on Rendell's readers is not so much her treatment of extramarital sex and how it can lead to murder, but rather her depiction of marriage itself. Few authors have captured the potential dreariness of wedded life as Rendell has. She paints with ruthless detail the ennui and mundane concerns that eat away at dreams of happiness; the unfortunate choices people make when they unwisely marry and feel constrained to live with their decisions; the mutual loathing that sometimes replaces whatever attraction caused two people to marry in the first place; the obsessive emotions of deserted spouses who cannot get beyond feelings of outrage and abandonment; and the bewilderment of children who can hardly understand what is happening around them as adult relationships unravel.

Rendell's fiction portrays the potential bleakness faced by most married pairs once the wedding is over. This is a literary motif that did not really enter literature until the romantic age, whose writings Rendell so often draws on. Wordsworth's idea of the "light of common day," which replaces in adult life the "celestial gleam" that surrounds every newborn ("Ode: Intimations of Immortality") virtually defines her treatment of most marriages. Her depiction of married life may be epitomized in *A Guilty Thing Surprised*. Wexford dismisses as a likely suspect in a murder a young man who had hoped the slain woman would sponsor his career as a pop musician. Wexford overhears Sean practicing his songs, immersed in a fantasy that would never be realized, and thinks of how he would continue to play-act until, one day, "some girl caught him and showed him how daydreams die." Throughout the series, Wexford remains devoted to his wife Dora, domestic life providing him with a refuge from the sordidness of his work, which brings him into constant contact with the cruelty family members so often visit upon each other. Still, in the early books in the series, Wexford too exercises fantasies of relations with young women he encounters. He is only too aware that his youth is behind him and that he is seeking respite from the daily routines of everyday life.

In modern fiction, the light of common day, rather than the grand dynastic ambitions that motivated ancient Greeks, will frequently lead to adultery and murder. In Rendell's short story, "People Don't Do Such Things," the first-person narrator whose wife proves unfaithful is a self-proclaimed conventional man, one who still experiences shame at memories of occasional pre-marital sex. He is probably too self-effacing when he says his marital life is a cliché, for people whose lives are true clichés are unlikely to recognize them as such. The story reveals some of the complexities of first-person narrations: Rendell has limited her point of view to that of a husband who is aware of his own boredom but fails to appreciate it as the source of his wife's infidelity. The story's surprise involves the cunning that can emerge when a slow, but not stupid, husband realizes he is being deceived.

The mundane routines that wear away at whatever romance initially drew two people together until the two live as virtual strangers, pale, however, in comparison with the mutual hatred portrayed in "The Fall of a Coin." When enmity leads to a divorce, it seems to take its natural course, but when a couple who should separate continue to cohabit, their hostility to each other can turn particularly ugly. Here, the wife is sexually frigid, a common enough excuse for a husband's philandering, but she is infuriated by his increasing unwillingness to balance her coldness with what she perceives as compensatory qualities brought to the marriage. The story's narrative point of view shifts between the two embittered parties until one of them begins to plot a murder.

A child who witnesses a dissolving marriage and an adulterous relationship will be immersed in another kind of mystery, often trying with little success to make sense of what is happening. In "The Orchard Walls," a fourteen-year-old girl is sent away from her family to a remote English countryside, as so many children were during World War II to keep them safe from the regular bombing of the cities. Her separation from her family and fears generated by the war would be trauma enough for a youngster. The disturbed family into which she is thrust, however, only intensifies her ordeal. Here, the first-person narration is Rendell's best choice, for it is the girl's innocence and confusion that create suspense. She knows something about adultery, that it is for example condemned in the Bible. But in her mind, it remains an enchanted subject, one attached to the romantic legend of Lancelot and Guinevere. She does not recognize that the legend obscures for her the commonplace situation she witnesses, which only deviates from the usual path because a murder takes place. Her innocence leads to her being implicated in the final catastrophe, and the guilt that pursues her into adult life can be read as the general damage done to all young children caught in events they scarcely comprehend. This vulnerability is even more pronounced in the story, "Mother's Help," where a little boy is used by his father to wield the murder weapon that kills his mother and makes way for his nanny to become his stepmother.

A particularly symbolic treatment of adultery and murder can be found in "Weeds." A couple whose private garden supplies visitors with a virtual tourist site charges admission for the privilege of viewing it. The husband obsessively tends his plants, challenging visitors to discover a weed among them. From the description of this neighborhood paradise as well as glimpses of the gardener's unhappy wife, it is possible to read the meticulously tended floral plots as domestic banality. The garden's neatness is described as "almost oppressive," some of the flowers appearing "as if they had been washed and ironed." Other blooms seem unreal, as if formed of wax. The weeds signify adultery and the disruption of the couple's domestic life, and the extra-marital love-making takes place not in a garden bower, but outside the confining walls, near the barnyard and sty. Rendell seems to have drawn on a vast literature—from Genesis to Spenser—in which true and false gardens abound. As if to emphasize this excursion into allegory, Rendell's narrator, a mere witness to the events leading to murder, is en route to a town called Diss when the garden visit takes place. There is a real town named Diss in England, and if it is the one Rendell had in mind, it is a place whose history involves a mixture of pastoral tranquility with barbaric pastimes, such as bear baiting. But the name also suggests the negative prefix found in such words as *discord*.

It is particularly interesting to recognize how Rendell effectively acknowledges the commonplace nature of adultery as a motive for murder that occurs in crime fiction. In "People Don't Do Such Things," the obtuse narrator and deceived husband proves surprisingly adept when plotting his revenge. What has led to his ingenuity is his extensive reading of mysteries. In another example from Rendell's short fiction, "Hare's House," a marriage begins to disintegrate when a couple given to reading mysteries take up residence in what appears to be a haunted house, once the scene of a murder. And although it is not adultery but growing mutual hostility that leads to attempted homicide, the story supplies another example of how crime fiction itself is thematically linked to a deteriorating marriage. The couple had given up reading mysteries when they bought the house, but now, a real mystery has virtually taken over their lives. Some literary critics might refer to these stories as self-referential, meaning that Rendell's story is not only about homicide but also about homicide as a literary subject.

Intrinsic to marital fidelity is the idea of sacrifice, for a faithful spouse must stifle sexual impulse aroused by another and relinquish transitory sexual satisfaction for the sake of the marriage (Wexford does this throughout the early

Kingsmarkham books with acute self-awareness that he is giving up immediate gratification for a longer-term good). Clytemnestra, who will not surrender either lust or ambition for the sake of her family, ironically invokes the subject of sacrifice as a defense of her adultery and subsequent murder of Agamemnon. Besides reproaching him for sacrificing Iphigenia, she projects onto him her own character weakness, accusing him of failing to surrender selfish goals and personal pleasures for the good of his family or even his people. *The Iliad,* it may be remembered, begins with the Trojan War coming to a halt as Agamemnon quarrels with Achilles over which of them would possess a slave girl. After the war, Agamemnon brings home the pathetic Cassandra as his unwilling concubine. But in *The Odyssey* Agamemnon portrays himself exclusively as the victim of Clytemnestra and Aegisthus. In Homer's epic, the ambiguity present in the tragedies is absent.

Traditionally, sacrifice involves the ritual slaughter of a living being, human or animal, for the purpose of honoring a deity or that deity's earthly surrogate. The ceremony is intended to appease the god, to deflect wrath and injury, or to ensure the preservation of something valued. Obeying the instructions imparted by the oracle, Agamemnon sacrifices his daughter Iphigenia to Artemis in exchange for the winds that would allow Greek ships to sail to Troy. Sacrifice always involves a substitution: one thing is destroyed or exchanged for the sake of something else that has or at least seems to have a higher claim. Agamemnon appears to have no choice in the face of a divine command, but in Euripides' play *Iphigenia in Aulis,* the reasons for his complying with divine edict are called into question. The catastrophe that can attach to a sacrifice is particularly obvious in Rendell's short story, "Fair Exchange."

In it, a young girl's life is sacrificed for her grandmother's, a woman so beloved by her husband that his devotion to her is unbounded. Frances, the wife of Tom Dorchester, is dying of cancer, and even the newest treatments do not seem to slow down the disease's inexorable progress. A desperate Tom locates a woman who is reputed to effect miraculous cures. She is described in such a way as to suggest a witch or powerful ancient deity, dressed so that she seems hardly to belong to this world, much less to the mundane place in which the story is set. Her name, Davina Tarsis, is anything but Anglo-Saxon and even evokes an image of Greece, as does the design on her tunic of a blazing orange sun. In Greek mythology, Artemis, to whom Iphegenia was sacrificed, was the twin of Apollo, who was the Sun God. Ancient myth, however, is not Rendell's only allusion. Her use of the word *weird* to describe Davina Tarsis evokes an image of the witches in *Macbeth,* the weird sisters, and is a reminder that in Old English, *weird* means fate. The entire story hinges on the ambiguous interplay of ancient beliefs and modern science, in this case medicine, with the additional interplay of fate with mere happenstance.

As Frances appears to get worse, Davina Tarsis asks Tom what sacrifice he would be willing to make for his wife, really asking whose life he would give for Frances's life. Tom, for his part, has come to think that this strange woman is a charlatan, and sees no danger in seeming to go along with Davina's suggestion that he exchange the life of his nine-year-old granddaughter Emma for Frances's. No wonder that when Emma accidentally dies and Frances recovers, Tom blames himself for his granddaughter's death. But it turns out that Davina has her own personal animus toward Emma, for the child had once been rude to her. Just as an implacable Artemis demanded the sacrifice of Iphigenia as retaliation for an injury done to her by Agamemnon, his killing one of her sacred animals during a hunt, so Davina is exacting vengeance. Moreover, the sacrifice of a child for a woman desired beyond reason suggests the exchange of Iphigenia for Helen. That the story is told from the narrative point of view of someone named Penelope only makes stronger the thematic connections between this story and the Trojan War.

The Trojan War supplies a thematic backdrop in Rendell's novel *Gallowglass*, where the sacrifice theme is subtly but fully developed. Here, Rendell leaves no doubt about her literary influences. A "Gallowglass" was an ancient Celtic mercenary or retainer whose duty, if necessary, was to sacrifice his life to protect his chieftain. Two characters in the book can be understood to be Gallowglasses, and it is the intersection of their lives that brings together various instances of substitution and renunciation—sacrifices of many sorts as well as the accompanying doubts and anguish that come along with them.

Gallowglass takes place during a time in which Italy was experiencing a rash of kidnappings. Wealthy people were seized and ransomed for enormous sums. Nina Abbott was (before the main story begins) a beautiful, famous model, who married a much older Italian prince and scion of a perfume empire. When kidnappers seized Nina, one of them, Sandor, fell in love with her. He thought she was his Helen of Troy. That she was a princess (even if only by marriage) only intensified the fantasy with which he surrounded her. During her capture, the terrified Nina tried to placate Sandor and thereby stay alive by becoming his lover. She also made him some promises revealed only at the end of the book to explain the course on which Sandor later embarked after Nina was returned to her husband. Meanwhile, sacrifice is piled on sacrifice. Sandor, having believed that Nina returned his love, had given up his share of the ransom money, a symbolic gesture that for him romanticized their sexual affair and, perhaps more important, that allowed him to retain his illusions. Nina's own sacrifice had been to surrender personal integrity in exchange for her life. Her surrender of principle will later exact a high price.

Released from captivity when *Gallowglass* begins, Nina had been twice widowed and had twice remarried. At the start of the novel, her third husband not only surrounds her with a bevy of servants but also turns them into bodyguards. Nina is terrified of being captured again, and she is distrustful of people, wondering how much or little money would make them betray her. One of the hired help is her driver, Paul, a former teacher whose wife left him, giving up custody of their seven-year old daughter Jessica in exchange for her own freedom from family ties. Paul and Nina fall in love and Nina begins to feel safe. But then Sandor arranges to have Jessica kidnapped, agreeing to return her in exchange for Nina. Paul must now decide whether he will sacrifice his daughter or Nina, much as Agamemnon had to decide between Iphigenia and—as the reason for the Trojan War—Helen.

One of Sandor's accomplices is Joe, a chronic depressive who is about to commit suicide when Sandor saves his life and takes him home. Joe, of course, has no idea that he is part of an elaborate plot to recapture Nina. In the course of the men's living together and passing time while waiting for their plot to hatch, Sandor tells Joe stories. One of these is the tale of the Trojan War. Sandor is described as having a "dreamy" look in his eye as he describes how Paris stole Helen, the most beautiful woman in the world, and in so doing, initiated a ten-year war. Sandor's fantasy, in which he is Paris and Nina is Helen, confuses and alarms Joe. But he intuits that when he has her, Sandor means to kill Nina. *Why* neither he nor, as yet, Rendell's readers understand.

After Jessica is kidnapped, her hair is cut off and is sent to Paul—to frighten him and to prove the kidnappers have his daughter. Although this was standard procedure during the Italian wave of kidnappings (the cutting off of John Paul Getty III's ear a particularly gruesome instance), there is a ritualistic element to the severing of Jessica's braids from her body. Joe's reaction to the scissors he uses, his beholding them with fear and awe, only intensifies the aura of a sacrificial ceremony. The role of hair in ritual and hair as a means of recognizing the person from whom it is cut are narrative elements in several ancient dramas about Agamemnon and his children.

Rendell emphasizes the pseudo-sacramental nature of cutting Jessica's hair by having the child relate to her captors an account of a more ordinary, mundane kidnapping. One of her classmates was forcibly removed by her father from her mother's house and taken to live in another country. The parents were involved in a domestic dispute over custody, and the mother had with great expense of effort and money gotten her daughter back. Divorce, however, almost always involves the sacrifice of children to one degree or another. This theme is implied in a Rendell short story, "Father's Day," in which a man is obsessed with the unfairness of modern British laws according to which custody is almost always given to a mother, so that a father loses not only wife and property, but also his children. Interestingly, the story is set in Greece and in a café named the *Agamemnon.*

Paul must choose between his daughter Jessica and not only his love for Nina but also his word, his earlier assurance that he would never betray Nina to potential kidnappers. His plight bears strong similarity to Agamemnon's in *Iphigenia in Aulis.* Of course, Helen was Agamemnon's sister-in-law (both his brother's wife and his wife's sister) and not just a woman he loved. Still, like Paul, Agamemnon must engage in the internal debate concerning how to choose between his child and some other commitment. Such an argument with himself would, of course, have to be dramatized. In Euripides' play, this dramatization engages the brothers Agamemnon and Menelaus in an argument over whether Iphigenia is to be in effect exchanged for Helen. At first, Agamemnon recoils from Artemis's demand that he sacrifice his daughter, and, in turn, Menelaus angrily reminds him that his reputation is at stake. Menelaus also invokes the loyalty owed a brother, and the preparations that have been made to set sail for Troy as well as the difficulties in calling off the troops. But then, moved by Agamemnon's grief, Menelaus changes his own mind.

But what has Helen
To do with this girl of yours? Disband
The host, I say, let it go from Aulis.

As to your share and mine in the oracle
Concerning your daughter's destiny, I
Want no part in it; my share I give to you.

In *Gallowglass,* Paul is both Agamemnon and Menelaus, their dialogue rendered as an internal monologue. He measures a father's duty against, not so much Nina herself, but his long-term chance for personal happiness with her. Here, once again, Rendell has created additional complexity to her story in her choice of names: in Spanish, Nina (niña) means little girl, and the resulting pairing of Jessica and Nina highlights the substitution motif. Neither Paul nor his lover had anticipated that kidnappers might find such an indirect way to get at Nina. Like Agamemnon, whose dialogue with his brother can be read as an argument with himself, Paul appears frozen by indecision. Eventually, like Menelaus, who was ready to sacrifice Helen and a chance to avenge the Trojan insult rather than see Iphigenia harmed, Paul chooses his daughter. But in order to do so, he unconsciously rationalizes his decision. Blaming Nina for his painful predicament, Paul finds his love for her diminished.

There are other narrative elements in *Gallowglass* that can be found in *Iphigenia in Aulis.* Agamemnon must lure his wife and daughter to Aulis, and he does so by deceiving them into believing that Iphigenia will marry Achilles there. Now he must tell Clytemnestra (in this play the aggrieved wife and mother she will claim to be in other tragedies less sympathetic to her) that it is a ritual sacrifice and not a wedding that will take place. Similarly, in *Gallowglass,* Paul cannot bring himself to tell Nina that Jessica has been taken and will only be returned in exchange for her. But Nina proves less passive than her tormented lover. It is she who firmly resolves to act, and in contrast to her, Paul appears contemptuously weak. The outcome of Nina's decision, however, is far more sad—tragic, if that word is used in a looser sense than the ancient Greeks would allow—than Rendell's readers are likely to hope. In many of her later books, of which *Gallowglass* is one, Rendell is more ready than she was earlier to withhold happy endings.

In any word match game intended to serve as a psychological Rorschach test, the word *sacrifice* is likely to be paired with the word *mother*. It is considered almost a feature of good mothering that a woman will surrender her own interests for that of her child. Conversely, a mother who pursues her interests at a cost to her child, as does Jessica's mother when she gives up custody of her daughter to live unencumbered by responsibilities, can be thought to have sacrificed her child. Comparing Rendell's fiction with ancient drama allows for a question the Greek playwrights were very aware of: how is it that Orestes and Electra, Orestes in particular, were allowed to live and possibly avenge the death of Agamemnon? In a family saga in which each generation retaliates for the atrocities of the previous one, it would seem strange that Aegisthus and Clytemnestra did not immediately rid themselves of Agamemnon's children. Neither Jocasta nor Laius recoiled from arranging the exposure and almost certain death of Oedipus, prophesied to slay his father. In the *Oresteia*, Clytemnestra claims credit for Orestes' safety, protesting a self-sacrificing mother's concern for her child.

Whatever the explanation, Orestes does survive and returns to Argos ready for the next stage of the family feud. His return after false rumors of his death supplies the Greek dramas with tension and suspense and makes possible the recognition scene that was a staple of ancient Greek tragedy. In Aeschylus, false news of Orestes' death proves a ruse used by him to get inside the palace and kill his mother. In all three Electra plays, Orestes must make himself known to his sister while remaining hidden from those he intends to kill. Electra's fears that he will never return or that he is indeed dead are resolved by a reversal in the fortunes of all the main characters, Clytemnestra and Aegisthus brought down, Orestes and Electra triumphant.

In each of the plays that treat Orestes' stealthy return to Argos, his strategies become central to the plot. In each, he counts on being thought dead. In Sophocles' *Electra,* Orestes explains how news of his death will further his plans to avenge his father, for his enemies will be disarmed by false rumors. He outlines his intentions to Paedagogus, the teacher who has returned with him from exile:

> Before now I have seen wise men often
> dying empty deaths as far as words reported them,
> and then, when they have come to their homes again,
> they have been honored more, even to the skies.
> So in my case I venture to predict
> That I who die according to this rumor
> Shall, like a blazing star, glare on my foes again.

These lines could be read as helpful advice to a mystery writer seeking an original twist to a frequently found plot element in mysteries. Missing, presumed dead, applies to so many characters in so many crime novels that not only the detective investigating a crime but also readers expect that the lost person has died. When the missing person proves, like Orestes, to be alive, the usual course of action has been altered. This is frequently a technique employed by Rendell, whose puzzle will often leave readers wondering *if*—rather than *when*—someone who has disappeared will turn up a corpse.

It is a narrative device that Rendell began to use early in her writing and still employs. In one of her first books, *In Sickness and in Health,* Alice Fielding, a wealthy woman, is newly married to Andrew, a man younger than herself who she can hardly believe loves her. Her friend and confidante, Nesta Drage, appears to be missing, and Alice sets out to find her. The search proves fruitless but information gathered in the course of it leads Alice to believe Nesta had become Andrew's lover and had been poisoned to ensure his new and wealthy wife never learns the truth. Because Alice herself feels unwell, she begins to fear she is Andrew's next victim, that she may be poisoned as well. The plot is unexceptional and what supplies this book with some enduring interest is that it foreshadows Rendell's brilliant portrayal of mounting terror in later writing. Alice undergoes her almost surreal experience when searching for Nesta, but after reaching an emotional breaking point, learns that Nesta is not dead at all but has only temporarily gone away to recover from some esoteric illness. No one has been murdered and—echoes of Daphne du Maurier's *Rebecca*—not only had Andrew not found Nesta desirable but rather had disliked her intensely. The book ends with all mysteries solved and the married couple likely to live happily ever after. Not much is being sacrificed here by revealing the book's ending. *In Sickness and In Health* displays its author's promise rather than fulfillment of that promise. In deference to Rendell readers who nonetheless treasure surprises, other examples below of the "missing, presumed dead" theme will be treated so as to preserve this particular mystery.

When Angela Hathall is murdered *In Shake Hands Forever,* Inspector Wexford is convinced her husband killed her despite Hathall's reputation for doting on his wife. In defiance of orders from a superior in the police department to desist from his investigations and to cease harassing the suspect, Wexford continues his sleuthing to the point of personal obsession. He even pays someone out of his own pocket to watch the wary and elusive Hathall. Meanwhile, another woman, Morag Grey, has disappeared. Her worried mother, rather than her ex-husband, instigates a search for her, which includes digging up ground where it is suspected she may be buried. Many characters enter the complicated story, and the novel's plot rests on who is actually dead and who might only be thought to be so—that is, who has been murdered and by whom, and who has not been murdered at all.

In another Wexford book, *Wolf to the Slaughter,* questions of missing persons are not spread over quite so many people, and the novel is consequently less tangled and perhaps more satisfactory. One Anita Margolis, also called Ann, a rich, beautiful, sexually promiscuous young woman goes missing. Her artist brother Rupert reports her disappearance to the police, less because he is worried than because he is inconvenienced when he loses her services as housekeeper. Wexford thinks there is reason to believe that someone named Geoff Smith has murdered her. Meanwhile, a gold cigarette lighter shows up under suspicious circumstances, inscribed "To Ann Who Lights My Life." But when the lighter is traced to the artisan who made it, it proves to be too old to have been crafted for Anita Margolis. Meanwhile, another Ann appears in the book, and Geoff Smith, when found, turns out to be an imposter. What makes this novel particularly interesting is not only the untangling of identities and the revelation that perverse sexual practices unite the otherwise seemingly unrelated characters, but also the conclusion in which the readers' assumptions concerning who the killer is and who has been killed prove incorrect.

Careful readers of Rendell books therefore learn not to reach hasty conclusions about missing characters. In *Simisola,* Wexford must learn a similar lesson, as the "missing, presumed dead" motif picks up additional significance. The Anglo-African Akandes are relative newcomers to Kingsmarkham. Dr. Akande is Wexford's personal physician and has replaced Dr. Crocker in the series. His wife Laurette had been a highly trained scientist in her native land, but in England she works at a far more pedestrian job. Kingsmarkham has changed, and racial diversity brings to the surface prejudices that the town had not formerly needed to confront. Wexford, too, must face his own latent racism, for when the Akandes report that their daughter Melanie is missing, and when, subsequently, the body of a young black woman is discovered, Wexford immediately jumps to the conclusion that the corpse is Melanie. Without investigating further, he prepares the Akandes for the ordeal of identifying their daughter's body at the morgue. And when the dead person proves not to be Melanie, Wexford must bear the Akandes' outrage and accusation that, had the body been that of a white woman, Wexford would not have so hastily jumped to his conclusions.

Matters of mistaken identity and the unmasking of imposters will frequently constitute compelling mysteries, especially when it remains unclear whether a missing person is dead. These plot motifs allow Rendell to do what she does best and perhaps wants to do most, explore the psychological reactions of her characters to the events around them. When a child goes missing, how its parents cope can prove more thematically significant than the absence itself. In *No More Dying Then,* a little boy disappears from the site where his mother could watch him from her window as he played with other children. His vanishing is particularly worrisome for the Kingsmarkham police, for they are still investigating the earlier mysterious disappearance of a child. Stella Rivers had been taken by her stepfather to a horseback riding lesson, expected to come back home on her own, but had never returned. Kingsmarkham fears the existence of a serial kidnapper and murderer. In this book, the missing person plot motif is explicitly linked to the sacrifice theme as Rendell introduces readers to one of the most chilling of the many horrific mothers to be found in her books. Stella's mother, Rosalind Swan, is so besotted with her new husband that she continuously fawns over and caresses him even while being interrogated by the police. So indifferent is she to the fate of her missing daughter that it is specifically said of her that she would *sacrifice* several children to her marriage. If Clytemnestra's union with Aegisthus were only what her daughter Electra believed it to be, then Rosalind Swan would be Clytemnestra.

In another Wexford novel, *Death Notes,* the internationally renowned flutist, Sir Manuel Camargue, is about to marry a woman considerably younger than his actual daughter, Natalie, from whom he has been alienated for many years. When the possibility for reconciliation comes about, he looks forward to a reunion with Natalie with the same joy that Electra experiences when Orestes comes home. But then things go wrong. When they meet, he decides that the woman who represents herself as Natalie is an imposter and he announces his intention of disinheriting her. Then, just before the wedding, Sir Manuel is murdered and Wexford is convinced that solving the crime is contingent on proving that the heiress is a fraud and that the real Natalie is dead. The novel is a variation on a situation popularized by *The Return of Martin Guerre* (although Rendell's specific reference is to the real case of the Tichbourne claimant, which influenced other writers as well). Identity theft is a problem with a long history. Much of Rendell's suspense in *Death Notes* hinges on whether or not Natalie is in fact who she says she is. What is particularly puzzling, however, is that she seems more amused than worried about the various tests she has to pass in order to establish identity. Eventually, a series of unexpected twists in the plot unmask more than one imposter.

Again, the "missing, presumed dead" theme is one that Ruth Rendell shares with countless crime novelists. As always, however, her readers are treated to unexpected developments in what would otherwise be a fairly conventional plot element. In a late Wexford book, *Babes in the Wood,* two adolescents and their babysitter disappear and foul play is suspected. As it turns out, only one of the three has been murdered and, in the meantime, the author has been allowed to develop her favorite theme, family pathology. As the parents respond to their fears and mutual blame, their already weak marriage further disintegrates in the face of their children's disappearance. Finally, in *The Monster in the Box,* in which two persons are missing and presumed dead, only one of them has been killed and not the one readers might expect to have been.

Today, a child's right to an emotionally secure home is deemed to be as much a child's birthright as the expectation of physical protection from danger. When not psychologically nurtured, children are easy to portray as their parents' sacrificial victims. At worse, they are left vulnerable to unspeakable dangers when, left inadequately guarded, they are abducted and hurt; or when they run away, joining the legions of missing persons who sometimes do turn up dead. And when they remain missing or are found dead, they can be thought of as not only sacrificed but as having been psychologically malnourished. No surprise, then, that food will prove to supply an important clue in *Babes in the Wood*, in which a gourmet food column is a plot element that becomes intertwined with a picture of children raised in an unhappy family. In *Portobello*, a petty criminal who seems more contemptible than evil is reluctantly given room and board by a relative who keeps him almost starved, and the lack of food is a sign of long-standing emotional deprivation. In the same book, a man with an addictive personality becomes so obsessed with buying, storing, and eating sugar-free candies that he comes close to wrecking chances for happiness in an impending marriage. This situation borders on the ludicrous, almost the parodic, but it does point up that, frequently, adults not only fail adequately to nourish their children but also destructively feed off each other.

In Book Eleven of *The Odyssey*, Odysseus descends to the underworld where he meets Agamemnon. His salutation to the dead hero as "Son of Atreus" prepares the way for Agamemnon's subsequent account of his murder. For in Odysseus's greeting is encapsulated the entire saga of Agamemnon's accursed family, beginning with the grisly feast at which Atreus butchered and cooked his nephews, serving them to their unknowing father, Thyestes, or even further back when Tantalus fed his own son to the gods. As if to emphasize these precursors to the family feud, Agamemnon recounts how he was murdered at a feast, this one prepared by Aegisthus with the help of Clytemnestra, a welcoming dinner at which not only Agamemnon but also all his followers were slaughtered: "You would have been sorry at heart for this scene, how we lay sprawled by the mixing bowl and the loaded tables, all over the palace, and the whole floor was steaming with blood." So, relates Agamemnon's ghost, were he and his men killed in the house of a man "rich and very powerful."

A similarly grisly sight greets the Kingsmarkham police in *Kissing the Gunner's Daughter*, when they answer the frantic call of Daisy, the only surviving member of the massacre in which her mother, her grandmother, and her step-grandfather were shot down as they gathered for the formal dinner they ate each evening. Daisy, although alive, is certain she is going to bleed to death. What greets Burden as he breaks into the locked house is comparable to what Agamemnon describes. A large table, set with glass and silver, is laden with food. The tablecloth is so stained with blood that the white damask seems to be dyed red, as if red were its intended color. On three plates are cold, congealed food, and Burden can barely stomach what blood had done to a bowl of pudding. For several pages, the ghastly feast and massacre are described in gory detail. For the rest of the book, the troubled relationships among the three murdered family members and the survivor, Daisy, will be explored. Not quite the House of Atreus, perhaps, but another of what Agamemnon describes to Odysseus—a rich and powerful family whose members are embroiled in unnatural relationships.

Burden had arrived at Daisy's home without Wexford because the inspector is detained by his own awful feast. His daughter Sheila is romantically involved with a Booker Prize finalist author, Augustine Casey, whose attitude toward her family is snidely patronizing. No one is killed at La Primavera, the Italian restaurant where the Wexfords have joined their daughter and her new lover, but the meal is as emotionally deadly for Wexford as the crime scene he will soon witness. Casey is either silent, as if bored with the provincial restaurant, or he pedantically shows off his erudition in an offensive manner. When he cannot get the mineral water he usually drinks, he orders brandy; he spits in his wine glass because he dislikes the wine; and after one mouthful, he disdains to eat the rest of their first course. And, finally, he has the effrontery to look down at Dora's pearls, worn for the occasion, as if they were as common and boring as everything else Sheila's family represents for him. By *Kissing the Gunner's Daughter,* Rendell had developed quite fully the characters in the Wexford family, to the point where their lives and interaction with each other often parallel the crime being investigated (see Chapter 9 for how Rendell alters the narrative patterns in the Kingsmarkham series). As Wexford's abhorrence of Casey alienates the doting father from Sheila, Wexford will seek a virtual substitute daughter in the young victim Daisy. But the horrible "feasts," at which Wexford and Daisy were present, will finally prove that what seem to be similar situations are anything but.

It is at a dinner party that a catastrophe leading to a murder occurs in *The House of Stairs.* Following the plot of Henry James's *The Wings of the Dove,* Bell and her lover Mark conspire to marry Mark to a rich older woman in order to gain her money for themselves. Food and gatherings at restaurants play frequent thematic roles in this book as the characters psychologically devour each other. In *Babes in the Wood,* another unpleasant dinner takes place in the Wexford house during Christmas. Sylvia's divorced husband, Neil, more referred to than present in earlier books, is nevertheless noticeably absent from the dinner table. Her sister Sheila is exhausted from giving birth to a second daughter, and Sylvia is obviously anxious. The bruise on her arm possesses an ominous significance that Wexford at first overlooks. Sylvia's new live-in lover is there and his horseplay with the Wexford grandchildren foreshadows his violence. On the whole, Wexford is disgruntled and even Dora is edgy. And, again, the scene inside the Wexford home parallels some of the action outside it. The young Sophie, implicated in a murder, is disgusted by a gourmet dinner she has read about. In her mind, the food is connected to her aversion to sex, but this does not stop her from using the meal described to fabricate an event that never took place. In so doing, she seriously misleads the police and impedes the progress of their investigation into a murder.

Most of Rendell's readers would certainly realize from personal experience that it is at family gatherings that intra-familial tensions are likely to erupt. This truth, however, does not fully account for the frequency with which eating disorders, dinners gone wrong, and human butchery are employed by Rendell as themes. In *Speaker of Mandarin*, Wexford and Dora visit China, and the inspector has difficulty with the unfamiliar eating habits of the Chinese. One of the tourists that comprise their group expresses an even stronger aversion, noting that the Chinese will eat anything that moves. "They'll eat mice if they can catch them." Tea being familiar to the English Wexford, he consumes it in great quantity even though it is not exactly like the beverage he is used to. Later, this variety of tea proves the source of his feeling seriously unwell and even hallucinating. In another book, one that is not part of the Wexford series, *Adam and Eve and Pinch Me*, a book that comes as close to farce as any that Rendell has written, one finds a "Jack Spratt" couple, Michelle and Matthew (the analogy to the nursery rhyme is mine, not Rendell's). He is a serious anorectic and the obese Michelle feeds him selected food of which he eats so sparingly that their meals are a virtual parody of the horrible feast.

Another Jack Spratt kind of pairing can be found in Rendell's novella *Heartstones*. Two sisters develop extreme but antithetical eating disorders after their mother dies. The story almost seems to illustrate the concept of inappropriate eating. Like many other mothers in Rendell's fiction, this one dies of cancer, which itself can be thought of as consuming the patient. Food, moreover, has come to play a significant role in her self-imposed treatment for the disease. Accepting the widely announced premise that certain diets place one at greater risk for the disease or, antithetically, are more conducive to cure than others, the patient rejects surgery and turns to naturopathy, a food plan restricted to raw vegetables. The narrator, one of the sisters, wryly expresses the view that the disease would scorn such food as an animal scorns a trap set with repellent bait. The patient does not live. Later, one of her daughters becomes seriously anorectic and has to be hospitalized. The other, who is younger and, as a result, experiences the loss of a mother all the more keenly, responds to the loss of nourishment ordinarily associated with the female parent by gorging herself on huge quantities of food. Her sister, who is no longer starving herself, wonders if there is an illness that is the opposite of anorexia, a sickness that is overtaking her sister. The story of these siblings will be returned to in Chapter 10, at which point it will be seen that the theme of food and inappropriate eating is woven through a story replete with references to Greek tragedy, and that the study of ancient literature is part of the sisters' education. The suspense in the novella reaches its climax with the question of whether one of the sisters, whose eating disorder is associated with her apparent descent into psychosis, intends to poison the other.

Poison supplies a common enough murder weapon in crime fiction as well as in ancient literature. In the face of slaying and dismembering the victim, however, it pales into insignificance as far as the human imagination is concerned. The butchery that characterizes Tantalus's feeding his son Pelops to the gods and Atreus's serving to Thyestes his own sons cooked in a stew, is played out almost literally in Rendell's *The Killing Doll*. Dolly is a very unhappy young woman who uses the dolls she makes in order to practice witchcraft—if to little success. Like Electra, she hates her [step]mother and wants her dead. Feeling powerless to act on her own, she incites her brother to kill their father's wife. This depiction of yet another of Rendell's unhappy families is paralleled by another story in the same book as Dolly is put on a collision course with a psychotic, out-of-work butcher.

When he is a young boy living in Northern Ireland, Diarmit Bawne witnesses his mother being killed by a bomb. An oblique reference to "he saw what happened to his mother" suggests that Diarmit's later mutilation of his murder victims is a re-enactment of that early experience. Among Diarmit's siblings, the most successful is a butcher in Belfast, who trains Diarmit in his profession. Later, his shop and an entire street are destroyed by a bomb, after which Diarmit, although physically unhurt, spends a year in a mental hospital. By the time he comes to London, he is both demented and dangerous, wandering through supermarkets looking for work. Ironically, it is in one of the recognizable trademarks of London, a green Harrod's bag (often containing purchases from its famous and elaborate food halls) that Diarmit carries about the city with the tools of his trade, long knives and a cleaver. By the time he murders a woman, a stranger to whom he has no connection, and dismembers her body, human beings and animals have no distinction for him.

In *The Killing Doll,* Ruth Rendell does what she is a master of, getting inside the minds of mentally deranged people like Diarmit, or of those, like Dolly, whose personalities are in the process of disintegrating. These interior portraits, when linked to murder, generate a horror that goes far beyond the feelings ordinarily aroused in readers by the thrillers that abound in the mystery genre. Rendell peels away layer after layer of madness and draws her readers into the psychology of killing that few authors since Dostoevsky or Poe have been able to depict. Rarely, though, are her books overtly political, although her social attitudes make themselves felt in her writing. But in *The Killing Doll,* the linking of murder and mutilation to the civil war and butchery in Ireland, as well as the emblem of London, England, as pictured in the Harrod's shopping bag, carry with them potentially strong political themes. War, Rendell may be implying, involves not only mutual butchery but also the sacrifice motif writ large.

This chapter has dealt with four inter-related themes that can be found in both Rendell and ancient literature: adultery and murder; the sacrifice of one person for the benefit of another; the uncertainty of whether someone presumed dead actually is; and the gruesome feast. What links these themes in Rendell's books is the prevalence in them of extremely disturbed families, another subject she shares with classical writers. The remaining chapters of this book (except the Conclusion) will be organized around the stories of Oedipus and Electra, each chapter emphasizing the impact of different family relationships on individuals—both killers and their victims.

CHAPTER 5

OEDIPUS AND THE SEARCH FOR IDENTITY

In *The Veiled One,* Jungian therapist Serge Olson describes the problems suspected murderer Clifford Sanders has had with his mother and asks Mike Burden—who had taken the case over from Wexford—if he had ever heard of the fallacy of the veiled one. A person is asked if he knows his mother. When he responds "yes," he is then asked if he can recognize someone who is veiled. When the answer is then "no," he is informed that his mother and the veiled one are the same. Fully knowing one's parents is a route to self-knowledge, affirms Olson, who goes on to invoke the words over the Oracle at Delphi: "Know thyself." He adds that it is an injunction few heed. The exchange between Olson and Burden involves the whole question of the self, one of the most complex subjects dealt with by Ruth Rendell in her fiction. For in exploring this subject, she reveals how being embroiled in family conflict strongly impinges on the development of that secure self-identity needed for psychological health.

Sophocles' *Oedipus the King* is about identity, about the identity of an unknown murderer, whose crime has brought a plague to Thebes, and about the identity of Oedipus himself. Raised by foster parents, Polybus and Merope, he learns from a drunken guest at a party that he is not their biological child. When they deny the truth, Oedipus is at first

81

reassured. But persistent rumors and his own uneasiness bring him to the Delphic Oracle, where he discovers he is fated to kill his father. Mistakenly trying to protect Polybus, he flees his home, only to encounter Laius, whom he takes to be a stranger and whom he slays. Trying to avoid his destiny, he runs into it. The most familiar episodes begin, therefore, with Oedipus's search for identity, and they reach their climax when Oedipus learns who his parents really are and, therefore, who he is. The Delphic Oracle had not promised that to "know thyself" would be a happy experience, and yet it appeared that it was a necessary one.

The extent to which selfhood is bound up with knowing one's parents—literally and symbolically—are ideas that inform several of Ruth Rendell's novels. In *The Master of the Moor*, Stephen Whalby is deserted by his mother when he is only six years old. He is raised by a seriously depressed father. To defend against feelings of abandonment and inferiority, Stephen not only fantasizes about his absent mother but also appropriates as his grandfather a well-known local author, Alfred Osborn Tace, to whom he has no biological ties. In Stephen's tortured mind, a connection to the writer, a local celebrity, confers upon him self-esteem that he cannot otherwise attain.

Stephen Whalby lives in a small community surrounded by a vast expanse known as the Vangmoor, where Tace had set his popular novels, his fiction televised in a series called *Bleakland*. For Stephen, however, the moor is anything but bleak. He writes a column for a local newspaper called "Voice of Vangmoor," describing its changing landscape, depicting its wild life, and generally creating anecdotes that constitute his musings on nature. In one column, he claims that Alfred Tace is his grandfather. In Stephen's invented scenario, when his grandmother worked as maid in the Tace home, she and the author had become lovers and from their union Stephen's mother was born. Stephen has effectively reversed Oedipus's story. Oedipus lived with people he mistakenly thought were his parents; Stephen lives with his real father and makes up an older male parental figure to whom he comes to believe he is related.

Stephen's fantasies began when his mother ran off with a truck driver. He consoled himself by imagining he was Prince of Vangmoor, a kingdom over which he had dominion. Later, aware that Tace is the most renowned person to come from the area, Stephen concocts the elaborate genealogy that links him to the author, whom he strongly resembles. A Tace biographer becomes fascinated at the prospect of interviewing this as yet undiscovered Tace grandson and thereby attaining new material concerning the author's life. With Stephen he reviews the chronology that was the basis for Stephen's fantasy, unwittingly supplying information Stephen does not know (just as Oedipus is confronted with unforeseen information about his foster and real parents). Tace had been on an American tour when Stephen's mother had supposedly been conceived and unless her mother, Stephen's grandmother, had accompanied the author, there is no way Stephen's construction of his antecedents could be true. The biographer does not say this to Stephen; he is too eager to find out what he can about this possibly unknown Tace grandchild and perhaps he himself had not fully worked out the time line. But Stephen understands only too well. In but a brief conversation with the Tace scholar, the reason for his "continued existence had collapsed." And by the time Stephen's self-created identity is destroyed, horrible events have turned him into a killer and have revealed some awful truths about the really significant male influence in his life, his father. (Stephen's disturbed relationship with his father will be discussed in Chapter 6.)

Stephen Whalby has good reason to wish he were someone else. The mother who had abandoned him came from a respectable but common family, and Stephen's more refined sensibility recoils at this hereditary connection. Then, at his grandmother's funeral, he meets the mother whom he has not seen for twenty-three years. She is not the slim, pretty young woman he remembers from an old photograph, but is rather an overweight, cheaply dressed woman, completely lacking in the refinement she might have possessed had she really been Tace's daughter. More important, she is completely indifferent to the son she had forsaken, expressing only the casual curiosity that could have been elicited by any person she remembered from her early life. In Ruth Rendell's rather extensive portrait gallery of awful mothers, Stephen Whalby's holds her own with the worst of them. Stephen, who effectively has twice lost his mother, who cannot get beyond the shadow of his father, and who has been deprived of the imagined identity he has created as a defense against his pain, begins to come undone (again, see Chapters 6 and 7 for more discussion of the Whalby family).

In *Grasshopper*, another young person, Clodagh Brown, must achieve some measure of self-awareness in order to develop at least that amicable relationship with her parents that would signal a true independence rather than a defiant distance from them. Clodagh's teenage rebellion against parental authority had led to the death of her young lover and to a profound alienation from her horrified and devastated mother and father. She comes gradually to self-knowledge by writing and rereading a diary in which she records the events in her life, although perhaps not all the feelings that accompany them. She had kept a diary ever since she had learned to write and, of course, most entries were made in the first person. But when she records the worst episode in that life, she does so as a short story, as if she were writing about another person. What becomes clear, however, is that, for Clodagh, the narrative she is writing in the first person, the book that is *Grasshopper*, the diary that supplies the memories she draws on, and the remote short story within the diary, become symbols of her attempt to know herself. At one point, she begins to refer to herself as "she" and quickly amends that to "I," musing on how "she" and "I" were the same person, not different ones. But her understanding of the simultaneous sameness and difference is not easily arrived at.

Clodagh's parents are benign, unexceptional people defined by their commonplace surname, *Brown* (Rendell frequently links an ordinary last name with an unusual first one, hence *Clodagh Brown*). Equally commonplace is their plight, driven to despair by a daughter they can neither understand nor control. It is possibly because of their conventional relationship to her that when *Grasshopper* opens, Clodagh has so little difficulty separating from them. Clodagh's self-identity is, however, not yet formed, and as she tells her story, she wonders at the difference between the person she was when she left her parents' home and the person she became after the incidents and relationships that will completely transform her life. With a more secure identity of her own, she forms a better relationship with her father and mother— perhaps never one of fully shared attitudes and values, but one in which she participates in pleasant family relationships. But before this reunion, Clodagh will have to experience tragedy, evil, and crime.

When Clodagh was a young girl, two conflicting experiences established the pattern of her early life. She learned to climb trees and discovered the pleasure of observing the world from a distance. Loving heights, she began at age twelve to climb pylons, thrilled not only by her ability to transcend the unexceptional, but also by the danger and power of the "grasshoppers" that supplied electricity to the surrounding area. After smoking became an expression of defiance, Clodagh began to light her cigarettes with the live wires. But another, contrasting, experience also had a profound impact on Clodagh. She had accompanied her father to an automatic car wash, of the sort that allows the driver and passengers to remain in the vehicle as it moves through a seeming tunnel, virtually attacked by the brushes and other devices that clean the automobile. Perhaps this journey was itself symbolic, and on some level, Clodagh recognized that the socialization that would turn her into her parents' good—that is, clean—girl could only be achieved by some attack upon her sense of self. In any event, she had been horribly frightened by the experience and had developed a form of claustrophobia in which it was not closets or small rooms that terrified her but, rather, underground spaces and tunnels.

Clodagh's youthful rebellion had included her boyfriend Daniel, and together they scooted around the countryside on his motorbike, making love in the fields. As she later describes it, she belonged to the generation affected by the changes that occurred in the 1960s and 70s. She realizes her parents should also have been influenced by those years, but from her point of view, the sexual revolution had passed them by. Consistent with Rendell's characteristic depiction of middle-class marriages, Clodagh has never seen them display any love for each other. As a result, they cannot provide her with a satisfactory model for a fulfilling life. Significantly, at the end of the book, Clodagh marries a man who has inherited a sizable fortune from his grandmother. The couple decides to give most of the money to the needy, but not all of it. The legacy is a paradigm for the break with, but also the continued attachment, real and emotional, to earlier generations. As Clodagh notes, they had "grown up." Becoming themselves, knowing themselves, involves the mature recognition and acceptance of what ties them to the past.

But long before this happens, a younger and more reckless Clodagh teaches Daniel to climb the pylons. Like her, he wants to light his cigarette with the electricity that surges through their wires. But in a horrible accident, Daniel is electrocuted, his death described in horrific detail as if he had been microwaved, cooked, so to speak, from the inside. Clodagh has a breakdown and undergoes psychotherapy for two years, after which she leaves her parents' home to go to London and, without motivation or enthusiasm, attend a course of study at a polytechnic college. Instead, in the main action of the novel, she falls in with a group of young people who prowl the rooftops of the city. Growing up for Clodagh is almost literally a matter of coming down to earth, which she does after another one of her climbing adventures involves her in another set of catastrophes, and after she confronts evil head on. Rereading her written account of her past, Clodagh can no longer explain even to herself what it was that lured her to London's roofs, nor what it was on them that she found so enjoyable.

As she records the events of her life, and as she describes the changes she goes through, Clodagh maintains a double perspective. As both narrator and character in her own narrative, she sustains for her readers the suspense engendered by her story and by the uncertainty concerning how she will and even *if she will* transform her life. The events of the past are described with the immediacy that accompany her transcribing them; at the same time, she is looking back and thereby assuring her readers that she has become in effect a different person from the reckless young woman courting danger. Perhaps Ruth Rendell took for her model one of her favorite authors, Charles Dickens, for the double perspective is one he employed when he allowed Pip to be his adult first-person narrator in *Great Expectations*. Like Rendell in writing *Grasshopper*, Dickens had to negotiate his way between portraying a young Pip whose actions sustain suspense, and an older Pip who, by virtue of having survived and morally matured, keeps readers comfortably certain that all would be well.

About midway through *Grasshopper*, Clodagh moves into an apartment inhabited by other young, disaffected people who will roof walk with her. Later she will become acutely aware that in her diary she has devoted ten pages to describing the flat and its inhabitants. For in rereading she realizes that only now is she really contemplating the "strange turns" her life had taken, the young lover who died, and the adults who had once thought her "wicked beyond redemption." Knowing herself, therefore, rests on Clodagh's being able to compare the self she has become from the young and distressed person who had—or so she then thought—been exiled from her family. The first word of the novel is

"They," a remote and detached reference to her parents, the effect being to distance them from Rendell's readers as well. "They" have sent her to college to be free of the daughter who has shamed them and who may be suffering from some essential moral flaw. Or "they" have sent her away so that she need not look at the pylons each time she leaves the house or looks out its windows. Even this is ambiguous. Are "they" protecting her from her own pain and remorse, following her therapist's advice, or do they recognize the continued attraction of the "grasshoppers"?

By the time Clodagh has lost interest in the pylons or any other heights, many years have passed, turning her into a happily married woman, a successfully self-employed electrician whose profession has transformed a former obsession into productive work, and a daughter her parents can be proud of. Her passages through time and change have been carefully recorded in her journal, and these supply the basis for her story. But while there are indications that she records feelings as well as events, her interior journey remains largely uncharted. For Clodagh seems to prefer maintaining the same emotional distance from herself that she once maintained from her parents, and from the very mundane world she climbed the pylons and rooftops to get away from. When early on, Clodagh muses on her belief that her parents truly view her as evil, there is sufficient vagueness in her contemplations to alert readers to the possibility that she is unable to free her identity from other peoples' views of her. She remains a not entirely solved mystery even to herself, one she may not wish fully to solve. She arrives at a significant point of self-awareness, that—again—where it comes to the most traumatic event in her life, she has written about herself in the third-person, as if having created a character in a story not about herself. Following this perceptual breakthrough, she can finally relate the girl who climbed the pylons to a more profound "I" than had been her point of reference in the process of diary keeping. For she now more fully knows who this "I" is.

Because Ruth Rendell is a master at getting inside a character's mind and representing for her readers the agonized twists and turns of psychological processes, her narrative method in *Grasshopper* has to be recognized as intrinsic to the themes she is working into her story. That Clodagh keeps a journal is reiterated throughout Rendell's novel. What she records are horrific events that this analysis of the novel will leave to the pleasure of Rendell's readers to discover. But if there are intimate self-revelations even in the secrecy of the diary, they are not shared. In the end, her ideal, imagined reader is the man she loves and marries. And so diary writing itself may come to an end. For just as Clodagh experienced a phobic response to tunnels and, in her early life, sought out heights, so she may have avoided a descent into the realms of the unconscious, into what one of Rendell's oft-quoted poets, Coleridge, called caverns measureless to man. For how deeply one should plumb their depths is a matter about which Clodagh remains skeptical. The psychotherapy she had received after Daniel's death had been intended to help her cope with the tragedy and to assume the daily tasks of living and preparing for her future. That she eventually comes to fully understand that the "she" and the "I" of her diary writing are one person perhaps brings her to an adequate end point of her psychological quest. For the psyche may be, like Coleridge's caverns, not only measureless, but bottomless, and it might swallow the person who endlessly plumbs its depths, destroying what Keats called the ties of humans each to each. Continuing self-analysis might work against what Clodagh has achieved—living with her feet planted firmly on level ground, secure in a loving relationship with another.

A few years before publishing *Grasshopper,* Ruth Rendell had in *No Night is Too Long* already taken up the relationship between recording one's life and self-discovery. Her protagonist/narrator writes the story of how he had come to murder his male lover, surprised that writing about these events, which he thought would be painful, proved quite the opposite. Not in the simplistic sense of relief or some kind of exorcism, but in gaining him an unsought-for "detachment." He says that he has found in writing a totally different "dimension" from the one involved in living and thinking. This novel will be discussed in detail in Chapter 6: it is being referred to here only to supply another example of a reiterated motif in Rendell's fiction: the arrival of self-knowledge by writing—about oneself or about one's family. It is a motif that dominates the narrative in *Anna's Book*.

The pivotal episode in *Anna's Book* closely reproduces the events of Oedipus' search for identity. In fact, on the very first page, the narrator says that she will be relating a "double detective story, a quest for an identity and a quest for a lost child." Again, Oedipus's crises begin at a party in what he believes is his parents' home, when a drunken guest informs him that Polybus and Merope are not his father and mother. Similarly, in Rendell's novel, Swanny Kjaer is about to host a party when she receives an anonymous letter informing her that she is not her parents' biological daughter. But whereas Polybus and Merope deny the truth when confronted by Oedipus, Anna admits that Swanny is adopted—although sometimes she retracts this admission. She then refuses to supply any additional information, either sloughing off Swanny's questions as ridiculous or supplying vague answers that only heighten Swanny's anxiety. On her side, Swanny feels as if her identity has been obliterated, finding it also ludicrous that this should have happened to her at the advanced age of fifty-eight. Rendell adds an additional twist to her plight: Swanny's mother Anna, who could have told the truth and spared Swanny her long period of anguish, consistently chooses not to tell. Rendell's readers must seek in Anna's diaries, written over many years and quoted from extensively in the novel, the clues that will not only reveal Swanny's identity but also the reason her mother refuses to respond forthrightly to her daughter's entreaties. Again, Ann, Swanny's niece and the book's narrator, writes at the start of the novel that she is going to be telling about "a quest for an identity."

That there are different kinds of self-awareness, different kinds of identities, and therefore different kinds of diaries (and different kinds of narratives) are among the themes of *Anna's Book*. Swanny suffers terribly because her mother's own self-esteem is so strong that it is virtually impossible for her to comprehend how tortured Swanny is over not knowing who her parents are and therefore who she is. Or possibly Anna's own self-absorption, reflected in her diaries' consistently subjective musings, renders her insensitive to Swanny's plight. Despite her love for Swanny and the pride she takes in her beautiful, successful daughter, Anna joins the ranks of Rendell's terribly destructive mothers— although she lacks the aggressive malice of some others.

Anna's Book covers three generations. Anna's granddaughter Ann is the narrator but not the main character of Rendell's novel, describing herself as a "privileged insider" but reminding readers that the story belongs to her aunt Swanny. Her grandmother, Swanny's adoptive mother, Anna Westerby, is a Danish immigrant in England whose diary covers sixty years of her life as a wife and mother. Her marriage has not been a happy one, but it was no worse than most women of her time experienced and was probably better. Although Anna records in her diary the disappointments that followed unrealistic expectations when she married Rasmus Westerby, he has provided well for his family. They have several children, but Anna's unconcealed favorite and her husband's least favorite is Swanhild. Anna claims Swanhild is their child, but it is a claim that Rasmus intuitively distrusts. It is, again, late in her life that Swanny, married to a Danish diplomat and childless, receives the anonymous letter informing her that she is not her parents' daughter.

When confronted, Anna rather dismissively and persistently conceals the story that is disclosed to Rendell's readers only in the book's last pages. It reveals a significant detail about which even Anna was ironically and even sadly ignorant. In any event, Anna, who could have prevented what the narrator Ann calls her aunt's "addiction," her obsessive search for her origins, refuses to take Swanny's dismay seriously. Even when Anna tells most of the truth, she does so in such a way as to cast doubt on her account. After Anna's death, Swanny discovers her mother's diaries, which she combs in hope of discovering the secret of her birth. One story her mother tells concerns a notorious crime that occurred in the neighborhood. A woman was brutally murdered and her eighteen-month-old daughter disappeared. Swanny's conviction that she is this child will lead her to increasingly bizarre behavior.

Before this happens, however, Swanny becomes immersed in the diaries for their own sake. She is gripped by Anna's writing, as if readng an absorbing novel. Realizing that the diaries possess extraordinary literary quality and narrative interest, she arranges for them to be translated and published. They prove enormously popular. Rendell's point of reference for this fictional success is the bestseller, *The Country Diary of an Edwardian Lady*. As Anna's editor and owner of the diaries, Swanny herself becomes a celebrity. Once a woman who, beautiful and wealthy as she was, had lived her life in relation to others, as Anna's daughter, her siblings' sister, Ann's aunt, or her husband Torvald's wife, Swanny begins to experience a new kind of limelight, celebrity, even if not a secure self-identity. Although Swanny is but the intermediary between Anna and the "cult" readers of her mother's diaries, who confer status upon her because she is Anna's daughter, it is her mother who has ironically supplied Swanny with interests and a new focus to her life after Swanny's beloved husband has died. Swanny, long the wife of a diplomat and thus living in his and others' shadows, is now a professional in her own right. But she nonetheless cannot relinquish her obsession and take her mother's legacy for what it is, because this gift was from her perspective only half of that legacy. Her niece Ann correctly believes Anna had driven Swanny mad. For Swanny's sense of herself was attached to a biological, rather than a psychological, truth.

Despite her newly achieved celebrity, Swanny remains convinced that self-identity is rooted in biological origins. Her thwarted search for the truth, however, only increases her conflicts. For as editor of Anna's diaries, she has a practical and vested interest in concealing the fact that she is probably an adopted child. Soon Swanny begins psychologically to disintegrate and to drift toward madness. Like Stephen Whalby, she invents an identity and begins to live it, believing herself to be the child who had disappeared right after the murder that *Anna's Book* relates in lengthy detail. Through periods of sanity and dissociation, Swanny oscillates between being her customary elegant self and the slattern she imagines she would have been if raised by what she deems her real family. It is as if—to anticipate the discussion below of *The Blood Doctor*—Swanny thought that all she was were her genes.

When Swanny dies, her niece Ann, the book's narrator, inherits all her property, and thus she becomes her grandmother's and her aunt's literary executors as well as editor of Anna Westerby's as yet unpublished diaries. She also inherits the family mystery and becomes the detective in Rendell's novel, one over whom the undisclosed Westerby secret takes increasing hold. At first, driven only by curiosity, Ann rereads the diaries carefully looking for possibly overlooked clues. She subsequently learns there are missing pages from the first diary and the importance of these involves Ann's own quest. Eventually, with the help of a man whose own family was involved in the murder of the woman whose daughter disappeared, the mystery of Swanny's birth is solved. No great inner transformation takes place as Ann investigates her family and its secrets. She, again, maintains her role as narrator rather than major character in the story she tells, an already reasonably secure self-identity allowing her to understand the difference. And if the complicated web of relationships that constituted her family has affected her personal life, she has not been irrevocably tangled in its threads. By the end of *Anna's Book,* Ann has achieved the contentment that had evaded both her grandmother and, once Swanny has had the mystery of her birth thrust on her, her aunt. This is perhaps too neat a conclusion on Rendell's part, but as is the case with the last play in the *Oresteia,* the conflicts that beset generations of the same family are nonetheless brought to an end.

A comparison between Clodagh's and Anna's diaries are significant. Sections from Clodagh's journal are referred to or paraphrased but are rarely quoted. In contrast, *Anna's Book* has as one of its main features the subject of writing itself. Even when Rendell presents the trial of the person accused of murdering the woman whose baby daughter disappeared, she creates a journalistic account of a trial that in her fiction is covered by the Famous British Trial series. This is as close to courtroom drama as can be found in Rendell's writing, and she models her prose on that series. Also, a large portion of *Anna's Book* consists of actual excerpts from Anna's diaries and a reiterated theme in the novel concerns diary writing itself. In Rendell's novel, another diary becomes a point of contrast that highlights the nature of Anna's. It is written by another Danish woman, who had lived in prerevolutionary St. Petersburg, and whose account of her life there was restricted to superficial events, such as clothing purchased and parties attended. But Anna's record of her life is consistently interwoven with contemplation of what diary writing itself means to her.

A natural storyteller, Anna writes because of the creative urge that impels any writer. Before her marriage she had kept diaries, but thinking that doing so was wrong, she began her new life by burning her premarital writing. But loneliness in a foreign country impels her to begin again and her notebooks are anthropomorphized, becoming someone to talk to, to share not only events and observations of life around her, but feelings. Some of these emotions seem forbidden and she remarks that her husband might murder her if he knew of them. Her diaries thus become a metaphor for a vicarious love affair, and she uses such words as *clandestine* and *passionate* when referring to them. In more dispassionate terms, she also says that she favors knowing the truth, and writing helps her deal with reality. It is ironic, therefore, that the central "truth" of her life and of the novel is what she never discloses in her notebooks, never fully discovers herself, and, to the extent that she does know the truth, consistently conceals from her imploring daughter.

Anna's diaries are also a continuing source of self-discovery. Rereading them, she in effect fulfills the injunction of the Delphic Oracle. As she notes in one entry, "keeping a diary teaches you to know yourself." (A journal is a very important feature of *The Birthday Present,* but it serves mainly to further the plot and to reveal the character of the journal writer, and it is therefore quite different from the diaries kept by Clodagh and Anna.) This self-knowledge may have as a negative side effect a noticeable self-absorption, and she admits more than once that the behavior of others often remains a mystery to her, the implication being that others do not concern her enough for her to make the effort to understand them. Had she, she might have responded differently to Swanny's entreaties. Still, diary writing can lead to self-criticism, and she sometimes thinks of herself as a bad wife and self-pityingly wonders if, after all, self-knowledge leads to improvement. Probably not, she concludes. Being honest in her diary, moreover, is difficult. Some recorded events will necessarily be painful, and to reread is also to relive the unhappy experiences and once again feel their sting. And, finally, she realizes that some emotions are too intense to put down. Among them, although she doesn't say so, must have been the death of the infant whose failure to move within her late in her pregnancy caused her such dread. When the changeling Swanny is placed in her arms, her adopted daughter comes to mean so much to her that Swanny commands more of her love than any of her biological offspring, including the narrator's mother, Marie. But failing to record some emotions does not mean that Anna has slipped into denial. She does indeed know herself. But, sadly, those feelings that remained too deep for written tears create the barrier that exists between her and her beloved Swanny. Her daughter, again, compounds the problem caused by Anna's silence by mistakenly and simplistically equating biological identity with self-identity.

The role of blood, that is genes, in determining that entity known as the self is a major theme in *The Blood Doctor*, in which Rendell has brought the quest for self-knowledge into the scientific world. For the novel asks about whether self-identity means familiarity with one's genetic inheritance, and then, about how much of the self can be explained by that biological continuity. In this novel, Rendell once again employs the device of allowing her protagonist, Martin Nanther, to learn about himself by narrating the process by which he sets out to write a biography of a family member. His subject is his great-grandfather, a specialist in hemophilia at the court of Queen Victoria. This was no abstract concern for the Queen, about whom it has been said that through her children and their marriages to royalty abroad, she spread hemophilia throughout the courts of Europe. As his biography takes shape, Martin faces the significance of blood—in its physical and its metaphysical sense.

By Martin's time, science had made significant discoveries and developed treatments for hemophilia to which his great-grandfather Henry had to his own great disappointment failed to come even close. But science had also transformed the terms according to which people thought about who they were. It would no longer be believed that a child enters the world as a blank slate upon which the environment imprints an identity. Rather, genes became a new kind of fate (see Chapter 11), affecting not only health but personality traits. It hardly seems a coincidence that Martin falls passionately in love with and marries a woman who strongly resembles the women his great-grandfather favored. But that some genes, such as the one that causes hemophilia, can spontaneously mutate, causing problems about which earlier generations had no reason for concern, only makes the new determinism that much more frightening. And the very scientific discoveries that offer hope, the chance to defeat "fate," come with their own self-altering dilemmas. The self as both subject and object of self-awareness must now negotiate its way to self-knowledge through a myriad of scientific and ethical considerations that are unprecedented.

Martin Nanther already has a strong sense of himself when *The Blood Doctor* begins, but his complacency is about to be seriously undermined. He is in his mid-forties; has had one failed marriage, although it was not a wrenchingly cataclysmic failure; has experienced a quite ordinary generational conflict with the son of that marriage, the nineteen-year-old Paul; and is deeply in love with his beautiful second wife, Jude. He faces only two significant problems. Reform of the House of Lords may deprive him of his hereditary peerage, reducing his income and, equally important, depriving him of a sense of entitlement that he will discover impacts more on his sense of who he is than he would have thought. In addition, he suffers Jude's desperation over a series of miscarriages and the possibility that she may never bear a child. He, Martin, is not only reluctant to begin a new family but is also rather smug in a mistaken belief that having successfully fathered a child, whatever problem that keeps Jude from carrying a child to term is hers alone. The usually self-assured Martin will find that he has reasons to grow less comfortable with himself and with his world.

In the course of *The Blood Doctor*, Martin will not only have to resolve the mysteries surrounding the life of the blood doctor Henry Nanther, but he will also have to cope with unexpected discoveries about his own character and have to wonder how many of them are inherited. It would be wrong to think that Ruth Rendell draws a clear line between nature and nurture. All but the most confirmed monists know that people are both their bodies and something not reducible to those bodies. Explaining Henry Nanther and his great-grandson

Martin does not involve nature and nurture in some simplistic either-or situation. It is perhaps in this book that Rendell's case histories begin to lose some narrative coherence as she refuses to neatly tie up all the loose ends she has created. She says as much, noting that even psychologists and psychiatrists cannot fully explain why people act as they do. The *whydunit* by now may require the admission that authors can claim omniscience only by falsifying reality. The mystery of Henry Nanther will, at the end of Rendell's novel, find a probable but less than definite solution.

By profession, Martin is a writer and when he undertakes to write about his great-grandfather, he will uncover many family secrets, including the significance of a murder in which Henry's fiancée is killed, her sister subsequently becoming Henry's wife. As clues begin to proliferate, some provided by family members Martin had never before met, Martin finds himself not only his family's memoirist, but also a detective intent on discovering the secret Henry wanted to be buried with him. When Martin finally has what he believes to be the revelation of the terrible deed that had blighted his great-grandfather's life and his descendents' lives as well, he decides to leave the family history unwritten.

Just as in *Anna's Book* missing pages from Anna's diary may supply clues to solving the mystery of Swanny's parentage, so in *The Blood Doctor*, does Martin find himself searching for missing notebooks that promise to supply the final pieces of the intriguing puzzle he is close to solving. And just as *Anna's Book* is based not only on a fictional diary but is also about diary writing, so *The Blood Doctor* has as one of its themes the writing of a book. Martin, a first-person narrator, starts out to write a biography but ends with an extended account of his investigations into Henry's life. Like any biographer, Martin is dependent on first-person sources and his great-grandfather's own journal promises to be a treasure trove, not only of information, but of the emerging portrait without which no biography can be of interest. Part of what Martin discovers are changes in the content and tone of Henry's notebooks. After the first truly catastrophic incident in Henry's life, the death of the close male friend whom Henry seemed to have loved more than any subsequent woman (see Chapter 11), Henry's journal entries become shorter and more perfunctory, void of emotions arising from recorded events. A missing notebook, never found but tantalizingly described by the person who inadvertently destroyed it, suggests a terrible confession by Henry about a terrible choice he had made in his life, and about his remorse at bringing profound suffering to the only other person beside his deceased friend he had ever deeply loved.

The Blood Doctor is another Rendell novel to take up the relationship of writing to self-discovery. Every person consists of many "selves" that coexist fairly comfortably or collide in extreme conflict. A diary may reveal the relative success or failure to integrate the disparate parts of the personality. Ultimately, each self-conscious individual will have to make choices to arrive at the point of saying, "This is who I am." Comparably, the biographer will sift through the evidence to conclude, "this is the essence of the person I am writing about." What, of course, becomes clear if more than one biography of the same subject is read is that, ultimately, the biographer's personality and the subject's are seriously intertwined, even if they are not ancestor and descendent, united by blood as are Henry and Martin. Rendell begins her novel by announcing that its theme will be blood and ends with an ironic play on words and a British vulgarism. The blood doctor, the Victorian expert on diseases of the blood, the ancestor whose blood is more a part of his great-grandson's heredity and thus identity than Martin Nanther comes to wish were true, is finally dismissed as "bloody Henry"—*bloody* possibly an epithet meaning no more than *damned,* or a stronger one equivalent to the *f*word. Martin chooses to leave his biography unwritten because, to finish what he is writing would be, he decides, to celebrate a monster, someone he does not want himself or his family to be associated with.

Who, then, is Martin Nanther? He is an upperclass Englishman and a self-acknowledged snob, although a self-aware one who also knows that snobbery can be ridiculous. For example, when a newly discovered American cousin, who not-so-coincidentally turns out to be a scientist studying hemophilia, responds to Martin's initiating contact with him by addressing him, "Hi, cousin," Martin is somewhat put off by the casual, intimate greeting. At the same time, the new reforms of the House of Lords, which will do away with most hereditary seats, involve a significant displacement of Martin from both his routine and also his role in English society. He plans to vote for the reforms but thinks of its outcome as a kind of self-banishment. He is increasingly aware that he falls between the cracks, as he puts it, neither a hereditary peer who can trace his title back for centuries, nor someone whose title has been won through some merit or achievement of his own in which he can take pride.

Martin has moreover had to reassess the relationship of his self-identity to his physical body. Immersed in Henry's scientific endeavors and aware of the way disease has worked itself through his family, he also self-pityingly thinks that Jude's determination to have a child reduces him in his own eyes to a mere sperm donor. At the same time, he rejects Jude's suggestion that he might find a surrogate, a woman who would bear his child and then give it to his wife. Blood still counts a great deal for him, although, ultimately, he will learn he is not as genetically pure as he assumed. His son Paul's easy and healthy birth is no proof of his ability to father a sound child. For the genetically based problem that is causing Jude to miscarry is one that both parents must share. Married to someone else, Jude probably would have no difficulty carrying her child to term. Once he understands this, Martin must think about whether an inherited disease or physical deficiency is some kind of original sin, something to hide, the source of shame or guilt.

In the end, Martin discovers that personal identity is not only a matter of blood but is also the product of interaction with others and with one's own other selves. Unlike his grandfather, and even unlike his beloved wife, when for a time she seemed to view him as reducible to his sperm, Martin sorts out the ways in which means and ends become confused in human relationships. It is because his great-grandfather lost sight of this distinction that he let loose on his own life and those of his immediate family and descendents the blight that had affected so many of them. Too late, Henry learned to love. And this is where his great-grandson is ahead of him. Loving his wife and son, and later the twin daughters he and Jude produce with the help of modern science, Martin does not confuse what he may want with who he is. *The Blood Doctor* portrays a character who, through the act of writing—or at least preparing to write—has satisfied the Delphic injunction to know himself—in part because, like Oedipus, if with a happier outcome, he has discovered some profound truths about his lineage.

Perhaps in no other Rendell novel is the theme of self-knowledge as compelling as in *The Chimney Sweeper's Boy*. Best-selling author Gerald Candless has died, survived by his widow Ursula and their two daughters, Sarah, a university lecturer, and Hope, a lawyer. From the novel's start, readers know that Gerald is homosexual and also that he is intent on having children of his own. After their second child is born, Gerald ceases sexual relations with Ursula. From their infancy, he appropriates his daughters' love and care to himself. Ursula truly becomes what the ancient Greeks deemed a pregnant woman, a sperm carrier and the "vessel" in which the seed matured. And she becomes as much a non-person in her daughters' lives as she is in Gerald's.

After her father's death, Sarah agrees to write a memoir of her life with him. Narcissistically, a decidedly daddy's girl who has never learned to love anyone else, including herself, she thinks of the project solely in terms of Gerald and herself until she confronts an unexpected mystery. Gerald Candless had invented his identity, including his name. Nothing the public or even his family thought they knew about the popular author is true. As Sarah embarks on a search for her father—a vicarious Oedipal quest—she begins to change. But Hope, also a devoted daddy's girl, resists learning what Sarah discovers in the course of her investigation into Gerald's origins. Therefore, Sarah's quest for the truth changes not only her relationship to her mother Ursula, but also to her sister Hope.

As was true of *Anna's Book* and *The Blood Doctor*, *The Chimney Sweeper's Boy* makes clear that in all written accounts of families in which the members are closely tied together, the story, so to speak, belongs to all of them. In her investigations into her father's life, Sarah is almost forced for the first time in her life to think of herself as her mother's and not only her father's child. The novel alternates between Sarah's attempt to solve the mystery of Gerald's past, and her mother Ursula's establishing her new-found freedom to finally become a person whose identity is free of her husband's cruelty or her daughters' obsessions with him. Through flashbacks that reveal the bleakness of Ursula's married life, and through the changes she makes after Gerald dies, Ursula's own story emerges to cast a light on Gerald that he would have extinguished if he could. Below, it will be suggested that the surnames *Candless* and *Wick* convey such meanings.

The Chimney Sweeper's Boy can be thought of as a hybrid, a story resembling Oedipus's quest for his father's and hence his own identity, and the obsession of Electra with her dead father. At first, Sarah's and Hope's attachment to Gerald—during his lifetime and after his death—leaves no room for their mother. About Ursula, their emotions range from indifference to, finally, in Hope's case, rage and rejection. But if Gerald is their Agamemnon, Ursula is no Clytemnestra. What is fascinating in this book is that the character from ancient tragedy whom Ursula most resembles is, in fact, Jocasta. For one of the most compelling features of *The Chimney Sweeper's Boy* is that it suggests what the Oedipus story might look like if it were related from Jocasta's point of view. Even more compelling, Rendell has, in a sense, broken the silence—both in Greek drama and among Freud and his followers (even among most detractors)—that has generally surrounded Jocasta. For, to repeat earlier arguments in this study of Rendell, Jocasta is virtually always the object and never the subject of her own story.

In Euripides' *The Phoenician Women*, the playwright comes closest among the ancient writers in asking his audiences to think about Jocasta's plight. But then, Euripides is renowned for his ambiguous and sympathetic portraits of women. He begins this play by allowing Jocasta to tell the story of her marriage to Oedipus and its terrible aftermath. At one point in her account, she too turns herself into object rather than subject, briefly switching from a first- to a third-person point of view. She seems to be trying desperately to distance herself from the worst event she has to tell about, that she unknowingly married her own son and had children with him.

> And so it happened.
> It was Oedipus, *my son*, who guessed [the sphinx's] song,
> So he became the ruler of this land
> and got the scepter of this realm as prize.
> The wretch, unknowing, wedded with *his mother;*
> nor did *she* know she bedded with *her* son. (Italics added)

(This shift in voice exists in the Greek as well as in translation.) Perhaps Rendell was influenced by Euripides' Jocasta when her own Clodagh Brown departs from the usual "I" in her diary to the third person to describe the worst thing that ever happened to her, as if she were alluding to someone other than herself.

In contrast, Ursula moves from object—her husband's wife, housekeeper, and typist, and the woman her children call mother, but whose existence they barely acknowledge—to subject, to someone who has to decide who she is, independent of the roles she has played. But when she attempts to take control of her own life, her daughters think she is betraying their father's memory. Even at the risk of alienating them, Ursula will not sacrifice her newly emerging self.

There are numerous echoes of the Oedipus story in *The Chimney Sweeper's Boy*. This is especially true if Laius's homosexual rape of Chryssipus (see Chapter 2) is taken into account. Both Laius and Gerald Candless are homosexual and both marry for socially acceptable and political reasons. Each wants children: Laius to perpetuate a dynasty, Gerald to fulfill psychological needs he thinks only a family can satisfy. It is, again, in Euripides rather than in Sophocles that Laius's dynastic ambitions are described in such a way that the drunkenness that leads him to impregnate Jocasta seems but an excuse to ignore the Oracle's injunction. Gerald also marries solely to have children; only later does he find his family image useful for promoting his books. Laius, to repeat, gets drunk one night and has intercourse with the otherwise celibate Jocasta. There is a comparable scene in *The Chimney Sweeper's Boy*. Long after Sarah and Hope are born and Ursula and Gerald have ceased sexual relations, he experiences a horrible nightmare and welcomes her into his bed. Later she mistakenly thinks she may be pregnant. More important, she understands that anyone could have comforted Gerald, just as it is likely that if lust alone had driven Laius to Jocasta, any woman would have sufficed. In both the ancient plays and Rendell's novel, the motives for marrying, for engaging in sex, as well as the problematic bonds that tie husbands and wives to each other form complex themes.

Ursula's thirty years of celibacy within marriage suggests what it must have been like for Jocasta, sexually frustrated and deprived of children so long as she and Laius obey the Delphic oracle. After Gerald's death, the widowed Ursula seeks a job as a babysitter, even though she is financially independent. She needs an outlet for her frustrated maternal feelings, and she craves the affection of a child. Whether Jocasta similarly experiences such feelings after having disposed of a child (she is Laius's accomplice in arranging the exposure and almost certain death of Oedipus), the ancient literature does not say. As she watches Oedipus's dawning horror at realizing that he has killed his father and has married his mother, Jocasta evinces a combination of wifely and maternal concern. But ordinarily, *her* motives are not that important. It is her husband and then her husband/son who is at the center of her story. Finally, just as incest provides the most renowned theme in the Oedipus story, so does it play a significant part in *The Chimney Sweeper's Boy*. Not only Jung's form of psychological incest, which binds Gerald's daughters to him, but a near-literal incest that is part of the mystery of Gerald Candless' real life.

In both *Oedipus the King* and *The Chimney Sweeper's Boy*, a game in the form of an ordeal figures prominently. In the Theban story, Oedipus solves the Riddle of the Sphinx. Had he failed, as others had failed, he would have forfeited his life, whereas his success earns him the rule of Thebes and Jocasta as his wife. In Rendell's book, Gerald and his daughters use a parlor game to humiliate those outside their self-contained circle and to demonstrate their supposed intellectual superiority. Jocasta's passivity in taking as husband the one who solves the Sphinx's riddle can be contrasted with Ursula's feeble protest against her own enforced passivity, for she refuses to play *the game*. When the young university student Jason, whom Sarah hires to help her look into the mystery of her father's origins, immediately gets the point of how the game is to be played, he demonstrates his intellectual capabilities. But he learns he is mistaken to think he is now a contender for the favors of, if not the queen, one of the princesses in Gerald's literary dynasty.

It is, of course, the search for the father's and hence one's own identity that most strongly attaches the Oedipus story to *The Chimney Sweeper's Boy*. In both works, a murder takes place. In both, the search for the father's identity is implicated in the searcher's quest for himself or herself. And in both the ancient tale and Rendell's novel, the wife is— to repeat—reduced to relative insignificance by the other characters. In a book entitled *Jocasta's Children,* French psychoanalyst Christiane Olivier portrays Jocasta as, historically, an archetypal woman in Western, male-dominated culture. She asks, "why this silence around Jocasta?," adding, "can she be left in the shadows she was hidden in by Sophocles and Freud?"—by which she really asks rhetorically, "should she be?" Ursula's daughters would reject the implications of the question: they would prefer their mother remain in the shadows. They resist her move from role of wife and mother to that of an individuated self. What only one of those daughters, Sarah, comes to realize by the end of that book is the extent to which her resistance has impeded her own development.

To make her move, Ursula must assume responsibility for her life and command respect if not love from her daughters. In short, she must assert her existential freedom. One of the themes that has for centuries occupied commentators on the Oedipus story involves the extent to which Oedipus acted with any degree of free will, once his destiny involved the curse laid upon Laius by Pelops and once the Oracle at Delphi had spoken. Oedipus and Laius meet by a seemingly random chance at a crossroads whose symbolism is clear. Similarly, Ursula thinks about how she had met Gerald Candless, who only by chance came to address a literary group to which Ursula belonged. For a long time, an unhappy Ursula thought of Gerald as being her "fate," and marveled that such happenstance could have shaped her life so irrevocably. Later, while her daughter Sarah investigates the mystery surrounding who Gerald really was, encountering dramatic surprises about his past, Ursula quietly puts her fate behind her and goes about remaking her life. She will not be drawn deeply into Sarah's investigations—and in truth, since she knew and understood so little about her husband, there was in any event not much she could provide to expose Gerald's secrets.

Once the parallels between Jocasta and Ursula Candless, or Ursula Wick (she will as a widow discard her married name as in their marriage Gerald discarded her) are recognized, it is easy enough to trace Ursula's emergence from the shadows. Her former name may be another instance of Rendell's symbolic use of names. Without a wick even the most carefully crafted candle will shed no light—nor allow any shadows to be cast. When Gerald *Candless* dies, when his literal self has been obliterated, his identity is obscured. Sarah's investigations are the result of a letter she receives that denies his claims to be who he says he is. At first, Ursula too remains obscured. Her husband's official obituary and the memorial service designed by his daughter Hope give her only glancing recognition. In a book replete with ironies, a final irony is only subtly apparent. Whereas by the novel's end, Sarah Candless has, as the result of her quest for her father's identity, achieved a better sense of her own self, Ursula has deliberately chosen to distance herself from her daughter's project. In no way must her emerging independence be affected by Gerald. By remaining indifferent to the question, "who was Gerald Candless?," Rendell's symbolic Jocasta has, by the novel's conclusion, successfully removed *herself* from the Oedipus story, the tale whose meaning had never yielded her much importance.

CHAPTER 6

FATHERS AND SONS

The Oedipus story involves one of the most notorious triangular relationships in Western literature. According to Freud, the son experiences a problematic relationship with, singly, his father and his mother, and, jointly, his parents as a couple. Each of these constellations involves its own dynamics, and it is possible to isolate the tensions among the parties. At the same time, the lines of conflict intersect so that each relationship bears the influence of the others. Some of Ruth Rendell's fiction reveals another dimension to these conflicts. If a father is dead and his wife assumes the dominant role her husband would have played in their son's life, the ensuing tension between mother and son will perpetuate the father-son conflict. The ghost of the father will be ever-present. For this reason, mother-son relationships will occasionally be treated in this chapter, separate from the focus on this pairing in Chapter 7. But the obverse situation also is part of Rendell's treatment of the father-son relationship, and Rendell ventures into a treatment of incest that was once virtually shunned as a subject of writing. If the mother has died, the son may become the object of his father's sexual needs, which the living mother would ordinarily be expected to have satisfied.

Ideally, fathers and sons should love each other, and a father should serve as a role model to the son he hopes will be successful and happy. But the inherent rivalry between fathers and sons can cause things to go very wrong. If the father himself suffers from low self-esteem, he may fail to serve as an adequate example to his son or may put pressure on the boy to succeed in order to make up for his own deficiencies. On the other side, a father might denigrate his son's aspirations out of fear that the youngster's achievements will point up his parent's shortcomings.

At the same time, the father is both specifically and abstractly a lawgiver, representing society's authority. In his relationship to his children, a generalized confrontation between the individual and society therefore comes into play. The father not only establishes the rules but also has the power to punish his son for transgressions. As a result, a series of problems affect the father-son bond: if the father restrains the son as a result of his own limited ambitions; if he denigrates the boy who does not measure up to his expectations; if he resents the son who will eventually succeed to his symbolic as well as real "kingdom," putting obstacles in the way of his son's successes; if he wields his authority with too much stringency or actually abuses it. As Rendell's novel *The Rottweiler* suggests, a father may even hurt his son by dying too soon in the child's life, for the son may become the sole object of his mother's love, unable to break free of her to create his own family. In her novels, Rendell has explored all of these possibilities.

Rendell's long story, "Piranha to Scurfy," exemplifies the Oedipal conflict, the widowed mother refusing to allow her son, Ribbon, to make his own way in the world, Ribbon unable to get out from under the relationship, referring to his mother even in middle age as "Mummy." As the ambiguous epithet suggests, the specter of the deceased husband and father hovers over this pathological relationship, and his absence, when joined to his wife's possessiveness, leads to Ribbon's sustained infantilism and psychological problems. Before his early death at forty-one, Ribbon's father had written textbooks whose royalties allow his widow and only child to live comfortably. But his estate will only pass to Ribbon if his mother leaves it to him and thus the authority over him that might have been wielded by his father is exercised by her. Ribbon, whose name suggests his feminization by his domineering mother, is prevented from going to school, his mother preferring he be educated at home.

His father's success nonetheless remains a constant challenge for Ribbon, who cannot find errors in his father's work, and who cannot himself write books. Instead he devotes his time to ferreting out errors in others' work and penning excoriating letters to authors and their publishers. He is, despite his own pretensions, an unpaid, glorified copy editor. This humiliation is intensified when he offers his services for hire to twenty publishing houses and none are interested. In the course of the story, one of the authors he despises becomes a stand-in for his father, first as an object of contempt because of his inferior fiction, finally as a source of terror. Ribbon becomes increasingly convinced that retribution is being visited upon him for daring to challenge the status of this popular author, just as he might have been cowed when challenging his father's authority.

In various ways, including her control over her husband's money, Ribbon's mother succeeds in tying her son to her. During her life and, even after her death, she remains his Mummy, just as he continues to think of his father as Daddy. His erotic attachment to Mummy is sustained after her death through the meticulous care with which he keeps her nightgown laundered and laid out on her bed, while his permanent celibacy emphasizes the meaning of this shrine to her. At the same time, he suffers her sustained contempt, for in her lifetime, Ribbon failed to earn Mummy's approval, being both a professional and financial failure. She thus becomes her husband's surrogate, punishing their son for his failure to match, much less surpass his male parent. Having symbolically castrated her son for years, she finally threatens the ultimate punishment, to disinherit Ribbon and leave the money that should come to him to a charitable foundation. To this potentially devastating injury, she adds insult. She reminds Ribbon that she has been his mentor and means of support, indeed supplying him with luxury, but that all her efforts have been in vain. For, she taunts him, he lacks "manliness." Her husband, Ribbon's father, is the model she invokes as she makes it clear her son has not lived up to it. Late in his life, Ribbon has to confront their triangular relationship, his dead father a rival for the only woman he, her son, has ever loved. And in the end, Ribbon has definitively lost the competition for her favor.

Stephen Whalby, the protagonist of *Master of the Moor*, experiences a similar plight, even though he has a living father. It is rather his mother who is gone, having left her son with her angry husband, who is given to the dark depressions that Stephen thinks might have driven her away. Whereas Ribbon's mother takes on the father's role in the Oedipal triangle, Stephen's father makes his son into a surrogate for the woman who abandoned both of them. The elder Whalby clings to Stephen—both figuratively and literally—and requires from him the kind of attachment a single mother might require from her child. Like Ribbon's mother, Stephen's father therefore combines the unhealthy aspects of both pathological mother-son and father-son bonds.

Stephen's father will not let his son replace the childish "Dadda" with Dad or Father. When Stephen reveals that his own wife, Lyn, has left him, the older man recognizes that history is repeating itself. But his response is to be exultant rather than regretful. Now he and his son will have only each other, be "all in all to each other." Throughout his life Stephen has lost each round in his efforts to be a free, adult man. "Dadda" has made all decisions about his son's education, and Stephen's ambitions to attend a university are thwarted. He works for his artisan father but lacks his parent's skills, reduced to transporting furniture and becoming at best a decent upholsterer. "Dadda" even chooses his son's wife, Lyn, a gentle and loving young woman who, unsurprisingly, physically resembles Stephen's mother. In this way, his father relives his own life through his son. It is hardly a surprise, then, that the son who has no identity of his own, and must live with the bleakness of his family life, creates another lineage for himself, living out a variation on what psychologists have called the family romance. This is the conviction that one's parents are imposters and that there had formerly existed in the world other people who would have cherished one had circumstances allowed. (See Chapter 5 for a discussion of Stephen Whalby's attempts to create a new identity.)

The most infamous aspect of the father-son-mother triangle in Sophocles' *Oedipus the King* concerns the son's incestuous union with the mother. In *Master of the Moor,* in which Dadda becomes a surrogate mother, there are strong hints that father-son incest has taken place, that Stephen has had to endure sexual advances by the elder Whalby. In the literature on parent-child incest, it is generally acknowledged that father-daughter incest is the most common form. The next most frequent form of incest occurs between brothers and sisters, and it is a subject that will be returned to later in this chapter. Mother-son incest is usually deemed relatively rare in real life despite its centrality in the Oedipus myth. It is usually acted out only symbolically when, for example, a woman acts inappropriately seductive toward her son or discourages his relations with other women. Father-son incest, however, is a subject about which relative silence exists, as if a particularly forbidden subject. In *Master of the Moor,* there are only hints about what Stephen Whalby has had to endure from his father, and it would be possible for readers to overlook rather oblique references to the apparent abuse of the son by the father.

After his wife leaves him, the elder Whalby frequently enfolds his son in crushing embraces that frighten the boy. Later in his life, Stephen will be sexually impotent, unable to consummate his marriage to Lyn, who eventually leaves him. Again, Stephen's father exults in the possibility that now Stephen will be exclusively his, and Stephen recoils from his father's unnatural response to his calamity, finding the horror of his present situation combining with memories of an earlier time. He recalls that when his mother first went away, he had been fiercely embraced by a half-mad, "gorilla-like man," whose feelings the little boy was reluctant to hurt. With love and with pity as well as with fear, he submits to the loathed embrace: "later on he had given way to Dadda in everything for the sake of peace and not to offend." Whether Stephen's sexual impotence has to do with incest with his father, or whether he has turned his wife Lyn into a mother-substitute, only to recoil from a kind of vicarious incest, remain teasing ambiguities in a book in which the Oedipal conflicts are heightened by treatments of gender confusion (see Chapter 7 for more about Lyn and Stephen).

By the time Rendell came to write *Grasshopper*, years after *Master of the Moor*, there were few if any forbidden subjects in literature. Father-son incest, if not deemed common, became a recognized form of sexual abuse. In *Grasshopper*, Jonny is the character who, among the roof walkers, seems to represent unmitigated evil. His attitude toward sex is only one, and perhaps not the worst, of his perverse view of things. He assumes women do not enjoy sex and use it to gain some other advantage over a man, and sexually preying on them becomes a justifiable revenge. A true psychopath, Jonny, lacking a conscience, also lacks the need to justify himself. But at this point in her writing, Rendell still seems intent on constructing coherent case histories. Jonny allows her to take up for her readers' consideration one of her favorite themes, the uncertain relationship of nature to nurture (Jonny will be discussed again in Chapter 11). Jonny's mother had been a heroin addict who used the drug throughout her pregnancy and who died when he was two. And from the time he was four, Jonny's father sexually abused him, later passing the child among his friends. In order to "secure his compliance," the father fed Jonny brandy and, in economically harder times, with methylated spirits so that the "boy was insensible when the abuse went on." Was it the pre- and post-natal chemical damage done to Jonny that did the most harm, or was it his environment with its grotesque variation on the Oedipal triangle?

Sex has nothing to do with the conflict between father and son in *A Fatal Inversion*. The part of the Oedipus story informing this novel is the murder of Laius by Oedipus and the latter's inheritance of his father's kingdom. The matter of property equaling power and, therefore, the question of who wields this power, engage Adam Verne-Smith and his father Lewis in an intense struggle. Their conflict appears at first less deadly than it is unpleasant, even distasteful. Yet their story involves a murder, one that had taken place years earlier, when the struggle between father and son had reached its most intense point.

When the body of a woman and infant, long dead, are dug up on the grounds of Wyvis Hall, a country estate in Sussex, the police intend to find and interrogate former owners. But Lewis does not wait for the authorities to locate his son, Adam, who at the time of the grisly discovery is vacationing with his wife and baby daughter in the Canary Islands. Smugly congratulating himself on obeying his civic duty, Lewis approaches the authorities and supplies the information that when Adam was a nineteen-year-old college student, he had inherited Wyvis Hall from a great-uncle. But, Lewis hastens to explain, his son had immediately placed the estate on the market, had never lived in it or rented it to others, and after only a few visits to assess its condition and value had sold it and returned to college. Adam, he assures the authorities, had certainly never given anyone else permission to inhabit it, including himself and Adam's mother. Lewis, of course, does not admit that being kept from the property had been a source of vexation and continuing resentment. Instead, he offers what he thinks is the helpful suggestion that vagrants may have lived in the house and committed a crime there.

The name of his son, Adam, suggests prototypical man and thus prototypical son (in Freud's so-called universal psychological paradigm), and when Lewis mulls over the

115

growing estrangement between himself and his male child, he thinks bitterly of the transformation of the loving, agreeable young Adam into the distant, secretive person he became. By seeing Adam in such a negative light, Lewis can justify his own bad feelings about his son, not facing his anger over it being Adam and not he who had inherited the property. He, of course, does not know the deadly secret whose revelation Adam has for ten years lived in dread of. The summer after he had inherited Wyvis Hall, Adam and a friend turned it into a kind of commune, not one based on some utopic idealism, but rather a place to enjoy a hedonistic summer holiday. In order to sustain this escape from ordinary life, Adam began selling off the contents of the house, such as silver, to buy food, wine, and drugs. Another man joins the group and several women arrive and depart, to sleep with the young men and in a somewhat desultory fashion do the necessary domestic chores. One of these is the psychopathic Zosie with whom Adam falls in love (see Chapter 8 for a discussion of Zosie and her type in Rendell's fiction). Another is Vivien, the only person who brings to Wyvis Hall a sincere desire to discover in their alternative lifestyle some meaning in her life. The young people call the estate Ecalpemos, *someplace* spelled backward, much as Samuel Butler's satiric treatment of utopias was about Erewhon, the reverse of *nowhere.*

From the very beginning of *A Fatal Inversion,* Rendell's readers know that at the end of the summer, a murder is committed at Ecalpemos. Three men who had agreed to leave the commune and refrain from any further contact find themselves drawn together again by mutual fear after the bodies are discovered. Not until the end of the book, however, are the identities of the victims revealed, or the motive for the murder, or which inhabitant of Ecalpemos is the killer, or even whether the authorities ever learn the truth about what happened at Wyvis Hall. A murder was committed, but it will turn out that the crime lacked malice. It is malice, however, that impels Lewis to get in touch with the police. And the source of his ill feelings has to do with his losing Wyvis Hall to his son and with that loss also losing power over Adam.

One way for a son to vanquish his father is to inherit his "kingdom" while his parent is still alive. Lewis Verne-Smith expected that Wyvis Hall would be his after the death of his childless Uncle Hilbert. Hilbert had frequently said it would be. Rendell portrays the family as minor gentry and describes how the country estate comes into the family. While the property is not particularly grand compared to some other British estates, the prospect of owning it looms very large in Lewis' mind. When he was a child, Wyvis Hall struck him as both impressive and beautiful. Later, dreaming of owning it, he realizes it can be a source of wealth and status. Unfortunately, his great expectations make him obsequious toward Uncle Hilbert, his ultimate gesture to name his son Hilbert John Adam—called Adam. Lewis soon realizes that his uncle is put off, rather that flattered, by this seemingly respectful gesture. Still, Lewis has no reason to anticipate Uncle Hilbert's ironic decision to bestow his home and its contents on his namesake.

When, ultimately, the nineteen-year-old Adam comes into his inheritance, Lewis is shocked, infuriated, and increasingly hostile toward his son. This antagonism is intensified when it becomes clear that his son has no intention of sharing the property and that Lewis would not inhabit the hall even as a guest. Adam has completely supplanted his father, intending to sell Wyvis Hall and profit from the sale. Thus it is with mainly an unconscious animus that Lewis does his civic duty and contacts the police when the skeletons are unearthed. Had he been able to, he would have been pleased to spoil Adam's holiday in the Canary Islands by contacting him about the grisly discovery (but he could not realize how such news would terrify his son). It is with bitter zeal that Lewis meets Adam at the airport to deliver the news. Lewis's barely suppressed anger at his son is only intensified by a renewed realization that Adam, now a husband

and father himself, has generally surpassed his father, living in a bigger house in a better neighborhood because inheriting and then selling Wyvis hall made this step upward possible. The normal order of things had been reversed, just as the name of the estate had been spelled backwards. Lewis, of course, does not know that, in the end, the inheritance would destroy his son's life, just as taking over the rule of Thebes after killing Laius had ultimately destroyed Oedipus's life. Still, when Adam benefits from his father's great expectations, he acts out the contents of Freud's castration complex, but in reverse. This time the son has castrated the father.

Strictly speaking, Freud's castration complex has to do with a young boy's fears concerning how his father might punish him for transgressions, particularly for desiring his mother and wishing to supplant his father in her bed. But obviously, every Oedipus who symbolically slays his father and marries his mother has, in effect, castrated his male parent by virtue of being his heir. In ancient Greek mythology, the first ruler of the universe, Uranus, was castrated by his son Cronus. Like Laius, Cronus was fated to be dethroned by a son, so he swallowed his children when they were born. Zeus survived because his mother had hidden and hence protected him.

It is the failure of a mother to similarly protect her son that informs the Oedipal triangle in Rendell's novel *Make Death Love Me*. Two inept bank robbers hold up the suburban branch of a major bank. At this point, the book's action divides into two narratives that come together in its explosive ending. Only one of these lines of action will be discussed here, because the unresolved Oedipus complex of the dominant robber, Nigel, will exacerbate the threat to the life of Joyce, the young bank teller kidnapped because she had seen the robbers' faces. As Joyce and the criminals are forced to live together, Joyce begins to fuel the fantasies and the anger of Nigel, who had turned to crime after failing to mature and to resolve his problems with his overbearing father and the mother helpless to shield her son from the pressures exerted by her husband.

Unlike the other robber, Marty, a working-class young man whose main ambition seems to be to avoid any real work, Nigel is the son of a doctor who enrolls him in a private school and expects his son to be a success. And when, early on, it becomes clear that Nigel is strikingly lacking in ambition, the father sends him to a psychiatrist, who fails to get to the bottom of Nigel's until-then passive rebellion. Thinking he can cut the sessions short by telling the psychiatrist what he wants to hear—or what Nigel thinks he wants to hear—he says he hates his mother, a claim that he admits to himself is untrue but that probably does express unconscious rage. On the subject of his father, he remains significantly silent. At some point, after attending a university, Nigel realizes that he could short-circuit the process of getting educated, finding a job, marrying, buying the inevitable house and new cars, raising children, and generally living out the dreary life exemplified by his parents. All he need do is quit school and live in a commune, one of those collectives in Rendell's fiction that for most of its inhabitants is detached from any ideology and supplies instead a place for shiftless youngsters to crash and avoid finding productive ways of living. In one way, however, Nigel differs from the pleasure-seeking young people in *A Fatal Inversion*, who live their hedonistic lives at Ecalpemos fully intending to return home and to inherit their parents' kingdoms—that is, replicate their lives. Nigel is unhappily insecure about his sexuality, desperately aware he has not succeeded in experiencing the unrestrained pleasure he thinks ought to follow his break for freedom.

Many young people who reject their parents' way of life turn toward social or political causes, in this way sometimes causing their mothers and fathers the same kind of disappointment and dismay as those who simply drop out of middle-class life, as Nigel does. They are probably examples of what are referred to in *Harm Done* by one of Kingsmarkham's policemen as "bolshie teens." But Nigel is too narcissistic to devote himself to anyone's welfare but his own, too self-absorbed even to adopt the rhetoric of an ideology of social progress. Instead, he seeks ways of exploiting agencies designed to help those truly down and out to get money, and under duress, he takes on menial jobs. When these fail to yield him enough money to enjoy himself, he turns to crime.

The bank robbery yields Marty and Nigel far less money than they hoped, but still several thousand pounds. Their big problem, however, is Joyce. They are thieves, but not yet murderers, and until they decide what to do with her, or find some way to get out of the country so that her reports to the authorities cannot harm them, they ironically become as much her prisoner and she is theirs. For they cannot leave her alone and therefore cannot enjoy their ill-gotten gains. It is the psychologically complex interaction among the robbers and their kidnap victim, as well as Joyce's desperate attempt to physically and psychologically survive her ordeal, that constitute one of the two parts of *Make Death Love Me*. At some point, Joyce, like Nina in *Gallowglass,* thinks that agreeing to sex with her captor will ensure her safety, and she and Nigel plot to get Marty out of the house so that they can go to bed together. Unlike Nina, however, Joyce is not beautiful; and unlike Sandor, Nigel is not in love with her. What Sandor and Nigel share, however, is the satisfaction that would come from their captor's submission, which feeds dreams of glory and omnipotance. Nigel, however, never anticipates that, despite her plain face, Joyce possesses a beautiful body, the sight of which will rob him of the basic dislike and contempt he feels for her. And without the ability to think of her as someone in all ways inferior to himself, a slave he imagines himself continually degrading, while at the same time she unendingly begs for his favors, he is rendered impotent. He is therefore humiliated when he finds himself unable to complete the act that she has steeled herself to endure. It is at this point in the novel that Nigel's sexual pathology is revealed to be rooted in a traditional Oedipal triangle.

Frightened by his sexual doubts and inadequacies, Nigel imagines that what he needs is an older woman, someone sexually experienced but also grateful for his attentions, someone with whom impotence would not be a problem. It is not difficult to understand that, in some way, Nigel links successful sexual experience to a mother figure. Joyce is younger than he, but what he perceives to be her unattractive looks render her unthreatening. In the meantime, although he does not consciously make the connection, Joyce has been surviving her ordeal by busying herself with tasks traditionally associated with housewives and mothers—with Penelope. She thoroughly cleans the filthy apartment that serves as her prison, and she has even gotten her captors to buy her yarn and knitting needles so that she may spend some of the long hours of her captivity with this traditional female occupation many people associate with their mothers. Moreover, during his frantic but failed attempt at sexual intercourse with Joyce, Nigel thinks of unattractive women he knows, including an acquaintance's drab mother.

Rendell has once again depicted the world as seen from within the mind of someone whose perceptions are consistently distorted. And most of the psychological clues she provides link sexual dysfunctionality to Oedipal themes. Nigel must repress his unconscious desire for his mother by debasing her. He does this when he lies to the psychiatrist in order to escape their unpleasant sessions. He may not in fact hate her, but he does need to transform her from the potentially powerful phallic mother into the inferior woman who had, in any event, failed her son in his struggle with his emasculating father. After Nigel's catastrophic attempt at sexual union with Joyce, who has actually fallen asleep during his futile attempts to penetrate her, Nigel has a flashback to a much earlier time in his life, perhaps to a dream rather than something that actually happened. He was being forcibly spoon-fed by his father, who was threatening him that unless he ate, he would never grow up to be a man, while his mother, crawling about on the floor, was busily alternating between wiping her son's face and cleaning up the food the young boy was spitting out.

The theme of Nigel's impotence, his symbolic castration, is worked out literally in *Live Flesh*. Victor Jenner, a serial rapist, and David Fleetwood, a young policeman, confront each other in the apartment of a young woman whom Victor holds hostage as the authorities close in on him. David tries unsuccessfully to talk Victor into surrendering, while Victor pleads for a short period of time in which to make his escape. During David's attempt to negotiate with the criminal, he does not believe Victor's insistence that the gun he is holding is real, not just a replica. When David is shot in the back, he is invalided for life and will have years ahead of him to contemplate his drastic error. One result of his paralysis is his inability to have sexual intercourse with Clare, the fiancée who loves him and intends to be his wife despite his disabilities.

The wounding of David is in *Live Flesh* the prelude to what ensues after Victor is released after almost a decade in prison and contacts David. The ex-policeman is a hero, a celebrity who has never lost the attention of the media, partly because his continuing treatments for his injuries keep the public abreast on progress in the treatment of spinal injuries and partly because David has written his autobiography. Victor, guilty but defensive about hurting David, is also paranoid, thinking the book has been written as an attack on him, when in fact it is one of those uplifting pieces of writing by and about a man who has managed to make a meaningful life for himself against the odds of his devastating paralysis. His name, Fleetwood, is almost an oxymoron, defining his strengths and the unfortunate course of his life. David is, moreover, in both interviews and also in his writing, explicit and open about the cessation of a normal sex life. But he refrains from assigning blame for his plight. Meanwhile, Victor is desperate about his wasted years in prison, believing that he was the victim rather than the perpetrator of the catastrophic events that ensued when he took a hostage. He clings to the idea that if he had been granted the very short time he had asked for to evade his captors, and if the police had believed that the gun was real, what transpired need not have happened. The distortions and self-deception that govern Victor's thinking are revealed once again when David and Clare agree to meet with him. For Victor comes to think of them first as friends, and then as an idealized family.

The odd relationship that springs up between Victor and David begins to resemble that between son and father. That is, if viewed through Victor's distortions, for David never thinks of Victor as a son. Nonetheless, the novel develops the father-son paradigm. Symbolically, it begins that way. David, the policeman, is the authority figure empowered not only to thwart Victor but also to punish him for his transgressions, which are specifically sexual in nature. Each of Victor's rape victims would, furthermore, evoke images of his mother, and as *Live Flesh* develops, Victor's early involvement in an almost classic Oedipal triangle would be made clearer. Moreover, several years before his death, Victor's father suffered a stroke and was confined to a wheelchair, which would link him in Victor's mind with David, who spends his life similarly confined. At one point, Victor begins using his father's chair as a regular place to sit, a sign of displacing the fathers, real and fantasized, in his life.

After his near decade in prison, Victor compares his life with David's much as a son might when he feels helpless to match an achieving parent, whom he therefore resents. David has the respect of the community, whereas Victor, hardly what his name signifies, is a former prisoner patronized by the social service agencies. David has material security and lives well in an attractive house, while Victor lives in a tiny room with a bathroom shared by other tenants. David has written a book that is already attracting attention, whereas Victor cannot even get a menial job. Even worse, Victor has been disinherited—not by his father, true, but by a wealthy relative who is contemptuous of him but nonetheless spends her life assembling a scrapbook devoted to his crime and punishment. And finally, to put the Oedipal triad together, David is loved by the lovely and gifted Clare, who wants to marry him and cannot be won away by Victor. Her position is like that of Victor's mother, who adored her husband with an exclusive passion that Victor believed—with some justification—left no place for him. As a young boy, he accepted the idea that his mother would prefer his father because he was so much older, bigger, and more powerful than Victor. When Victor becomes an adult, the Oedipal rivalry turns pathological.

Live Flesh, especially in a significant section describing Victor's childhood, can be read as a complete case history of an unresolved Oedipus complex that resulted in Victor's becoming a serial rapist. If anything, it is a weakness in the narrative that Rendell cannot rely on her readers' possessing sufficient knowledge to understand Victor. Through his propensity to read pop-non-fiction, Rendell lets them know, for example, that Victor's early witnessing of his parents' lovemaking is known in psychiatric terms as the "primal scene." In any event, Victor's earliest memories of his parents are of a pretty woman forever caressed and kissed by the husband who never seemed to be in her presence without in some way touching her. In his recollections, which he recognizes as possibly faulty, Victor could not recall ever being alone with his mother. The resultant rivalry with his father would later resurface when he tries to win Clare away from David. His parents had seemed all in all to each other and, clearly, sex was a crucial element in their love.

It was also a subject on which they uninhibitedly instructed their son, probably imparting more information than their quite young child needed to know. Not surprisingly, despite their attempts to be frank and enlightened, Victor never thought of sex as having anything to do with them, although two incidents in which he witnessed their lovemaking would have a profound influence on his becoming a rapist. In one of these, he passed his parents' bedroom and heard the audible sounds of their sexual intercourse. In another, he had crept out of his own bed to find the Christmas present he knew they had hidden for him and witnessed his father, naked from the waist down, "humping" on top of his mother, who was lying with her skirt up and her blouse undone. On that occasion, too, it was the noises they made more than the activities visible to him that were to influence his future.

Victor, of course, would not be the first child to misunderstand what he took to be the violence of sexual intercourse. But this perception would be compounded by his mother's special way of expressing sexual pleasure: a protesting of the heightening sensations until her climax was reached and she uttered an animal-like howl. Just before that, she seemed to implore her husband to stop: "Don't, don't—Oh, no, no, no!" No wonder that years later, when Victor was given to raping women as part of a violent attack on them, he would hear that same protest—"Don't, don't, don't—Oh, no, no, no!"—but not understand the difference in meaning between what his victims were uttering and what his mother had cried out in pleasure. When, after a few rapes, Victor makes the connection, he represses it. And Rendell leaves it to her readers to understand that in raping women, Victor is acting out his early erotically charged desire for his mother as well as his rivalry with his father, who he thought had kept her love from him.

Victor's symbolic castration of David Fleetwood, the injury that made David sexually impotent, can thus be understood as the fulfillment of childish wishes, except that even in Victor's tortured psyche, which provides most of the book's narrative point of view, Victor never comes near understanding his need to replace his father in his mother's love. When he tries to win Clare, to take her away from David, whom Victor had rendered unable to give her what Victor realizes is a large part of what kept his mother bound to his father, he fails—just as he had earlier failed to vanquish his father and have his mother to himself. It is when the extent of his second failure is driven home to him that Victor once again begins raping women. These attacks were always and still are his way of acting out the violence of his parents' lovemaking and the violence of his own consequent anger and jealousy.

The Oedipal relationships in *No Night is Too Long,* one of Rendell's most complex and brilliant novels, are so thematically intertwined that discussion of this book will be divided between two chapters: this one and the next (Chapter 7). For now, it is the pseudo-father-son paradigm that will be looked at. Tim Cornish is a graduate student in a university creative writing program, and Dr. Ivo Steadman, a neighbor, is a paleontologist who spends his summers lecturing on cruise ship expeditions to Alaska. At the beginning of the book, Tim remembers killing his homosexual lover Ivo, and he is tortured by imagined hauntings by Ivo's ghost. He is writing his account of what happened in part to exorcise the psychological furies that pursue him.

At the center of Rendell's plot is a significant episode from the Oedipus myth, inverted, however, as is often the case in Rendell's use of literary sources. When Laius and Jocasta fail to heed the Delphic Oracle's injunction not to have children, and when Oedipus is born, they arrange for him to be abandoned in the wild, exposed to the elements so that he will perish. As it turns out, he survives to be raised by foster parents. In *No Night is Too Long,* Tim leaves Ivo on a desert island to die of exposure. But this time, it is (figuratively speaking) the father who is exposed to the elements by his son.

Tim had been Ivo's lover in a relationship that became irksome in part because of Tim's immature attitudes toward love, in which to be loved by a partner was to lose interest in that partner, and in part because Tim rebels against what he perceives an older man's patronizing attitude toward him. Ivo had assumed the role of would-be mentor dealing with a rebellious and recalcitrant child or student. When, for example, he tries to instruct Tim in areas of scientific knowledge that Tim is ignorant of and indifferent to, these lessons begin to remind Tim of similar sessions with his father. But this growing area of difference is only one that emotionally separates the pair. As the relationship begins to break down, Ivo, deeply in love with Tim, becomes frantic as Tim, in turn, becomes increasingly indifferent to Ivo's despair. Moreover, Tim falls in love with a woman, Isabel, and in a last-ditch effort to reverse the course of events, Ivo threatens to reveal to her their homosexual relationship and thus ruin Tim's hopes for his future. After Tim renders Ivo unconscious on the remote Alaskan island where they had angrily fought, and Tim leaves Ivo there to die, Tim begins receiving anonymous letters that are actually accounts of famous shipwrecks and castaways—for example, that of Alexander Selcraig, the model for Daniel Defoe's Robinson Crusoe. These letters and short narratives are quoted in the course of Tim's written account of his relationships with Ivo and Isabel, and of what happens after he leaves Ivo on the island. It is clear that someone knows what Tim has done, but who that person is and how he or she knows, is the mystery toward which the book moves. (A weaker version of this plot element can be found in *The Birthday Present*).

In *No Night is Too Long*, again, Tim consciously perceives his relationship with Ivo in terms of an Oedipus complex. In this novel, which combines elements of the Oedipus myth with an increasingly antagonist homosexual relationship between a young man and his older lover, there may be echoes of the rape by Laius of Chryssipus. At one point, when Tim wants to end his relationship with Ivo, he no longer wants his body to be penetrated by Ivo and requests that they restrict their encounters to external, intracrural sex, which in ancient Greece was the common form of sexual practices between older men and young boys. Perhaps Laius had not restricted himself to this way of satisfying his desire for Chryssipus, for the young man's suicide suggests a possibly more forceful act on Laius's part. Similarly, in Rendell's novel, Tim's attempt to limit the boundaries of sex with Ivo invokes the latter's scorn

This is not to argue that Rendell would have had to be familiar with the Laius and Chryssipus episode to depict an intrinsic Oedipus complex between two male partners, one of whom comes to resist the other. Still, it is striking that in two of her novels, *The Chimney Sweeper's Boy* and *No Night is Too Long*, explicit elements from the Oedipus tale are combined with a homosexual theme. And in *No Night is Too Long*, another motif from the Laius-Chryssipus story can be found. Although Ivo does not literally kidnap Tim when the two of them go to Alaska, Tim is reluctant to go. And when in Juneau, he tries to return to England, he discovers that his special fare airplane ticket—purchased by Ivo—will not allow him this escape.

It is interesting to discover in a lengthy study of ancient Greek homosexual love the speculation that where an older man becomes a younger boy's lover, his feelings for the youth are essentially fatherly. The argument is that because of a division between the world of men and the domestic realm of women, men were excluded from the lives of their family and had little contact with their children. An affectionate bond with their youthful male lovers compensated for the separations from their young sons. But even if Tim resentfully casts Ivo in the role of a father, Ivo appears to have no fatherly interest in the young man he loves. At one point, when Tim is petulant because he cannot get Ivo to take him on a vacation, Ivo responds with scorn: "Look at you, making faces because Sugar Daddy won't take you on holiday." Ivo is only ten years older than his lover, but from Tim's point of view, he is too much a father figure, "*the* father," the "archetypal parent" who wields authority, demands submission, and punishes transgressions, thinks Tim. As the power shifts between them, however, Ivo loving Tim more, Tim desiring Ivo less, their roles are reversed: the father emotionally becomes the son, the son the father.

As Ivo and Tim enter troubled water, the father-son aspect of their bond dominates Tim's perceptions of their affair. Even retrospectively, after he has exposed Ivo on the island, Tim, writing his memoir, thinks of the two of them as a "young, not very strong-minded penniless boy and a clever, comfortably off, dominant older man." He remembers thinking of Ivo's intellect towering over his own and thinks of how frequently Ivo made him feel like a "bimbo." No wonder, then, that fears of castration had entered into Tim's responses to Ivo: he writes now of feeling his "maleness being sapped." It is therefore Tim who retrospectively defines their hostility as an Oedipal struggle. He does so derisively—"Oedipus, Eyedipus"—recognizing that he does indeed hate his "father" but also understanding that the ancient drama and Freud's theory are inadequate to explain the murderous rage he begins to feel toward Ivo or to account for the outcome of that rage. *No Night is Too Long* is one of Rendell's most elusive novels, its narrative twists and turns, its psychological complexities, and its ambiguous ending never yielding the neat case history available in *Live Flesh*.

Another theme from the Oedipus story proves important in *No Night is Too Long*, the theme of incest. This too is implicated in the novel's ingenious plot complications and will be discussed in the next chapter. For now, what is notable about how Ruth Rendell has drawn on the Oedipus story and Oedipus complex in her fictional treatment of fathers and sons is her ability both to isolate a part of the Oedipal triangle and create a story around it, and also her skill in integrating into her plots other intersecting features of the psychological configuration. This chapter has focused on fathers and sons and their struggle for dominance, their rivalry for the mother's love, and the conflict between mothers and sons when the former are effectively stand-ins for absent or dead fathers. The next chapter will focus on that other part of the Oedipal triangle, mothers and sons and their sometime surrogates, sisters and brothers. It is this sister-brother motif that incorporates the incest theme into *No Night is Too Long*.

CHAPTER 7

MOTHERS AND SONS, SISTERS AND BROTHERS

In *Death Notes* and in *The Face of Trespass*, Ruth Rendell invokes Freud's claim that the mother-son bond is "the most perfect, the most free from ambivalence of all human relationships." Freud's ideas about mothers and sons are developed in an essay paradoxically entitled "Femininity." Its essential premise is that a "mother is only brought unlimited satisfaction by her relationship to a son," for she can "transfer to her son the ambition that she has been obliged to suppress in herself." Contemporary feminists have exposed the crippling results for women, for marriage, and for society in general of accepting such ideas about female psychological development. For the mother-son relationship is presumed by Freudians to be based on an essential deficiency on the woman's part, the lack of the male phallus, symbol of power, which supposedly elicits what Freud calls penis envy. Only through the men in her life can a woman vicariously possess the penis. But because of the inherent tensions in the marital relationship, it is not her husband but her son who allows her the satisfactions she would otherwise fail to experience.

Rendell's novels actually parade before her readers a plethora of pathological mother-son relationships that nonetheless confirm the Freudian claim that women need men for their own, vicarious satisfactions. Even hemophilia, the subject of *The Blood Doctor*, ultimately depicts a mother-son bond gone wrong—however unintentionally. For although women can experience symptoms of the disease, such as unusually heavy menstrual bleeding or serious bruising from a relatively minor injury, only sons experience the full-blown illness, transmitted by their mothers. But this is an unusual variation on mother-son pathology in Rendell's fiction as, almost in defiance of Freud, the author reveals the pernicious results of women turning to their sons for their own fulfillment.

In *An Unkindness of Ravens,* murder results from the unleashed fury of a young woman who reacts against her mother's obvious investing all of her affection and ambition in her son, despising the daughter whose goals she will not support and would even sabotage if she could. Joy Williams' sole happiness in her life comes from her son's weekly phone calls from college, and there are few more chilling scenes in Rendell's fiction than the mutual hatred expressed when Wexford gives mother and daughter the news that their husband and father, Rodney Williams, is dead. Rendell's novel reveals how difficult it is to portray the mother-son tie without revealing the complexities of the mother-daughter roles—especially if a daughter/sister is involved in the family constellation. It will be argued below that Rendell supplies a way of looking at mothers' desire to bear sons that Freud has omitted from his account. For cultural reasons, many women may not want sons so much as they *do not want* daughters. Without anticipating too much of Chapter 10 of this study, which focuses on the mother-daughter relationship, this discussion will nonetheless contend that why mothers may not want to give birth to daughters is very much bound up with how they interact with their sons.

Defenders of Freud point out that the idea of penis envy will appear less susceptible to criticism and even ridicule if the concept itself is understood symbolically. It is not the penis, but male power and status, that a young woman seeks. Still, every baby girl would then be thought to have been born with a cultural, rather than a physical, birth defect.

The "castrated" girl becomes aware of her low position in a patriarchal society. (*Patriarchy* is a term rarely found in a Rendell novel, and it may be for her another instance of jargon that reduces, rather than enhances, meaning.) She also recognizes her mother's similar plight and may even be angry with her mother, who seems willing to participate in her daughter's socialization, encouraging her female child to accept her "disability," the essence of her femininity. To see the matter this way can suggest another—very significant—way that Rendell views Freud's argument that women long for sons. It may be less that they wish to give birth to the child through whom they can fulfill themselves, than that they do not wish to bear an infant who comes into the world with predetermined handicaps. Especially since, again, such a birth forces the mother to raise her daughter by perpetuating the very pattern that has frustrated her own life.

This less common way of understanding the preference of a pregnant woman for a son is evidenced in *An Unkindness of Ravens.* Jenny Burden experiences a deep depression when the results of prenatal tests indicate she is to give birth to a daughter. Mike Burden's second wife causes him concern and distress when she expresses hatred toward the unborn child, because he cannot understand her antipathy. Having both a son and daughter from a previous marriage, he is very content to have another female child. Both Wexford and Burden are particularly puzzled because Jenny is a feminist. At first she does not even understand her own responses, speculating that the traditional desire for a son is rooted in what Jung called the collective unconscious. It is Wexford who immediately (and probably correctly) speculates that Jenny does not want to play the role of teaching her daughter to adapt to a male-dominated society, one that still deems strong and ambitious women inappropriately lacking in femininity.

Sylvia, Wexford's feminist daughter, expresses similar convictions in *A Sleeping Life.* She tells her father she is glad she only has sons, for if she had had daughters she would "feel sick with despair." She asks her exasperated and defensive male parent if he had not realized that she and Sheila would live their lives "exploited and humiliated" by men. Nor, given the Wexford series, is she entirely wrong. If Clytemnestra typifies the angry mother in conflict with her children, and Dora the contented Penelope who keeps the home fires burning, Sheila can be thought of as Dido (there is a little dog named Dido in *The Face of Trespass*). The beautiful Carthaginian queen committed suicide when deserted by Aeneas, who left her to pursue his manly destiny and found Rome. Sheila proves similarly vulnerable to male ambition. Although beautiful, successful, and renowned in her career as an actress, Sheila is twice in the Wexford books left by a man with whom she is having an affair, a man whose own professional goals take precedence over his attachment to her. One instance can be found in *The Veiled One*. More telling is *Kissing the Gunner's Daughter,* where Sheila has taken as her lover a celebrated author of avant-garde fiction. The inspector fears that Sheila may marry her lover or follow him to America, where he has obtained a prestigious university teaching position. But just as Aeneas fails to take Dido with him to Rome, so the author elects to go to America without Sheila.

While neither Jenny Burden nor Sylvia say so, they seem to fear that a daughter might hate them for passing on woman's inferior position in a man's world. Freud understood this could happen but tended to slight its importance: the end point of a woman's psychological development would be to transfer her affections to her husband, who would assume the authoritative role formerly held in her life by her father. Two examples of how this might actually work out in a Rendell novel will make her point clearly. In *The Best Man To Die,* Nora Fanshaw is encouraged to engage in intimate confidences by her mother, who has lived her life exacting expensive gifts from a constantly philandering husband as payment for looking away from his infidelities. During one of these supposedly close talks, Nora confesses to an unhappy sexual affair in which her lover deserted her. Instead of sympathizing, Nora's mother turns on her and betrays her to Nora's father. The parents go on to berate their daughter for a loss of purity they still believe is essential to her future ability to marry. When the angry and now contemptuous Nora relates this history to Wexford, and he remarks that her father's promiscuity hardly allowed him to be so judgmental, he anticipates Nora's response that things are different for a man. Then there is the domestic violence that is horrifically detailed in *Harm Done*. An upper-middle-class woman is repeatedly hurt so badly by her husband that one would think any parent would immediately offer her shelter and help her rid herself of the fiend she married. Instead, hers deny their daughter's reality, telling her she is making too much of what she claims is happening, or insisting she must have done something to provoke this supposedly ideal husband and father. These are the fathers and husbands into whose hands women are to entrust their lives.

This is, again, not the place to explore at length the mother-daughter relationships that will be the subject of a later chapter. For now, it suffices to say that a mother's presumed preference for a boy child can be understood in ways Freud never seems to consider, and, again, it is possible to read Rendell's portrayal of mothers and sons as a challenge to the rather smug Freudian premise that she on two occasions quotes in her fiction—that mothers and sons form the most perfect of family bonds. To continue with her ironic response to Freud, it will be helpful to review an aspect of Sophocles' *Oedipus the King* that has so far not been discussed. Despite the incest theme, the play does not really depict a mother-son relationship. Or rather, one way of looking at Sophocles is to say that as the action proceeds, a husband-wife drama turns into one concerning a mother and her son. And what ensues points directly to the kinds of mother-son bonds (or lack thereof) that Rendell portrays.

Oedipus's final ordeal and the play's catastrophe begin when Oedipus tries to discover why a devastating plague is decimating his people. This leads him to the necessity of solving an earlier puzzle, the mystery of his own origins. To recapitulate the plot, when Oedipus learns he is fated to kill his father, he leaves the home of Polybus in the mistaken belief that he has averted fate. When, therefore, he must identify Laius's murderer in order to save Thebes, he at first has no reason to think he is the very killer he seeks. As the investigation takes place, Jocasta is the wife who allays her husband's growing fears that he is on the verge of a terrible discovery. Then, after the messenger who gave the infant Oedipus to Polybus and Merope tells the story of how the baby fell into his hands to begin with, Jocasta is the first to recognize the truth and kills herself. But the revelations that devastate Oedipus have not yet concluded.

For Oedipus must also learn that he was, in fact, the intended victim of infanticide, and that it was his mother specifically who gave him to the shepherd to do away with. With dismay, Oedipus asks, "she was so hard—its mother?" This disbelief is based on precisely the same assumptions concerning the mother-child bond that appears to make matricide an especially heinous crime. For a mother is defined as a nurturer. It is she who carries her child within her body, ordinarily feeds and cares for it after its birth, and as a result is thought to have a special relationship to it. Oedipus's shock can be used to illuminate the feelings of Stephen Whalby in *Master of the* Moor when his mother, who had deserted him when he was six years old, later meets him again at the funeral of her own mother and greets him with no more interest than if he had been a distant acquaintance whom she barely recalled. Neither the young mother Jocasta in the ancient plays, nor Mrs. Whalby (or a slew of other mothers in Rendell's fiction) come close to possessing what may be called maternal instincts. Ironically, it is only after an adult Oedipus begins to endure the agony of a slowly dawning understanding of his situation that Jocasta begins to assume the role she turned away from at his birth—that of the protective, nurturing mother. But now she is helpless to allay his fears.

The son who kills his mother invokes in some, therefore, even more horror than the mother who kills her son. For psychologically, it is possible to argue that the devouring, possessive mother who seeks her satisfactions through her son in a sense kills him over and over. But because the murder is more symbolic than actual, it may not be seen in this light. Some psychoanalytic critics have argued that it is not the relationship between Jocasta and Oedipus that exemplifies a mother-son problem, but rather the pairing of Clytemnestra with Orestes. In the *Oresteia,* Clytemnestra describes the bond presumed to link mother and son:

> It is strange—
> This motherhood; for sons of one's own bearing,
> However ill entreated at their hands,
> One cannot muster hatred.

When she pleads with her son for her life, she denies Orestes' accusations that she was never motherly. She had, she says, shown love for him by sending him into exile to protect him from the ongoing carnage of the House of Atreus. But when she claims that he had fed at her breast, which is unlikely, given the use of wet nurses by aristocratic women in ancient times, she resorts to the seductiveness that in many mother-son relationships substitutes for literal incest. For the argument has been made by some psychoanalysts that in killing his mother, Orestes finds a successful solution to the universal Oedipus complex. The sword Orestes plunges into Clytemnestra is symbolic of the actual intercourse Oedipus enjoys with Jocasta.

In *Master of the Moor,* Rendell juxtaposes the themes of incest and impotence. Stephen Whalby has already been discussed in earlier chapters, this Rendell novel ingeniously interweaving narrative motifs that can be understood singly, but that take on additional complexity when looked at together. As a defense against his mother's abandonment and his father's devouring love for him, Stephen invents his own identity. His resemblance to the famous author he fantasizes to be his grandfather is based in part on what his own mother looked like when she was young. That his own wife Lyn, chosen for him by his father, looks like that young mother, and that he suffers from being motherless most of his young life, encourage him to treat Lyn as a substitute mother rather than as a wife.

When *Master of the Moor* begins, Stephen and Lyn have for four years existed in a celibate marriage that has never been consummated. Stephen is either impotent or repelled by sex because of childhood images of his mother being "mounted" by his father or by the truck driver she eloped with. Even more significant, their marriage seems based on Lyn's playing the part of Stephen's mother, and as such, she may be sexually off bounds for him. When Stephen brings to Lyn the story of discovering a murdered woman on the moor, he is portrayed as a child carrying bad news to a parent from whom he seeks reassurance and comfort, rather than as a husband whose concern for his own wife might be aroused by fears of danger to unprotected women in the neighborhood. And when Lyn finally leaves Stephen, she timorously suggests that he no longer needs a mother. The situation between Lyn and Stephen is rather the reverse of the one between Euripides' Electra and her farmer husband. The farmer's character is ennobled because he thinks himself too lowly to force sex on a princess, even though she is his legal wife. In contrast, Stephen claims for himself a higher social status than he actually enjoys, and in his preoccupation with his own fantasized identity, he remains unconcerned that he is depriving his wife of a normal life. In one case, sex is permissible but, according to the farmer, unseemly. In the other, the role Stephen casts Lyn in makes sex impermissible.

Like all immature "sons," Stephen cannot imagine that his substitute "mother" may have needs of her own: that she may feel physically frustrated; that she cannot hope to have children with him and must be content with his gift to her of a kitten; that she would experience shame if her situation were known to others. Occasionally he realizes that his real mother may have left his father to escape Dadda's dark depressions and domineering personality, but he also knows that she left with another man. The result is extreme confusion about his relations to the women in his life. His transferring of his need for a mother from his real one to Lyn only intensifies his Oedipal conflicts. The idea of his mother's sexual relations with his father and with her lover causes him to explode in murderous rage when Lyn tells him that she has become pregnant by another man. Again, *Master of the Moor* illustrates the argument that links Orestes to Oedipus as representing a different side of the same psychological coin: the helpless inability to break out of the Oedipal triangle and the violent rage turned on the wife and/or mother.

In an earlier novel, *The Face of Trespass,* Rendell never suggests that Graham Lanceton has experienced any primal scenes. But his meager income comes from royalties from the only novel he has so far written, and that book is described by an acquaintance as obviously autobiographical, "about a sort of hippie Oedipus." Nor is Graham's sense of abandonment by his mother based on any literal desertion by his female parent, as was Stephen's. But when Graham was fifteen and traveling with his widowed mother, to whom he was deeply attached, she met and married a French waiter. Graham resented the significant disruption in his own life occasioned by his mother's remarriage, the disruption only exacerbated when she moved to France. Thereafter, Graham splits her image between the former mother who kept home for him and welcomed his friends, and the mother who he thinks has rejected her son, her country, her friends, and her religion for what Graham perceives as an ugly and ridiculous Frenchman.

Only after Graham becomes thrall to a seductive and amoral woman, Drusilla, and comes close to being involved in murder, does he appreciate his mother's attempt to have a life beyond that of good parent, including a sexual relationship. In contrast to Stephen Whalby's fury, Graham's realization leads him out of the Oedipal triad. Where Stephen is ready to kill, Graham declines the role of murderer, shrinking from Drusilla's demands that he kill her husband. It is, moreover, because he does not confuse mistress with mother that he does not perceive the husband as a formidable rival. Working through his early conflicts, he has no need to play Oedipus to Laius, the older man who stands between him and his love.

Throughout much of *The Face of Trespass*, however, Graham appears stuck in the difficulty of integrating the two parts of the split image of the mother who nurtured him and then, he thinks, abandoned him. His arrested development may be intended by Rendell to explain his fatal attraction to a woman with whom he cannot hope to achieve any satisfactory future. It is Graham who consciously mulls over Freud's theory that the relationship "between mother and son is the most complete that can exist between human beings," adding for himself that it is also perhaps the bond that is the most easily destroyed.

For some psychologists, this destruction must take place—a symbolic matricide—for a son to pass through the Oedipus complex. Again, to employ the language of psychoanalysis in order to see Orestes' murder of his mother in some positive light, Orestes has both freed himself from his infantile attachment to his mother or to the idea of a mother (for they were separated when he was a baby), and also has given up fantasies of being Clytemnestra's lover. At the same time, in revenging the murder of his father Agamemnon, Orestes has actually surpassed him. In the course of his own psychological journey, Graham peacefully comes to terms with his mother and stepfather. His suffering comes about not because he is stuck in his Oedipus complex, but ironically because he has come through it. To contrast Graham once again to Stephen Whalby, the latter remains infantile, ready to kill his wife/mother Lyn because he cannot get beyond his early psychological fixations on his abandoning mother. His father's destructive clinging to him, moreover, deprives him of an appropriate male model. It is, moreover, precisely because the elder Whalby could not hold on to his wife that he fails even as a potential rival for Stephen to overcome.

What remains as a psychological task for Graham Lanceton is to free himself from his mistress, the projected evil side of his mother created when he split her into the good and bad female parent. More will be said about this relationship in the next chapter, for *The Face of Trespass* is one of Rendell's earliest treatments of a man enthralled by an almost mythic femme fatale. Treating this literary theme would eventually lead Rendell to her masterpiece in the genre, *The Bridesmaid*, a novel warranting a brief mention here because it portrays a son who has received enough good mothering—or perhaps has had what the English psychiatrist Donald Winnicott calls a good-enough mother—to allow him to pass rather easily through the Oedipus complex, only mildly uncomfortable when he imagines his mother in the arms of a lover. But like Graham, Philip Wardman must confront the negative side of the archetypal mother figure, as the woman he loves requires him to kill for her. As the next chapter will argue, both Graham and Philip in a sense play a reluctant Orestes to a murderous Electra. In the character of the dangerous temptress, the anguished "sister" merges with the good/bad mother to represent what is for the son the confused and divided image of woman herself.

Between *The Face of Trespass* and *The Bridesmaid*, Ruth Rendell wrote *The Lake of Darkness*, which also combines two themes: the problematic relationship between a young man and his mother and the thralldom of a lover infatuated with an amoral femme fatale. This time, however, Rendell has divided her narrative and portrayed two separate characters so that her readers need not work out why, specifically, a person experiencing an unresolved Oedipus complex is particularly susceptible to the predatory wiles of a dangerous woman. In one of these narrative lines of action, Finn is a hit man for hire, a sociopath whose bond with his mother is one of the most extremely pathological in Rendell's fiction. In the other narrative line, Martin Urban is an ordinary man with some quixotic impulses—such as sharing the winnings from a lottery ticket with the needy. For example, he buys a flat for a stranger who cannot afford a decent place to live. Martin falls in love with Francesca, a woman whose secretive life draws him into a nightmarish existence. The separate stories of Finn and Martin move along separate narrative lines in *The Lake of Darkness* until the two narratives converge in a catastrophe. Like Graham and Drusilla, Martin and Francesca will be discussed again in Chapter 8. For now, Finn and his schizophrenic mother Lena are another example of Freud's supposedly ideal mother-son bond gone wrong.

Lena, already a psychologically fragile person, conceives Finn when she is over forty and her husband is terminally ill. Unable to care for her infant, she takes him to live with a cousin, Queenie. Not much about the triad of Finn, Lena, and Queenie is described to account for what will eventually transpire, but there is enough to suggest that from the beginning, Finn's attachment to his mother is threatened by their relative. First, the childless Queenie tries to claim Finn for herself, hoping that he will come to prefer her to his mother. Her behavior toward Finn is at first glance appropriate as she provides the mothering he does not get from Lena: Queenie takes him on outings, reads him appropriate children's stories, and cooks tasty meals. But apparently these benefits are outweighed by a seemingly small but psychologically significant act on Queenie's part. She prevents Finn from following his own inclinations to sleep in his mother's room, arguing that it is wrong and silly, particularly because there are enough rooms in her house for him to have his own. Meanwhile, Lena watches the "theft" of her son with silent anguish and Finn must find his way in the dark to his mother's bedroom. Not only does Queenie come between Finn and Lena, but she also mocks their shared belief in spiritualism. Mother and son are convinced that there exist transcendent influences and poltergeists in the universe, and they are influenced by the Rosicrucians and Madame Blavatsky, whose books are eventually destroyed by Queenie. At some point, the now grown Finn decides to kill his mother's interfering cousin and, after two years of contemplating the deed, he seizes his chance and repeatedly strikes Queenie with a poker. Unfortunately, Lena witnesses the murder but nonetheless hides the signs of her son's crime so that the police never suspect Finn. But the horror of what she has seen finally sends Lena over the edge on which she had teetered for so long. In the hospital, she is diagnosed as schizophrenic, and after her release, she and Finn continue to live together. But Lena is constantly fearful of her son's murderous propensities. And Finn, as protective of his mother as she was of him when he killed Queenie, now has two concerns as he kills people for money. One is to evade suspicion and capture; the other is to protect his mother from her fears concerning him, to the point of hiding newspapers whose accounts might alarm her.

Finn is a noticeably asexual person, conforming sufficiently to societal taboos by repressing not only early Oedipal desires for Lena but also—and probably consequently—sexual feelings for any other woman. In a less pathological guise, he is the familiar figure of a man so tied to his mother that he cannot commit to a normal relationship with another woman. In that latter guise, he has a counterpart in one of Rendell's short stories, "Loopy." Its title is ambiguous, referring as it does to eccentric and dotty behavior that is benign compared to the psychopathology that binds Finn and Lena, and also to *loup*, the French word for *wolf*, the werewolf being a traditional image of a human being who has shed— to use Freudian terminology—all vestiges of a superego to revert to pure id. As the story puts it, the werewolf is "that animal part of man's personality that detaches itself and wanders free while leaving behind the depleted human shape."

"Loopy" features a common enough triangular relationship: Colin, an unmarried man in his 40s; Moira, the

exasperated fiancée whose engagement has been so pro-
longed that an actual marriage seems unlikely; and Colin's
widowed Mother, unnamed so that she can be thought of as
the prototype of the female parent whose hold on her son
appears unbreakable. What brings them into conflict is that
Mother wants to live with her son and daughter-in-law after
they marry, only to help and serve as their housekeeper, she
says. But Moira knows better. She is aware that she is caught
in the throes of a full-blown Oedipus complex and alludes
at one point to Freud's theory. In an unguarded moment,
she says that she wants to make a man out of Colin, to which
his mother responds wryly that this will be quite an under-
taking. At one and the same time, Mother has kept her son
from becoming a man and also expresses contempt for his
failure.

In his leisure time, Colin engages in some amateur acting,
which Moira understands allows him to become someone
else for a while and escape that part of himself that causes
him discontent. When he is given the role of the wolf in
Little Red Riding Hood, his mother makes his costume out of
a fur-like fabric. She is particularly excited by this particular
role because when he was a baby, she used to "play animal,"
a game that, whatever its contents, her husband put a stop
to. He was either exercising his role as enforcer of socially
appropriate behavior in his home, or, with a new son in the
family, he wanted to make sure that his wife did not encourage his son to become his rival. The story leaves it to readers
to interpret the early versions of a game that will dominate
the life of Colin and Mother after he gets to be wolf in the
play. For Colin begins to put on his costume at home, in
secret, enjoying, as does the werewolf, the throwing off of
inhibitions. Even the idea of sex, which he usually tries not
to think about, begins to appear desirable rather than something to dread as an impending marriage and honeymoon
approach.

One day, Mother comes across Colin playing animal,
and aroused by this chance to re-engage in the game, makes

herself a costume and joins him in the play that involves their vaguely embracing. At first they pretend to be animals at home, but soon they take rides into the country and "[roam] wild among the trees." The former triad of Colin, Moira, and Mother is reduced to the pairing of mother and son, Mother now Queen of the Beasts as she had managed for years to be queen of Colin's household. Moira is forgotten or at least pushed out of his mind, and after a while, the line between Colin's human, socialized self and the uninhibited animal begins to blur in his everyday life. When Moira finally forces herself back into the exclusive relationship of mother and son, they treat her as another animal, but this time as the prey they had pretended to hunt and kill during their play. The inevitable happens and Colin recounts his life and its final events from the safety of the psychiatric hospital in which he is confined after the catastrophe. But because he experiences partial amnesia and only *thinks* that he and his mother had at one point embraced, readers cannot be sure at the story's end whether actual incest had taken place, whether mother and son had crossed the line between symbolic games and literal acts.

The domineering and the sexually seductive mother are split in *The Veiled One,* in which Clifford Sanders discovers in a shopping mall the body of a murdered woman he at first mistakes for his mother. Clifford has already been discussed in Chapter 3. Like Colin, he lives with his mother at an age when many sons would be on their own. Seriously disturbed—Burden and Wexford come to realize he is insane— he appears to be undergoing the wrong therapy (Jungian) for his problems, because a Freudian approach based on the universality of the Oedipus complex might better have helped him break the hold his mother has over him. Clifford thinks of his mother as exercising a bad influence, responsible for his "shadow," the negative side of his personality. Consistently, he has lived with the double messages she sent him. On one side she had, from his childhood, exercised an "icy authority" over him. On the other, she had encouraged

higher education, if not his independence, working at menial jobs to support the two of them.

Dorothy Sanders is a cold, dour, rigid, and unhappy
woman who had once been a servant. Decidedly unpleasant,
she is one of similar mothers to be met with in Rendell novels, mothers who, as members of a social underclass, are protective of a damaged child because the son's or daughter's
deficiency is a sign of injury done by society to the mother.
Defending the child against the outside world becomes one
of the ways the mother has of reacting against her self-per-
ceived victimization. Wexford does not at first see Dorothy
as a protective mother, but he comes to understand that he
is mistaken, that he has misinterpreted her seeming hostility
to her child and her obvious *self*-protectiveness.

Although Dorothy Sanders has much in common with
the mother in "Loopy," there is no suggestion of sexual
abuse by her of the son, Clifford, whose hatred of her is a
major theme in this Wexford novel. Yet incest is a subject in
The Veiled One, thereby becoming another element to think
about as an explanation of mother-son pathology. Important
clues to the murder being investigated come from a maga-
zine column in which readers write for advice to someone
known as an agony aunt—what in the United States is typified
as Dear Abby. One letter is the part-confession, part-plea of
someone who admits to having forbidden sexual desires for
her own teenage son. The letter that actually leads Wexford
to solving the crime is another one; still, if obliquely, the
column has raised incest as a suggestion, if indirect, about
the basis for a disturbed relationship between mother and
son. Another possibility is that if incest, even in some symbolic form, was *not* part of the psychological mix that held
Dorothy and Clifford together, then Rendell, like Jung (see
Chapter 3), may be casting doubt on an unresolved Oedipal
complex as the only or the *essential* basis for understanding
the mother-son relationship gone wrong.

In another of the Wexford novels, *Wolf to the Slaughter*, can
be found what might be designated *indirect incest* involving a

brother and sister. The Kingsmarkham police discover that Anita Margolis is missing when her brother, the renowned artist Rupert Margolis, comes to the police station, not to report her absence but, astonishingly, to ask where he can find a housekeeper. His sister had kept house for him and with her gone, he finds himself needing a replacement to perform the duties she ordinarily assumed. At the same time, it turns out that Anita is a sexually promiscuous woman who only requires physical pleasure from the men she picks up almost indiscriminately. Whatever love she is capable of is bestowed only on her self-absorbed brother. If analyzed carefully, *Wolf to the Slaughter* suggests an idea found in two other Rendell novels in which psychological brother-sister incest can be found. Anita Margolis, by caring for her brother, effectively serves as a mother figure, one who truly loves her brother/child. But whatever the sexual component of this love for a sibling, it has been repressed, acted out by the promiscuity of a woman who has split off sex from love. The inference may be that she has thereby protected herself from a forbidden relationship. If the inference is valid, then her acting as her brother's housekeeper reinforces the argument that incestuous feelings between a brother and sister are an extension of the erotic mother-son bond defined by the Oedipus complex.

Overt mother-son incest is held by experts on the subject to be very rare. In contrast, incest between brother and sister is a more common form (father-daughter incest is the most common—see chapter 9). If, in fact, brother-sister sex is frequently a substitute for an even more forbidden mother-son incest, then it is appropriate to include a discussion of it in an analysis of the mother-son paradigm.

From her first published novel, Ruth Rendell used unconventional sexual relationships as direct or indirect motives for crimes. In *A Guilty Thing Surprised*, an early book in the Wexford series, Elizabeth Nightingale is found murdered. She was the wife of an affluent businessman, Quentin, and sister of a Wordsworth scholar, Denys Villiers, whose recently published book *Wordsworth in Love* supplies Wexford with a clue to solving the crime. Wexford had thought Wordsworth a rather dull subject for a biography, but reading Villiers' book piques his interest. He had not known, for instance, that the poet had been in love with a French girl involved in the Revolution. Unnamed in Rendell's novel, she was Annette Vallon, whose surname resembles *Villiers*. Before beginning *Wordsworth in Love,* Wexford steels himself for a tedious few hours, wishing that Wordsworth had been more like the notorious Byron, among whose scandalous exploits was a reputedly incestuous relationship with his half-sister Augusta Leigh. When he finishes Villiers' book, Wexford rebukes himself for his ignorance. For he learns that rumors of incest are also attached to Wordsworth and his sister Dorothy. After years of separation from her brother, Dorothy came to live with him, devoting to Wordsworth her life as well as frequently serving as his muse and even a source for his writing. It will turn out that brother-sister incest involves the mystery at the heart of Elizbeth Nightingale's murder.

In the writings of nineteenth-century authors, as well as in their lives, there are many brother-sister relationships that at least imply incest, literal or psychological. In *Judgment in Stone,* a horror-inspiring novel in which most members of a family are massacred by a servant because she cannot read, seventeen-year-old Giles and his twenty-year-old stepsister Melinda are among the victims. When Giles makes Melinda the object of his youthful infatuation, the book's omniscient narrator points out that there were no sexual prohibitions to stand in the way of a relationship between them and that the parents might actually have welcomed it, because Giles was a disaffected, maladjusted youngster about whom they worry. But Giles is also a romantic; that is, like the romantic writers in rebellion against bourgeois society, for whom incest was one expression of revolt, Giles relishes the forbidden aspect of his desire for Melinda. He longs for prohibition; he wants them to be like Byron and Augusta Leigh, except that he imagines a transcendent, spiritual love, never sexually consummated, whereas the poet and his half-sister are generally believed to have been lovers.

Beyond the well-known examples of Byron and Wordsworth are other writers to whom rumors of incest have been attached. The guilty but undefined secret that forms a reiterated motif in Nathaniel Hawthorne's writing has been argued by at least one critic to be his incestuous relationship with his sister Elizabeth. Edgar Allan Poe supplies another instance, Poe having married his very young cousin Virginia, whose mother, Poe's aunt, was a woman to whom he was extremely attached in a quasi-mother-son connection. Incest is a theme frequently associated with *Wuthering Heights*, a novel that strongly influenced Rendell's *Going Wrong*. Two particular works of fiction seem to have significantly influenced her treatment of incest in her own novels. Edgar Allan Poe's renowned short story, "The Fall of the House of Usher," although unmentioned, makes itself felt in *A Guilty Thing Surprised*. And a very strange work by Herman Melville, *Pierre: Or the Ambiguities*, which scandalized the nineteenth-century American reading public, appears to have left its mark on Rendell's *No Night is Too Long*.

Melville's novel has, as one of its notable themes, the inference that brother-sister incest might be the expression of an unresolved Oedipus complex (obviously, Melville would not employ a Freudian frame of reference, but as Freud himself claimed, literary artists had preceded him in his insights). Briefly summarizing these works of American literature will make clear how they influenced Ruth Rendell's treatment of brothers and sisters.

In Poe's classic story, the narrator has been summoned by a former school friend to visit his ancestral family home. The House of Usher—both the dwelling and the last two descendents, Roderick and his twin Madeline—are marked by severe decay. The house and grounds are described with such adjectives as *dreary, bleak,* and *vacant,* and they radiate an *irredeemable gloom.* Rodney appears to be suffering from some "acute bodily illness" and presents a "wan being," possessed of a "cadaverousness of complexion" and "emaciated fingers." Madeline, who later will be mistakenly thought to have died during the visit, is ill with an undiagnosed disease, both siblings afflicted with a vague "family evil." They are probably suffering the results of inbreeding, their incestuous origins described so cryptically by Roderick Usher that any potentially shocked Poe readers could overlook it. "The Usher race . . . had put forth, at no period, any enduring branch. . . the entire family lay in the direct line of descent, and had always, with very trifling and very temporary, variation, so lain." Being each other's sole companions for years, Roderick and Madeline may themselves be lovers. At the end of the story, the sister who had been buried alive claws her way out of her tomb and seeks out her brother. Enfolding him in a ghastly embrace, she falls upon his prostrate body and they die together.

It would be surprising if any author writing in the mystery genre were not influenced by Poe's fiction, by his Auguste Dupin detective stories (among them, "Murders in the Rue Morgue") and his Gothic tales (for example, "The Fall of the House of Usher"). Nor is it unexpected that the Poe influence would be felt most strongly in the early works when an author was in a sense experimenting with her art and acquiring experience in the genre. *A Guilty Thing Surprised* is one of Rendell's earliest novels. There is even a decaying house in the novel. Quentin Nightingale, out of respect and fondness for his scholarly brother-in-law, Denys Villiers, restores for his use a dwelling called the Old House. It is a shaded place where the "sun never penetrated" and where Villiers (like Roderick Usher) applies himself to esoteric studies. In particular, he is drawn to the life of Wordsworth, a poet whose relationship with his sister he believes parallels his own with his sister, Elizabeth. Meanwhile, the physical aspect the scholar presents to the world seems modeled on Roderick Usher. When Wexford first interviews Villiers, he assumes the man is ill. His once good looks had been drained by some illness—Wexford is reminded of dying cancer patients—so that he presents a "dusty parched look, yellowish-grey drawn features, blue eyes bleached a haggard grey. He was painfully thin, his mouth bloodless" (vampire stories have been invoked by critics in their analysis of "The Fall of the House of Usher"). Villiers' looks reveal him as haunted, not by disease, as Wexford would eventually learn, but by guilt and remorse—emotions that also ravage Usher.

Because Villiers is known to have intensely disliked his sister, a feeling she reciprocated, he is one of Wexford's suspects. But a more likely one is Sean Lovell, a young man about half the age of Elizabeth Nightingale, with whom he had a very close and—given their class differences—unlikely relationship. When Burden expresses disbelief over Wexford's early theory that the gardener's boy might have entered into an illicit affair with his older employer, Wexford scornfully reminds his less well-read colleague of D. H. Lawrence's Lady Chatterley and her gatekeeper. But sex is not what most draws the young man to the older woman whose age he had in fact underestimated. Rather, he views Elizabeth as a benevolent older sister who has promised to support his ambitions to become a pop music star. But the confusion of mothers and sisters is quite apparent in Rendell's portrait of Sean. His real mother, referred to as Mrs. Lovell, is a character who would be reborn in a later book as Eileen, mother of the sociopathic Teddy in *A Sight for Sore Eyes*. Both women are grossly obese, their lack of care for themselves and physical self-indulgence extending to their indifferent attention to their sons. Their surroundings are squalid as they live in unhealthy, filthy dwellings they cannot bother to clean.

Eileen, who had had no prenatal care and had eaten no nutritional food during her pregnancy, had gone so far as to chain smoke her way through her labor, and neglect is probably too slight a word to describe her indifference toward her son after he is born. But whereas Eileen views sex as something to be endured, not too bad if it didn't hurt, Mrs. Lovell reveals a voracious sexual appetite that she takes no pains to hide from Sean. For she needs him out of the way as she entertains her many men and earns herself the reputation as the village trollop, and she makes no excuses for why her son's presence is unwelcome. *A Guilty Thing Surprised* does not describe how his mother's sexuality impacts on Sean, although his situation at home makes clear why Sean is drawn to the seemingly respectable Mrs. Nightingale. When interviewed by Wexford, Sean reveals, however, that he had not been totally lacking in erotic feelings for his benefactress, for the woman who took a real interest in his life as his own mother never did. He contrasts the attractive Elizabeth, who spent an inordinate amount of time and money on her appearance, to the slattern who was his real "old lady." When Wexford reminds him that Mrs. Nightingale had not been that young, a "brilliant seeping of color came into the olive-gold cheeks." Sean protests that Elizabeth was only about thirty, hardly that old (he is off by a decade). Presumably, whatever desire Sean felt for Elizabeth would have been particularly disturbing if he had to place her in his mother's generation, rather than think of her as a supportive older sister.

In Melville's nineteenth-century novel *Pierre*, an equally young-looking woman makes it possible for her son to think of her as a contemporary rather than a parent. In its time, *Pierre* was a complete fiasco for the author. One of Melville's reviewers called it the product of a diseased imagination, and in recent times, John Updike deemed it the most insane novel ever written. The theme of incest pervades the work. A young, beautiful widow flirts with her son and on his behalf takes great care of her appearance and dress. Mother and son consistently address each other as "brother" and "sister," and Pierre believes that "much that goes to make up the deliciousness of a wife, already lies in the sister." When an actual half-sister, Isabel, the illegitimate child of his father, makes herself known to Pierre, much of his attachment to his mother/sister is transferred to this long-lost relation. Pierre rationalizes this diminution of regard for his mother by focusing on the impossibility of her accepting into the family his newly found sibling. Moral and social concerns as well as a constant reminder of her husband's betrayal would make a united, happy family out of the question.

Pierre's solution is astonishing. Since no one knows of Isabel's connection to him, he will marry her and they will live chastely as loving brother and sister. Allowing for centuries of writing in which spiritual love is described in sexual terms, the language in which Pierre imparts his idea to his sister reveals unconscious desires he cannot rationalize away:

> "Brace thyself: here let me hold thee now; and then whisper it to thee, Isabel. Come, I holding thee, thou canst not fall." He held her tremblingly; she bent over him; his mouth wet her ear; he whispered it. The girl moved not; was done with all her tremblings; leaned closer to him, with an inexpressible strange-ness of an intense love, new and inexplicable. Over the face of Pierre there shot a terrible self-revelation; he imprinted repeated burning kisses upon her; pressed hard her hand; would not let go her sweet and awful passiveness. Then they changed; they coiled together, and entangledly stood mute.

And in the unlikely event that Melville's shocked readers overlooked the theme of incest, there is also in the novel a reference to the Cencis. Beatrice Cenci, a Renaissance beauty, had been sexually abused by her father and conspired with her mother to kill him. The two women are executed, their story dramatized in Shelley's play *The Cenci*. In *An Unkindness of Ravens*, Sheila Wexford plays the role of Beatrice in a production attended by her parents. (See Chapter 9 for further discussion of Sheila's role in this play.) In the same book, Sara Williams tells her mother that her father has abused her, but Joy Williams is no Countess Cenci, for rather than coming to Sara's aid, her mother accuses her of seducing her father. In any event, these cross-connections between nineteenth-century literature and Rendell's fiction serve to highlight her use of the incest theme for readers who follow her allusions. And, again, Melville's novel in particular makes mother-son and sister-brother incest closely related subjects.

Evidence for the influence of Melville's novel on *No Night is Too Long* can be found in Rendell's themes and in her choice of a name for Ivo's sister. When Ivo is left by his lover Tim to die on a remote island off Alaska, Tim does not realize he has been engaged in an affair with Ivo's twin sister Isabel. It is not the name Isabel alone that is striking— Rendell had used it before in her fiction—but Isabel's surname, *Winwood.* In Melville's book, Pierre learns his family history from two sources, one of them his half-sister Isabel, who reveals herself in a letter to Pierre, another a cousin named Ralph *Winwood.* But beyond this borrowing, Ruth Rendell's treatment of incest takes a different turn. Whereas Ivo Stedman unwittingly becomes a father figure for his homosexual lover Tim so that the two become engaged in an Oedipal struggle (see Chapter 6), Isabel Winwood, although several years older than Tim, is in no way either a symbolic mother or sister to the man with whom she engages in a brief but intensely passionate affair. What is unique in Rendell's treatment is that Tim, as lover of both Ivo and Isabel, in effect sexually links the siblings in indirect incest.

Like Roderick and Madeline Usher, Ivo and Isabel are twins whose attachment to each other is therefore especially close. And like Melville's Isabel, who in a letter informs Pierre of their relatedness, Rendell's Isabel also writes to her brother, in part to express her love for him, and in part to express guilt over how she had betrayed him by entering into a sexual relationship with Tim, the man Ivo loved. Tim did not know that Isabel was Ivo's sister when he met her in Alaska, but Isabel knew who Tim was. These revelations come late in *No Night is Too Long,* but Rendell has not violated the rules of fair play adhered to by good crime fiction writers. Her readers have had clues to the brother-sister relationship.

While he was Ivo's homosexual lover, Tim was aware that a sister from America had visited Ivo. As Isabel and Ivo later realize, however, Tim was so self-absorbed that he had no curiosity about his lover's family. Later, Rendell's readers will be aware that, after Tim and Isabel have become lovers, Ivo knows more about Tim's possession of a scarf owned by Isabel than he could have known if the two were strangers. But only after he returns from Alaska to England will Tim learn the truth about how Ivo and Isabel are related.

Isabel's letter to her dead brother is an attempt to explain—and at times to rationalize—how it was that she became Tim's lover, one of her excuses being that because Tim was gay, she thought that although she found him almost irresistibly attractive when she first met him, nothing could result from seeing him frequently. Her letter comprises a long chapter in the novel, and it is striking how incest enters into her narrative as a repeated theme. She begins by expressing her love for her brother, in language less torrid than Melville's in describing Pierre's intention to enter into a celibate marriage with his sister, but nonetheless suggestive of an attachment beyond that ordinarily used to express affection for a sibling. "My dear, my darling. We were so close," she reminds him, adding that they had never quarreled. Their early love for each other had continued into adulthood, until Ivo had learned of her betrayal. When they met, Isabel reminds Ivo, "For the first time . . . you didn't come to me and take me in your arms and kiss me."

Isabel's husband Kit, a jealous, abusive brute from whom Isabel is separated when she goes to Alaska, had on occasion accused Isabel of committing incest with Ivo. Kit is a highly unreliable character in the novel, but his jealousy allows Rendell an opportunity to make explicit what Isabel's language would otherwise only imply. These twins, unlike Roderick and Madeline Usher, have not been involved in a sexual relationship, and only in part because Ivo is unambiguously homosexual. It is nonetheless striking that in one of her references to her husband's unfounded accusations,

Isabel takes up her husband's charge. She treats incest as both a punishment for what she conceives of as an even worse sin committed against Ivo, her love affair with Tim, and also as a way of reuniting with her brother after she betrays him and he reproaches her for that betrayal. "When you were standing there, killing me with your eyes, I thought, now if I could, if you'd said to me, let's do it, why not, I'd have gone with you and loved you any way you'd wanted."

As this incest theme is woven in Isabel's letter with her description of meeting Tim and becoming sexually aroused by him despite her knowing that her brother loves him very much, Tim as a sexual link between brother and sister becomes apparent. At different points in the book, both Ivo and Isabel are at first attracted by Tim's beauty, which arouses lust in each of them. For both, lust is followed by sex, and then an emotional involvement that leads to love. If the siblings' love for each other is threatened by their connection to Tim, it also brings into the open, at least in Isabel's letter, feelings between brother and sister that were probably too threatening even to contemplate before Tim entered their lives.

Although Rendell has drawn on ancient tragedy for themes and perspectives on family relationships, rarely does she seem to aim at writing in a tragic vein. *No Night Is Too Long* is an extremely complex novel, in which human relations verge on tragedy, not in the popular but rather in the deepest sense of that word. In the end, it is not the rupture between Tim and Ivo that strikes deepest, but the one between brother and sister, between Ivo and Isabel. Sibling relations are important in Rendell's fiction. And, again, brothers and sisters can mimic the conflicts expressed by their parents and aroused by their parents.

In *The Killing Doll*, for example, can be found a story strikingly close to that of Orestes and Electra, who not only depended on her brother to avenge their father's death but also transferred to him the love she had for Agamemnon. In Rendell's novel, Dolly, a deeply unhappy young woman, similarly tries to convince her brother Pup to kill their stepmother. What is perhaps only implied in the ancient tragedies is much more obvious in *The Killing Doll*. Pup is unquestionably the most important man in Dolly's life, and she lavishes on him love more appropriately given to a lover or husband. These characters exemplify how brothers and sisters can mirror other familial ties in which sexual desire may be present but is usually repressed. Further discussion of *The Killing Doll* will be postponed to Chapter 9, whose subject is Rendell's treatment of fathers and daughters, and the way in which brothers can become surrogate fathers to their sisters.

CHAPTER 8

ELECTRA AND RENDELL'S FEY GIRLS

Oedipus makes himself felt throughout Ruth Rendell's fiction, sometimes in direct references, such as Tim's scornful allusion in *No Night is Too Long* to "Oedipus-Eyedipus," as his anger mounts against his lover Ivo, whose paternal role Tim bitterly resents. And, of course, the Oedipus complex itself, even if not specifically cited, supplies a distinct and well-known psychological paradigm for understanding the mother-son, father-son relationships. Electra is another matter. Although there are in Rendell's novels references to Clytemnestra, the most obvious in the humorous situation in which Wexford and Dora care for a pesky dog of that name while Sheila is on holiday (see Chapter 2), Electra is not specifically mentioned in Rendell's fiction. The Electra complex, moreover, never successfully established a paradigm for understanding female psychological development, for reasons discussed in Chapter 3. In challenging Freud's emphasis on the Oedipus complex, Jung never went on to develop the Electra complex as a rival theory. Even contemporary Jungians, who urge women to get in touch with their feminine selves by identifying with the Great Mother archetype, and to bond with other women, avoid mentioning Electra in their writings. Jungian psychologists stress the danger to women in being the "daddy's girls" Freud was content that they be until husbands replaced fathers in their lives. And Electra was precisely that, not emotionally her mother's daughter, but her father's; and her hatred of Clytemnestra and complicity in her mother's murder makes her a strongly negative image of women's relationships to other women.

If Electra makes herself felt in Rendell's fiction it is—as has been argued in earlier chapters—because few authors have captured mother-daughter conflict, even unbridled hatred, as Rendell has (also see Chapter 10). In that sense, Electra casts her shadow over much of Rendell's writing, which draws so much of its inspiration from ancient Greek literature. It would, however, be a mistake to concede that Electra is not among the characters from ancient tragedy that seem to have influenced Rendell's fiction. What this chapter will in fact argue is that to study the three Electras portrayed by Aeschylus, Sophocles, and Euripides is to find in their portrayals a female figure that bears strong resemblance to several characters in Rendell's fiction. She calls one of them a "fey girl," and this designation can be extended to others in her work. This chapter will look at Rendell's fey girls to explore their resemblance to the Electras of ancient tragedy. This will establish the significance of Electra and, by extension, an Electra complex as a psychological pattern for discussing—in the following two chapters—Rendell's treatment of fathers and daughters, and mothers and daughters.

In one of Rendell's short stories, Wexford attends the wedding of Mike Burden to his second wife, Jenny. The inspector recalls how, when the widower Burden was still grieving for his first, he had a love affair with Gemma Lawrence, whom he met when investigating the disappearance of her young son. She was a "red-headed woman, wild and sweet and strange, gone now God knew where." Their brief passion is a theme woven through the novel *No More Dying Then*, in which Burden, lonely and sexually frustrated, is irresistibly drawn by Gemma, whose desperate emotions only heighten her allure. But Rendell readers familiar with how frequently in the series the conventional Burden plays Watson to the more liberal Wexford's Holmes will recognize that the relationship is doomed. From the perspective of Kingsmarkham in this early book, Gemma *is* a decidedly strange woman, better suited to London, from which she had moved with her son after her husband divorced her to marry another woman.

The world Gemma left behind consisted of actors and dancers, a bohemian society inherently unsuited to Burden's temperament and need for an orderly domestic life. Gemma is indeed, as Wexford remembers, sweet, gentle, naïve, almost childishly innocent. She is also beautiful, Rendell's description evoking the exotic women in Rossetti or Klimpt paintings. What immediately marks her as different from most Kingsmarkham women is her clothing. She wears long, flowing skirts, and instead of sweaters, lavish shawls punctuated with exotic jewelry. Similar garb is described in a more negative fashion when Francesca in *The Lake of Darkness* is described as dressing "like the hippies," usually wearing jeans, skirts with uneven hemlines, shapeless tunics and cardigans, shawls, and scuffed boots.

In dispassionate moments, Burden connects Gemma's attire to everything he disapproves of, such as her impossibly bad housekeeping. He must repress his fear that, however good she may appear, Gemma is essentially outside the world he wishes to inhabit. And when she leaves Kingsmarkham to go to some unknown place, Gemma disappears from Rendell's books. The character who most resembles her is Vivien in *A Fatal Inversion,* the gentle, sincere hippie in the pseudo-commune where every other member is merely playing at what she truly embraces as an ideal of communal living.

It is not that "wild" and "strange" women disappear from Rendell's books. To the contrary, some of the author's most memorable characters belong to such a group. But they are neither sweet nor good, and if their enthralled lovers think they are, it is because these men are deceived or are self-deluded. The short story in which Gemma is referred to is part of a collection of Rendell's stories entitled *Means of Evil,* and evil is probably an appropriate epithet for Drusilla in

The Face of Trespass; Francesca in *The Lake of Darkness;* Bell (Christabel) in *The House of Stairs;* Zosie in *A Fatal Inversion;* and Senta in *The Bridesmaid.* Each lacks a conscience, so that good and evil are not categories she recognizes. Over a span of years with long intervening periods, Rendell seems to have rewritten the character, as if she were a problem to be solved. After creating Drusilla and Francesca, Rendell waited seven years to portray in rapid succession Bell, Zosie, and Senta.

But whereas literary femmes fatales are characteristically dramatic, commanding figures, Rendell's ordinarily appear as wraiths, fairy-beings who seem on the verge of disappearing if looked at too closely. This fragility is part of their deception. In *A Fatal Inversion,* Zosie is perceived by another character to be "fey-faced, nymph-like, unreal." "Fey" is derived from the French word *fée,* meaning fairy— not a Tinker Bell or other diminutive supernatural being likely to enchant children, but rather a seductive creature who is dangerous if for no other reason than she belongs to another world, one that tempts people away from everyday concerns. In a short story, "Thornapple," Rendell turns *fey* into a noun, *feyness,* denoting a quality otherwise hard to define. In the story, a young woman who had been christened with a quite ordinary name, Brenda Margaret, had renamed herself Mirabel. Possessed of a "brooding sadness," she proves to be a poisoner.

The Greek tragedians did not portray Electra as evil, although they understood that in her obsessions she was dangerous. But early commentators on the plays were inclined to find evil in her: one late nineteenth-century critic went so far as to call her a *teufelin,* a she-devil who egged on her brother Orestes to kill their mother. Later commentators softened this view, finding in Electra a person driven by circumstances and her family history to madness: they perceived her to be a strange, alienated, neurotic, and perhaps even psychotic woman, who lived on the fringes of her society, partly because she had been exiled, and therefore only partly by choice. In Sophocles in particular, her obsessive hatred of her mother leads those around her to think she is crazy. In Euripides, both her plight and also her defiance of those who forced exile upon her are reflected in her clothing. She has been demoted from princess to the wife of a poor farmer. It is striking that her ragged garments and short haircut create a character who could easily be transported across the centuries, becoming the recognizable hippies or fey girls who appear in Rendell's books.

There is, of course, one significant difference between Electra and Rendell's fey girls. Electra is a virgin, even in Euripides, where her marriage to the farmer makes it impossible for her children to be contenders for the kingdom seized by Aegisthus and Clytemnestra. But the farmer has never claimed his marital rights, his delicacy signifying nobility of character despite his lowly origins. Ironically, as a virgin, Electra is precisely the kind of woman some of Rendell's ordinary men, perfect victims of her fey girls, hope their wives to be. In *The Lake of Darkness,* Martin Urban, one of the most conventional of them, is dismayed to learn that Francesca has been married and has given birth to a child. But he nonetheless continues to daydream that she is the virginal bride he would marry in church.

Rendell's fey girls are, instead, sexually promiscuous. Sex is for them an appetite, a weapon, a bargaining tool, a way of escaping painful reality, or a ploy for achieving ruthless ends. Even when they appear to crave affection, theirs is a clinging, devouring, self-absorbed love. Often very beautiful, sometimes exotic, they are driven by their narcissistic needs to seduce men. To claim their resemblance to Electra might be to say that they possess the characteristics that for centuries were attributed to her mother Clytemnestra, attributes that *she* attributes to her mother. Despite her aversion to Clytemnestra, Electra cannot avoid a resemblance that suggests she is a split-off aspect of her mother: ruthless, full of rage, and driven to achieve her ends by virtually any means available to her.

As mother and daughter, Clytemnestra and Electra are of course intrinsically bound to each other. This inherent connection, a biological reality, burdens many of Rendell's female protagonists. When in *The Tree of Hands*, Benet repeats almost as a mantra, "I must not hate my mother," she is not only affirming her desire to act in an appropriately daughterly fashion toward her schizophrenic and destructive parent, but is also distancing herself from the tangled web that is made up of mother-daughter histories and feelings. Electra experiences similar emotions. In Aeschylus's *Libation Bearers*, she is sent by Clytemnestra to perform religious rites over the grave of Agamemnon. Among her prayers, she utters the wish that she not be like her mother. In Euripides' play, Electra responds to Clytemnestra's insistence that the murder of Agamemnon was just revenge for the sacrifice of Iphigenia by retorting that if Clytemnestra's vengeance is justified, so then is the retribution Electra and Orestes are soon to exact. It is not merely logic that drives Electra's argument but her awareness that both their lives have been shaped by the intra-familial hatreds that are destroying the House of Atreus.

Electra must therefore prove as fierce as her mother. As she rages in Aeschylus, her curses match the ferocity of those who murdered her father: she will fight evil with evil. In Aeschylus, she disappears from the play after she obeys Orestes' instructions about how to lure their mother to her death. In Sophocles, she remains obediently outside the palace in which the slaying of Clytemnestra takes place, venting her rage when she calls out that Orestes should strike twice. In all three plays, she eagerly seeks Clytemnestra's death, but only in Aeschylus does she spell out a deadly inheritance from her female parent: "The savage cubs the she-wolf bred / Are like their mother."

In all three tragedies, Electra—again—lives on the fringes of the society into which she has been born. In Aeschylus's *Libation Bearers*, the chorus of slaves reinforces the image of Electra's demotion in her own land. She needs Orestes, not only to avenge their father's murder, but also to rescue her from virtual exile within the palace. Like a pathetic Cinderella, Electra utters lamentations over a parent's grave, mourning Agamemnon and expressing resentment at her denigration in her own home (in Sophocles, she alludes to step-siblings, the offspring of Clytemnestra and Aegisthus, who have been raised in status above her). Alone, Electra is helpless, driven frantic by the false news of Orestes' death, and it is when he reveals himself to her that Electra herself creates the simile of the she-wolf and her cubs to represent Clytemnestra and her vengeful children.

In Sophocles, the chorus consists not of slaves but rather of Electra's social peers, the ladies of Mycenae. The chorus thus highlights Electra's partially self-chosen alienation. For the women possess a comfortable role in society that they think could be Electra's if she did not disdain taking her place among them. The major confrontation in Sophocles' play is between Electra and Clytemnestra, the latter insisting that if Electra were more daughterly, she would be more motherly. But Electra is obsessed with Agamemnon's murder and with revenge. As the chorus entreats her to give up her compulsion, she responds that they should let her rave. To Chrysothemis, her sister, who similarly asks Electra to accommodate herself to Clytemnestra's rule, Electra admits that she is intractable: "I am mad . . . I shall never be free from distress, and laments numberless."

A critic who says of Euripides' Electra that she posseses a tortured psyche has not adequately distinguished Euripides' portrait of Agamemnon's daughter from Sophocles' portrayal. For it is not a near insane but rather a defiantly proud and alienated Electra who is found in Euripides. In his version, Clytemnestra and Aegisthus have married Electra to a farmer, and Euripides' chorus is made up of countrywomen, neither slaves nor highborn women. In their attempts to aid Electra, they only emphasize that her isolation is at least in part self-chosen. She expresses deep resentment, not only because her father has been murdered and because her mother and stepfather have cast her out of the palace, but also because she is helpless on her own to alter her existence.

Euripides' Electra expresses her pride and defiance when she refuses to attend a festival of Hera because she lacks proper clothing, refusing the chorus's offer to lend her the appropriate attire. Her own clothing is makeshift and ragged and her hair is shorn and dirty (Rendell's Zosie closely resembles her). What Electra wears therefore becomes a symbol of a plight thrust upon her yet defiantly self-maintained. When she asks a stranger whom she does not yet recognize as Orestes to carry a message to her brother, she says, "Tell him firstly of the sort of clothes I wear," reinforcing their symbolic importance to the audience.

To summarize this composite portrait of Electra, she is a descendent of the House of Atreus, born into one of Western literature's most disturbed families. Her father has been murdered and her mother has cast her out of her home, reduced her royal privileges, or raised over her in importance children she bore to Aegisthus. Unmarried, Electra is also childless, bereft not only of the comfort a child might give her, but also of the roles that bestowed status on women in ancient Greek society. As a princess, she has not only lost the privileges that belong to her, but has been further humiliated by marriage to a lowly farmer. In Euripides her reduced status is reflected in how she looks and dresses. Isolated, in part by circumstances, in part by choice, Electra also lacks the support she might expect from father, husband, sister, and the brother who, either dead or still in exile, is her only hope. Her situation has either driven her mad or enraged her, and she clings to her obsessions as a defense against her past and her present situation. Given the opportunity, Electra proves devious, for example by serving in Aeschylus to lull Clytemnestra into false security and thereby to lure her to her death; or in Euripides by lying to her mother by falsely claiming that she has given birth to a son and needs her own mother's help. In so doing, Electra perverts an essential bond that links mothers and daughters. Electra may be no femme fatale, but as Clytemnestra's daughter and Helen's niece, she carries with her associations with the fatal woman.

The composite derived from the three versions of Electra's story dramatized in ancient Greek tragedy also reveals a significant ambiguity that resonates in the mysteries of Ruth Rendell. The Electras of Greek drama raise questions concerning heredity versus environment, fate versus free will. Does her membership in the House of Atreus reflect an ancient variation on the idea that character and personality result from the transmission of inherited traits—as is suggested by the image in Aeschylus of savage cubs that resemble their mother? Or is she, instead, rather a product of her disturbed family and of a culture that equates personal vengeance with justice? Does her psychological profile doom her, or is she a free agent who persists in making deadly choices despite the advice others (for example, the choruses) give her?

Rendell effectively adds another question to this list in her portrayal of her fey women: how unique is Electra? Take her alienation from society, her rebelliousness, her obsessive personality, and actual or potential madness, her strange garb and short (read *punk*) haircut, transport her across centuries, and it would be possible to find in Electra a prototype of the female hippies who were so large a part of the cultural landscape in the 1960s and 1970s when Rendell's early books were published. In *A Fatal Inversion*, it is said of Zosie that while striking, even beautiful in appearance, although odd in behavior, she is hardly unusual. Thousands like her could be found on any day in any English shopping mall. As Rendell begins to explore the potential such young women offered as literary characters, this plethora of Electra-like young women becomes in itself a frightening vision of modern life.

Again, it is not being argued here that a necessarily straight line exists between the three ancient Electras and Rendell's fey girls. It is arresting to note, however, that despite the influence of classical literature, Rendell never specifically alludes to Electra, to the woman who, unlike Benet in *The Tree of Hands,* has no difficulty surrendering to hatred of her mother. It is as if the conflicts that beset mothers and daughters are more potentially threatening than the incestuous wishes that bind mothers to their sons, so that Electra becomes an even more problematic figure than Oedipus. In Rendell's fiction, mothers and daughters are frequently tied together by fear, dislike, or outright hatred. Chapter 10 will explore the perhaps culturally determined problems that affect the mother-daughter bond. The ghost of Electra haunts Rendell's books, but she seems kept at a distance, filtered through other, similarly destructive female figures drawn from Rendell's vast reading. Similarly, the ghost of Orestes hovers over her fiction, as brothers and lovers merge with each other as characters trapped by the obsessions of the women they love. Because these other literary characters have so obviously influenced Rendell's creation of her fey girls, some of the following discussion may seem to have strayed from the Electra motif that is the focus of this chapter. Other strands of literary influence will be followed; at the same time, themes derived from the composite portrait of Electra will be found in them. By the end of this chapter, the path of discussion will return to Electra.

Rendell's first novelistic treatment of her fey girl can be found in *The Face of Trespass.* Drusilla Browne becomes the obsession of Graham (aka Gray) Lanceton. She is the "succubus" who appears in his dreams after their brief but intense affair has ended. Most of the novel is narrated in flashbacks from the time when Gray loses Drusilla because he will not agree to help kill her wealthy but boring husband. The book's suspense is generated by the uncertainty about whether this most ordinary man, whose character is reflected in his name, will finally accede to his lover's demands and kill for her.

A Rupert Brooke poem serves as the novel's epigram, invoking a well-established literary tradition for *The Face of*

Trespass. Brooke's speaker is an anguished man describing the end of a love affair, undecided about whether he has lost a "high goddess" or a "dull, slight, cloudy naught." At the end of the poem, he admits about himself that whether the woman was "foul or lovely," he had been a fool to love her. Brooke's dualism is paralleled in Rendell when she names her fey girl. Drusilla Browne is almost an oxymoron, especially if the final –e is removed. That her real surname, her husband's, proves to be Janus (the mythological god who simultaneously faced forward and backward) only reinforces the duality.

The fair/foul woman is a well-established character in folklore and literature, especially in English medieval and renaissance writing. Briefly, to summarize the fair/foul motif, a besotted young man is seduced by what he perceives as an alluringly beautiful woman. Then, either by happenstance or because some set of circumstances removes the woman's power to deceive, she is revealed in her true colors, often as an ugly hag. In Chaucer's *Wife of Bath's Tale,* a knight agrees to marry a loathly lady because she can help him save his life, and because of his submission to her will, she is transformed into a beautiful lady—or so he sees her. Some commentators have pointed out that in the Middle Ages, it would have been obvious that the knight, like Rendell's Gray Lanceton, is a victim of his own distorted perceptions. In Rendell's novel, however, Drusilla suggests other characters found in English literature. In Book II of Spenser's *Faerie Queene,* the Red Cross Knight is enthralled by a seemingly fair lady Duessa, until one day he discovers her to be a foul, hideous creature.

The name *Drusilla* also suggests a combination of Duessa and Camilla, the famous vampire of gothic literature. Drusilla wears an exotic perfume whose name translates as dangerous bait. She is described as *foxy,* a common enough term for a seductive woman, but also evocative of the shape-shifting fox-woman who, in folklore and literature, belongs to the fair/foul catalog of literary characters. David Garnett wrote a novella about such a creature, *Lady into Fox*, depicting in detail the nature of the fair/foul lady, and Rendell may have read this work by a member of a famous English literary family. Finally, when Gray calls Drusilla his succubus, Rendell also invokes the fair/foul elements of dream lore. The incubus or succubus (the demon can take either male or female shape) seduces its prey with its beauty, but its real nature is epitomized by the ugly, malevolent imp in Edvard Munch's famous painting, *The Incubus*. In it, a sleeping woman expresses both the ecstasy and the terror that the demon evokes. So, conversely, do Rendell's fey girls inspire such contrary emotions in their enthralled lovers.

To conclude this brief excursion into folklore as well as medieval and romantic literature, Gray's surname, Lanceton, brings to mind the knights of King Arthur's round table. One of these, Gawain, encounters a fair/foul lady in two stories. *Sir Gawain and Dame Ragnell* is another version of *The Wife of Bath's Tale*. And in one of the most famous works of English medieval literature, *Sir Gawain and the Green Knight*, the image of fair and foul is split between two women, Lady Bercilak, the beautiful temptress who covets Gawain's body because she wants his soul; and the ugly Morgan le Fay who utilizes the wiles of her beautiful counterpart in order to trick Gawain and shame Arthur's court. Given her wide and varied reading, Ruth Rendell was almost certainly familiar with these stories, staples of English literature, and she almost certainly saw that the fair-foul motif reflects the ways in which human perception could be distorted, so that fair and foul become indistinguishable. In her novel *Anna's Book*, one of the characters alludes to an Edgar Allan Poe story about a man who is "too vain to wear glasses," and who courts his own great-great-grandmother, mistaking her for a young girl.

Names—again—are frequently thematic signifiers in Rendell's fiction. Gray, which is a shortening of Graham, also suggests a man whose commonplace existence is evidenced in its most colorless form. A similarly descriptive name, Leonard Dunsand, is given to a dull husband in *Some Lie and Some Die*. As Lanceton (i.e. Lancelot), however, Gray possesses sufficient imagination to turn foul into fair. For Gray, Drusilla's delicate beauty signifies all that is ethereal and reminds him of the lovely fairies that can be found in illustrated books. This inchoate imagination had made it possible to write the novel whose royalties supply his income. But Gray cannot escape his conventional roots (see Chapter 7). When Drusilla arrives for a dinner date, Gray experiences difficulty reconciling her clinging purple dress matched by purple lipstick with his fantasies about her essential innocence. He muses that it would be difficult for a casual observer to see her dressed as she is and still recognize her "underlying naivety."

It is, of course, Gray who is naïve. He interprets Drusilla's voracious quest for experience as childishness, and when she tempts him into procuring drugs for them with a promise that their love making will become even more exciting, he tries not to face the implications of her demand. Drusilla herself admits she wants to do "decadent" things—that is why she must be rid of her dull husband—but Gray translates decadence into instability. When he procures LSD for her but declines the drug for himself, his reluctance foreshadows his later disinclination to help kill her husband.

In *The Lake of Darkness*, Martin Urban proves even more conventional and stodgy than Graham Lanceton. Gray's aspiration to be an author at least suggests a struggle against the ordinary. Martin Urban is, in contrast, completely without imagination or excitement, as his name suggests. But Martin is essentially decent, and when he wins a great deal of money in a lottery, he seeks out people who desperately need help: for example, he pays for one of them to have heart surgery. But someone close to Urban and unidentified until late in the novel resents his windfall and arranges for him to meet and fall under the spell of the fair/foul Francesca.

Unlike Drusilla, Francesca has no rich husband to support her at all, much less extravagantly. She must work. Her employment places her in a flower shop, predisposing Martin to make Gray Lanceton's mistake as he equates Francesca's beauty with the symbolic innocence of fresh blooms. Later, he will be shocked to discover that she has a two-year-old child, not only because she has deceived him by withholding the information, but also because motherhood implies sexual experience and is at odds with his rather prudish ideas about her. Confused, he cannot untangle the contrary threads that make up her personality. Like Drusilla Browne, Francesca Brown's name implies duality, and like Drusilla, Francesca can be traced to the fairy folk, who, Rendell tells her readers, are likely to vanish in daylight. Another folktale may supply an even closer analogue, one known generically as the Vanishing Hitchhiker. She can be found in stories of a woman who, after an encounter with a man, seems like a sprite to vanish entirely.

For Martin does not know where Francesca lives; taxis spirit her away after she refuses his offers to take her home. Much of the novel involves Martin's attempt to find her and the readers' puzzlement over the scheme that requires Francesca to seduce Martin although she finds him insufferably boring. For Rendell, this virtually double puzzle requires a narrative sleight of hand for the disclosure of the solution. Late in the novel, Rendell alters her narrative point of view. Until then, readers have remained in the dark with Martin, because Francesca only exists through his befuddled experience of her and is only on the scene when he is. But then an omniscient narrator takes over and readers are allowed to see the real Francesca and her accomplice working their plan to gain access to Martin's wealth. This shift in narration from limited to full omniscience is a structural weak point in the book, but it does afford Rendell a chance to employ dramatic irony. The tension involves when and how Martin will come to know what Rendell's readers have already learned.

Suspense in *The Lake of Darkness* and *The Face of Trespass* has to do with how a deceived man will come fully to grasp the foul nature of his seemingly fair lady. Martin Urban is not asked to commit a murder, but he is nonetheless a pawn in a criminal scheme, drawn by his fey girl into a plot of which he remains ignorant until the novel's end. To trace Rendell's fey girl sequentially through several of her works is also to see how Rendell deepens her treatment of these themes. Again, several years would intervene between the early portrayals of Drusilla and Francesca and the later portrayal of Bell in *The House of Stairs*. In that time, Rendell had more fully mastered her craft and the fairly straightforward femme fatale tradition had given way to a far more subtle exploration of character and circumstance. Literary allusions, however, still supplied her book with crucial thematic glosses. Bell, short for Christabel, is one of Rendell's most allusive as well as elusive fey girls. No longer would a neat fair/foul dichotomy suffice to describe her, for Rendell has now decidedly moved her fey girls out of the realm of wickedness into that of psychopathology.

Rendell's most obvious literary borrowing in *The House of Stairs* is Henry James's novel *The Wings of the Dove*, which she summarizes in detail. Two people, in love but too poor to sustain the lifestyle they aspire to, plot to marry the man to a dying heiress. When Rendell's first-person narrator, Elizabeth, summarizes the plot for Bell, she has no way of predicting that Bell will concoct a similar scheme that will eventually lead to murder. Early in the story, Bell and Elizabeth live in the same house, another of Rendell's hippie hangouts (despite its elegance), supported by an older woman, Cosette. Widowed, rich, and weary of her past conventional life, Cosette tries to recapture her youth, surrounding herself with offbeat characters who randomly enter and exit the House of Stairs. One of these is Bell, who introduces her brother Mark to Cosette, whom Bell believes to be suffering from cancer. If Mark marries Cosette, he is likely to become her heir. When the conspiracy fails, a crime takes place. But all of this has already happened when the book begins and Bell has been released from prison. Who she has killed is the mystery not revealed until the book's conclusion.

Whereas James's novel and its thematic role in Rendell's story must be made clear to her readers for them to follow her own plot, it is not necessary for them to recognize the significance of Bell's changing her name from its original, Christine, to Christabel, of which Bell is the diminutive. Christabel is the title character in one of Samuel Taylor Coleridge's major narrative poems. Coleridge's story tells of an innocent young maiden who encounters a strange, fair/foul woman named Geraldine, whose influence over her will prove highly ambiguous. Geraldine may be a witch, a vampire, a lesbian, or someone divinely entrusted to rescue Christabel from impending danger. At some point, Coleridge's innocent Christabel begins to take on the malignant characteristics of Geraldine, especially after a particularly erotic scene in which the two women share a bed. In *The House of Stairs,* Elizabeth and Bell are lovers.

That Coleridge's poem strongly impressed itself on Rendell's imagination can be discerned by skipping ahead several years to the writing of one of the later Wexford books, *Simisola.* Ingrid Pamber is one of those pretty, flirtatious, self-absorbed, even scheming young women to whom Wexford is sometimes briefly attracted. It is Ingrid's startlingly blue eyes that the inspector finds most striking, but when he comes to understand that her fresh prettiness only conceals a blatant self-interest, he is struck by the way those sparkling eyes had become "dull as stones." The description echoes an image from Coleridge's poem, in which Geraldine is described with the serpent imagery that is threaded throughout the poem. Like a snake's eye, which blinks "dull and shy," Christabel, now under the influence of Geraldine, absorbs those "shrunken serpent eyes," and "passively did imitate / That look of dull and treacherous hate!" But Rendell also rewards with a joke those readers who have picked up her literary allusion (a clue is the name *Christabel* given to a teddy bear coveted by Ingrid). Nothing unearthly or supernatural accounts for the transformation of Ingrid's eyes from brilliant to dull. She has merely removed her contact lenses.

No joke, however, attaches to the influence of Coleridge's poem on *The House of Stairs*, where everything appears to be seen "inside out," and the name Christabel is a signal for constant transformations. Bell's form of dress consistently indicates her strangeness. It is not only that she almost always dresses in blacks, browns, and grays, but also that her clothes are unlike anyone else's dress. Shortly, however, they would, as the book's narrator observes, "become wildly fashionable in the alternative mode," the virtual uniform of those who thereby announce their scorn of all that is conventional. As Bell will say about herself at one point in the book, a "woman who has done murder [has] put herself outside the pale of any civilized society." Here she might even be describing Electra, whose alienation leads her to murder and thereby further isolation from what Bell calls civilized society. That thousands of young women will engage in self-exile, defining themselves by their dress, becomes a reiterated theme in Rendell's fiction—although, of course, most of them will not become murderers.

Cosette, who is Bell's benefactor and intended victim, also uses clothing to cross the boundaries between her former traditional existence as wife of a wealthy businessman and her present, freer life. The House of Stairs, in which she supports hangers-on who pretend to an ideal of communal living, is her rewriting of her life. At one time, her attire was conventionally appropriate and consistently drab, even her wedding dress. But now she has become almost defiantly trendy in her quest for renewed youth, for experience, for love, for sex. Even so, her new mode of dress is not that of the hippies who inhabit the home she so generously provides them. For Cosette never fully leaves behind a moral realm she would never abandon. Rather, it is Bell whose attire consistently announces her moral and psychological alienation. At a dinner party that foretells the collapse of Bell's scheme to marry Mark to Cosette, Bell is described as being the worst dressed person there, her clothing a metaphor for her status as dangerous outsider.

Bell's slender, almost wraithlike figure appears to belie the tenacious self-interest that consistently drives her. She is, again, one of Rendell's psychopaths, a woman without morals, whose narcissism makes it possible for her to exploit anyone who passes her way and seems to promise something to gain. The extent of her moral and psychological pathology is revealed as the book progresses, so that her release from prison and insinuation once again into Elizabeth's life is increasingly horrifying (Huntington's disease, which renders Elizabeth vulnerable to Bell, and which supplies a major theme in this book, will be discussed in Chapter 11). For the novel is not only about how Bell binds unsuspecting men to her, although there are many of those in the novel, but—consistent with Coleridge's poem—also how she seduces Elizabeth.

The lesbian theme in "Christabel" has been part of the controversies surrounding the poem. Unlike Coleridge, however, Rendell was free of constraints when she wrote *The House of Stairs,* and the sexual relationship of Elizabeth and Bell is both explicit and detailed. Bell has no boundaries in her own life, sexual or otherwise. No specific definitions therefore apply. Her sexuality is as much a matter of indifference to her as everything else, mattering only if her narcissistic ends are served. For Bell, every relationship involves an act of absorption, of incorporating her surroundings into that self beyond which she cannot, in fact, see. Or perhaps, psychologically, she has no self, and like Francesca in *The Lake of Darkness,* her psyche is as wraith-like as her body, always on the verge of disappearing. *The House of Stairs* suggests that a possible bad seed had from childhood shaped Bell's personality and character. Similarly, by the time Rendell created Zosie in *A Fatal Inversion,* her fey girl appeared as much the victim of her birth and environment as the perpetrator of harm. Fair or foul, good or evil, nature or nurture, all seemed as dichotomies to be inadequate as explanations for human action.

In his writing, William Blake, another writer who exerted a strong influence on Ruth Rendell, exposed the limitations of these either-or pairings by advancing a different set of seeming contraries, innocence and experience, both of which were essential to human existence. Innocence is the childlike perception of beauty and goodness in the world that some children are privileged to experience and sometimes too ready or too reluctant to abandon in adulthood. Experience roots people in the world, which too often not only destroys the remnants of innocence but also mires them in an environment inimical to human fulfillment. Blake first asserts the importance of environment in human development, but then, because of the social conditions of his own age, exposes its devastating effects. In his *Marriage of Heaven and Hell*, Blake creates a series of proverbs, uttered by the Devil, whom Blake completely redefines as a source of wisdom and energy, challenging society's conventional—and for Blake, too often hypocritical—codes of behavior.

Frequently these proverbs are also puzzles: one of them supplies a striking analogy to the plots of *The House of Stairs* and of *A Fatal Inversion:* "Sooner murder an infant in its cradle than nurse unacted desires." To take Blake literally would be to read that he advocates murder as an act of individual will, urging one to kill rather than repress the impulse. Bell would seem to have done just that in her early life when she murdered her infant sister. For anyone who studies the effects of the environment on the individual, however, the proverb could be understood to say that the way society severely represses all human instincts is so damaging to the evolving adult that children might as well be killed while they are still infants.

There is in this proverb, moreover, an ambiguous use of the word *nurse,* which in addition to its association with *nurture,* also points to the social disparities among English classes. The nursemaid became an increasingly problematic and often alienated character in romantic and post-romantic literature, her own thwarted maternal instincts often leading to a disturbed relationship with her infant charge. These narrative, cultural, and psychological motifs surround the murder that takes place in *A Fatal Inversion,* whose catastrophes are triggered by the virtual death of a baby in its cradle and the coincidental employment of one of the characters as a kind of nursemaid.

A Fatal Inversion begins ten years after a crime has been committed and the bodies of a woman and her infant are dug up on the property of what had for a disastrous summer been the site of an impulsively created commune. The three men who lived in it had promised never to contact each other again, but when the corpses are discovered, they are drawn back into each other's lives. Only at the end do readers learn the identities of the victims and the killer. Zosie is the fey girl who wanders into the commune to become the lover of young Adam, who had inherited the house from his uncle and was thereby free to live a summer devoted to enjoying an unconventional, irresponsible life of drugs and sex (see Chapter 6). Like Graham Lanceton and Martin Urban, Adam is enthralled by his fey girl but eventually alarmed by her amorality. Zosie lies about almost everything, so that she seems to lack substance, an ephemeral wraith. She also consistently steals without guilt. More significantly, she steals other women's children because she so desperately wants a child. When she enters the story, it is not clear whether she has been released from a mental institution or has run away from a home for unwed mothers. If the latter, it is a sign of her amorality that she cannot muster empathy for the mothers whose children she wants to take because her own had apparently been taken away from her. Because of Zosie's obsession with having a child, a murder takes place and several lives are ruined.

Of all of Rendell's fey girls, Zosie most resembles Electra. Her shorn hair and her makeshift clothing account for some of this resemblance. That Zosie bitterly resents her mother is another point of similarity. But that Electra is unwed or is a virgin, whereas Zosie is sexually promiscuous, rather than differentiating them, points to the same end: both are childless and both suffer from the lack of children or the status that accrues to being a mother. That both are also likely to be horrendous mothers is implied in both Rendell's novel and Euripides' *Electra*, whose endings bear comparison. After Electra and Orestes kill their mother and stepfather, Electra marries her brother's friend Pylades. This appropriate union, so at odds with her marriage to the farmer, suggests a "happy ending" whose ominous undertones require that Euripides' audience recall the generational conflicts besetting the House of Atreus. As Pylades' wife, Electra is likely to become a mother and her doomed family history may be perpetuated in her children. Similarly, Rendell leaves the readers of *A Fatal Inversion* with a horrifying future to contemplate. For despite the catastrophes that follow Zosie's acting out of her obsessions at the summer commune, she seems to have survived the ordeal that led to others' death and suffering, apparently becoming the smug wife of a wealthy man and mother of many children (Rendell is both clear and teasingly vague on this denoument). What these offspring may have inherited from their mother, either via nature or nurture, will leave Rendell's readers with a decided chill as they close the covers of her book.

As a psychopathic kidnapper of children, Zosie proves to be both victimizer and victim, thereby rendering *A Fatal Inversion* a novel in which environmental factors help explain her behavior (they are not, however, self-sufficient explanations). When she shows up at Adam's makeshift commune, she virtually disappears from the family she was ostensibly going back to after giving birth. There is no indication, however, that her indifferent mother has made any attempt to look for her, something about which Zosie is very bitter. Moreover, it may be her stepfather who made her pregnant with the infant Zosie has given up. There is no question that even if Zosie is mad, she has also been the product of a terrible family life. But—again—neither is there a question that Zosie, for all her longing for a child, could be a fit mother. She is like countless other young, emotionally deprived young women who hardly distinguish infants from dolls. Desperately wanting love herself, she is ill equipped to bestow it. And so the final horror of the book is, to repeat, that after nemesis has overtaken most of the commune members, Zosie seems to have survived and to have indulged over and over her desire to have babies.

In introducing environmental factors into her portraits of her fey girls, Rendell has created in Zosie one of the most ambiguous of them. Senta Pelham of *The Bridesmaid* is Rendell's most frightening. She also may also be Rendell's final word on her type, for to date no other book written by Rendell has appeared to add to the group being studied in this chapter. Some of the similarities between the psychopath Senta and the unconventional but otherwise gentle and sweet Gemma Lawrence close the circle of characters that this chapter has designated Rendell's fey girls. (See Sources and Additional Comments for a consideration of Rendell's choice of names, *Senta*.)

When Philip Wardman's sister Fee gets married, the groom's cousin Senta is one of her bridesmaids. At the end of the wedding, Senta arrives at Philip's house and, in his room, strips off her attendant's dress. The rather ordinary and less than tasteful dress would be the last conventional garment Senta would wear. Her discarding of it is a characteristic Rendell signal to readers that the ensuing love affair between Senta and Philip is fraught with peril. Near the conclusion of *The Bridesmaid*, when things have gone horribly wrong and Senta's madness has fully emerged, terrifying Philip, he leaves Senta, withdrawn into herself and draped in the kind of shawls that typify the dress of Rendell's fey girls (including the harmless Gemma Lawrence). As Philip leaves, Senta falls asleep curled "foetuslike" on her bed with the shawls spread over her.

Philip Wardman is another of Rendell's basically conventional men, his surname reminiscent of Martin Urban, in both instances evoking images of the ordinary, colorless realms these men literally and symbolically inhabit. Philip resembles Gray Lanceton even more, each of them at least capable of imagining a life at odds with the one he actually lives, and tending to fantasize about it. Here again, Rendell plays with names, once again reversing their potential meaning. Philip has two sisters, one of them the bride at whose wedding Philip meets Senta. Her name is Fee, again, close to the French word for fairy, but she could hardly be farther from Rendell's fey girls, looking for nothing more out of life than the unexceptional and dreary married existence Rendell is so adept at portraying. If anything, it is the other sister, Cheryl, whose amoral hippie way of living appears a backdrop for the more extreme character of Senta. Once again, Rendell is turning things inside out, revealing ambiguities through ironic contrasts. Both Cheryl and Senta live at or beyond the fringes of conventional society. But whereas Cheryl is prone to commit petty crimes such as stealing clothes, Senta's self-proclaimed rebellion against conventionality might be phrased as *I murder, therefore I am*. (This formulation is mine not Rendells, but she defines Finn in *The Lake of Darkness* by alluding to Descartes: "I kill, therefore I am.") It is perfectly consistent with this philosophy that Senta demands from Phillip as proof of love that he kill someone for her—anyone will do. And she, in turn, will kill for him.

Senta holds Philip in thrall because of her beauty, her seemingly dependent fragility, her craving for love, and her insatiable desire for sex. Rendell is uncharacteristically explicit about the couple's lovemaking. They spend most of their time in bed, and Philip is amazed by the ease with which he is able to physically satisfy Senta. If his sister Cheryl is a compulsive gambler, Philip is addicted to sex with Senta, fearing only to lose the ecstasy that he mistakes for love. At the same time, the image of dirty sheets thematically undercuts these erotic scenes, and Philip must repress his aversion to Senta's filthy apartment (much as Mike Burden had been repelled by Gemma's capacity to live in a messy and unclean house). In one instance, when Senta has temporarily thrust Philip out of her life and only appears in his dreams as a succubus, he awakens immediately to launder his bed linen. There is a sordidness about their union that only begins fully to dawn on Philip when he realizes that Senta is not merely playing a game when she demands each should kill as a sign of love for the other. Who the victims are does not matter; what is important is that the murders take place. And in this way, Senta proves far more frightening than Drusilla, whose desire to be rid of a boring and rich husband is almost simple in motive; than Francesca, whose moral indifference allows her to be used in a criminal scheme that really does not interest her very much, despite the promise of money; than Bell, who readily kills to gain something she wants but would be content to get it some other way; or than Zosie, whose obsessions do not require murder but nonetheless result in one.

In horrific contrast, Senta raises murder to a philosophical, Nietzchean level. She and Philip will kill to prove they exist above the herd, to demonstrate that morality has nothing to do with them. Senta is astonished to discover that Philip is disturbed by his sister's petty thefts. All that matters, she tells him, as if it were self-evident, is that Cheryl not be caught. At first, Philip rationalizes such attitudes, pretending that he need not take Senta seriously. She is an actress by profession and mundane reality often has little meaning for her. But when Senta begins psychologically to disintegrate, Philip is terrified by the demonic look he occasionally sees in her eyes, wondering, when it is gone, if he had only imagined it. Eventually, he cannot pretend any longer that the woman he thought he loved and who seems to crave his love so desperately is anything but completely insane.

Philip could not have become Senta's prey, however, if his own tendency to fantasize and thus confuse illusion and reality was not already deeply ingrained. He is Rendell's narrative point of view, his fluctuating emotions, his uncertainties, dilemmas, fears, hopefulness, ecstasies, terrors, and revulsions portrayed in great detail as he succumbs to Senta's madness. Philip is torn between his rootedness in conventional life and his yearning to transcend it. His conflicts intersect disastrously with Senta's immunity to all conflict, and ironically, it is she who often appears the more clear-eyed and consistent, often having to explain to Philip that she had already told him something he only later realizes she really meant.

Before meeting Senta, Philip's fantasies had been centered on the statue of the Roman goddess Flora that his deceased father had bought his mother on their honeymoon. Philip is so taken with this beautiful objet d'art that he determines that if he ever meets a woman who looks like the statue, he will fall in love with her. Meanwhile, he trains to be an interior designer, lives at home with his mother and sisters, whom he feels responsible for, and, although not entirely satisfied with his limited expectations, hopes for little more than his modest ambitions are likely to yield him. Then he meets Senta, who recognizes as readily as Philip that she looks like Flora. And like Martin Urban, who thinks that the flowers Francesca sells reflect her essential innocence, so does Philip attribute to Senta/Flora a similarly illusory freedom from guile. At first, her minor lies disconcert him, but he relegates them to the realm of harmless fantasy. When he finds out, however, that some of what he assumes are fabrications are in fact truths, he feels guilty about mistrusting her and becomes that much more vulnerable to her ploys. Finally, when Senta demands he murder for her, promising to do as much for him, he chooses to see her scheme as a merely playful game. He will not take her seriously. In, again, another of Rendell's ingenious and ironic narrative twists, Philip's ultimate fantasy is that Senta at her most deadly is but a fantasizer.

The Bridesmaid is—again—the culmination of Ruth Rendell's treatment of the fey girl. Masterful at getting inside the psychopath's mind, Rendell elects this time to instead tell her story through Philip, whose own mental equilibrium is endangered because he complicates what is in fact quite simple—if frighteningly simple. Dealing with his sister

Cheryl's problems parallels his mounting concern over Senta, but because Cheryl's difficulties obviously belong to the domain of psychologists and social workers, Philip mistakenly thinks his sister is the more serious problem in his life. It will take him a long while to recognize that it is Senta's insane otherworldliness that makes her the more dangerous of the two young women. The brother-sister pairing of Philip and Cheryl as a gloss on the lovers Philip and Senta suggests once again the complex relationship between Orestes and Electra. Agamemnon's daughter has only one living man in her life she could love and depend upon, her brother (that in Euripides she marries her brother's close friend reinforces this connection). And if she does not demand that Orestes kill to prove his devotion to her, her reasons for egging him on to murder their mother when he hesitates to do so are in the last analysis self-serving, allowing her, like Senta, to carry a personal obsession to its horrific conclusion.

CHAPTER 9

FATHERS AND DAUGHTERS

The plot of *Death Notes* rests on the nineteen-year alienation of renowned flutist Manuel Comargue and his daughter Natalie. Over her father's objections, Natalie had given up her studies in music, married, and had gone to live in America. Despite letters from him, even the news that her mother is ill with cancer, Natalie does not respond until she learns he is about to remarry. For this places in jeopardy her inheritance of his estate, and when Comargue is murdered before his scheduled wedding, suspicion falls upon Natalie. During his investigations Wexford contemplates the father-daughter relationship. He thinks of Sylvia and Sheila, his pleasure in them, and theirs in him, and how they had never seriously quarreled. But as he muses on Freud's theory concerning the ideal bond between mother and son, he draws the logical conclusion that "father and daughter is not the perfect relationship." In this, the eleventh of Rendell's twenty-two Wexford novels, the inspector does not realize that his words are almost prophetic and that in the future he will find far fewer reasons to be complacent about his family.

Freud critics frequently note that, in attempting to formulate a female Oedipus complex, the psychologist had not adequately accounted for the transference of the young girl's attachment from her first love object, her mother, to her father. The bond with the caretaking mother is one boys and girls share, and it is a natural connection that Clytemnestra invokes when in Aeschylus she pleads with Orestes for her

185

life. Freud argued that, unlike their brothers, girls must experience two shifts in affection, first from mother to father and then from father to husband. The girl stuck in her Oedipal phase, however, did not face too serious a problem, because her husband would take over her father's role. The more difficult and ultimately controversial issue for Freud to explain was her moving away from mother to father to begin with.

Chapter 7, on Rendell's mothers and sons, discussed Freud's arguments and how they failed to adequately explain why both Burden's wife Jenny and Wexford's daughter Sylvia view with repugnance the idea of giving birth to daughters. The psychologist had accounted for the transfer of a girl's affection from mother to father in terms of a deficit in her female parent, the absence of a penis or what that symbolizes, her lack of status and power in a man's world. But there is an additional problem in explaining the father-daughter bond, for in the Victorian and early modern periods in which Freud lived and wrote, and earlier, when men's work took them outside the home, the traditional role of a man usually distanced him from the domestic sphere and thus from his children's daily lives. Unless one speculates that it is the father's general remoteness that allows his daughter to romanticize him, it is difficult to imagine Freud's typical husband and father taking over feedings and changing diapers, assuming a share in his daughter's care and thereby cementing their affection for each other. The conventional situation is illustrated in *A Sleeping Life,* in which Sylvia's emerging feminism reflects her growing dissatisfaction with her marriage. Her distress and her anger are so obvious that Wexford feels compelled to explain apologetically that although his work keeps him occupied and frequently away from home, he hopes he is never too busy to talk to his daughters and be there for them when needed.

Later in this chapter, both Sylvia's feminism and also her difficulty with men will be attributed to disappointments concerning Wexford. Where it comes to fathers and daughters, or so post-Freudian writing instructs, a young woman may be in trouble if she is too close or insufficiently close to her male parent. Gender conflict may be particularly grievous in father-daughter relationships, because both a woman's relatively limited choices about her life and also her burgeoning opportunities in a more liberated era may lead to confusion and make her more vulnerable than a man to her father's early treatment. In *An Unkindness of Ravens,* Jenny Burden recites a list of "gross exploitations" that is woman's lot: "pornography, degradation, career prohibition or curtailment, rape, [and] father-daughter incest." In short, contrary to Freud, a woman stuck in an Oedipal conflict experiences not a relatively unimportant crisis but rather a particularly aggravated one, paradoxically as her choices about her life have expanded.

At its worse, the Electra complex can destroy a woman. At one point, Sylvia muses on the psychological dangers of modeling oneself on the opposite-sex parent. The ancient tragedians obviously understood this, for to read the Electra plays is to realize (to reiterate an earlier discussion) that she is driven less by love of her father Agamemnon than hatred of her mother Clytemnestra. Depending on the play in question, Electra's anger is fueled by resentment over her exile from the palace and its prestige, or marriage to a lowly farmer, or a life of near-poverty, all of which she blames on Clytemnestra. Her dead and significantly long-absent father exists less as a formerly doting parent than a symbol of the power she herself lacks, and she depends on Agamemnon's surrogate, her brother Orestes, to supply what was lost with her father's death.

The narrative pattern involving a woman filled with despair and mounting rage, deprived of the support she should be able to expect from a father, and therefore dependent upon her brother whom she invests with powers she herself lacks, can be found in Rendell's *The Killing Doll.* Dolly has many reasons to be deeply unhappy. She was born with a disfiguring birthmark that repels many who see her, and as much as possible, she hides from the world. Her mother had made her leave school and trained her as a dressmaker, work Dolly could do at home. As a result, she has no friends. Dolly is in her mid-twenties when her mother dies and her father, oblivious to her misery because he escapes from his own by constantly reading historical romances, marries his next-door neighbor, Myra. His new wife finds his children's presence in the house intrusive. She virtually banishes them to the top floor so that contact will be minimized—much as Electra is banished from the palace.

Dolly's only solace and companionship is her brother Peter, called Pup. That she both depends on him but also thinks of herself as his mother speaks both to her powerlessness and also her need to feel important. Her unrealistic view of their eternal bond, exacerbated by her daily consumption of full bottles of wine, causes her life to spin out of control. She knows that when he was still young, Pup had promised his soul to the devil in exchange for some added inches to his short height. When he eventually grew to a normal if not tall size, he continued his arcane studies, turning his room into a temple where he practiced what he called white magic. With Dolly, he attends séances, and eventually he joins the Temple of the Dawn, a well-known society devoted to esoteric knowledge and practices. At one point, Dolly is about to urge him to magically erase the disfiguring mark on her face when she thinks of a more compelling challenge, killing Myra. Nervous, Pup distracts Dolly by promising instead to "clobber" their father's new wife.

Effectively playing Orestes to Dolly's Electra, Pup ritually plunges a knife into the stomach of a doll that Dolly has fashioned to look like her stepmother. He hopes this vicarious murder will pacify his sister. When Myra actually dies, however, of a pregnancy she tries to abort herself, Dolly is convinced her brother caused the death and that his powers are unlimited. Eventually, Pup realizes Dolly's long-term emotional problems have evolved into a serious mental illness and that she is in dire need of help. The novel moves toward its horrific climax, depicting what might happen if a woman could no longer get her father to protect her or her brother to kill for her, and thought she had to commit a murder herself.

All of the ancient tragedians who dramatized Electra's joy at her brother's return from exile understood that Orestes was a stand-in for their father Agamemnon. In Sophocles, in fact, Electra maternally assumes the role of Orestes' protector, sending him out of the country and away from the never-ending ravages visited on the House of Atreus. Now she must wait for him to act against their mother. It is Euripides who introduces into his play a mysterious element concerning parent-child bonding. When Clytemnestra confronts her angry daughter concerning Electra's grievances, the queen remarks that some children seem to be born preferring their mothers, others their fathers. Electra, she contends, is one of the latter. Even allowing for rationalization on Clytemnestra's part, the ancient plays suggest that in the father-daughter relationship, there is interplay among emotional bonds that defy explanations based on either biological or cultural determinants. Rendell's fiction reflects the range of possibilities that bind fathers and daughters—or that alienate them.

It would be difficult to recall strong examples in Rendell's fiction of positive father-daughter relationships with the exception of the Wexford books, and these, as will soon be seen, become more problematic as the series progresses. Of course, it is difficult to find in her fiction good parent-child relationships, a sadly ironic instance occurring in *Not in the Flesh,* in which a small girl is taken away from her doting parents because of a practice Somali immigrants think will secure her future well-being but which is illegal in England. In *The Lake of Darkness,* a two-year-old girl annoys her mother with her reiterated whine, "I want my daddy," her very plaint revealing conflict with her mother. Chapter 3 introduced Sara Williams, who in *An Unkindness of Ravens* falsely accuses her father of incest, perhaps to mask an unconscious sexual attraction to him. In that novel, Wexford's solution to the murders he is investigating is based on what he knows of Freud's rejection of his seduction theory and the psychologist's explanations for why so many of his female patients claimed to have been forced to submit to incestuous relationships.

But Sara has a more obvious and immediate reason to obsess over her father. She is extremely ambitious, hoping to enter medical school, and neither of her parents offers her the slightest support for her goals. Her mother seems to nurture antipathy toward her daughter, her love exclusively given to Sara's brother. But it turns out that it is her father and his bigamous existence that proves the greatest stumbling block in Sara's way as she strives toward professional success. For without her father's assistance when she fills out application forms, she will not receive the financial aid she requires for her education. Her father, in turn, has his own hidden reasons not to help her. But—consistent with Rendell's habit of exploring all permutations of family relationships—it is just the opposite set of circumstances that sets Sophie Dade against her father in *Babes in the Wood*. Sophie despises the father who is always nagging at her to study and makes it almost impossible for her to have friends. But it is not just his relentless pressure that turns Sophie against him. He is a hard, cold man who shows no love for his daughter and therefore elicits no affection from her.

There is no obvious reason why in the short story "Almost Human" a woman hires a hit man to commit murder. The killer assumes she wishes to be rid of a husband or lover, but the story's surprise is that the intended victim is her father and that unless he died on the designated day, there would be no point at all in killing him. The inference is that the father is about to take an action that would diminish or prevent his daughter's inheritance of his wealth. Equally antagonistic to their fathers are Rendell characters who feel burdened by them. For the position of an unmarried woman with a widower father dependent on her may be unbearable.

The assumption is that she, and not her married siblings if she has them, will be his caregiver, and often his needs render him demanding and quarrelsome. In one of Rendell's earliest novels, *The Secret House of Death*, Magdalene Heller seems to have married to escape from the father invalided by multiple sclerosis, and the letters in which she describes duty rather than love for him supply important clues to solving a mystery. Similarly, a father in *A Sleeping Life* complains querulously about his neglect by his daughter. Although he had thwarted her hopes for an education, he now expects her to care for him after her mother dies, and is particularly resentful when her winning the lottery does him no good. And in *The Veiled One*, the husband of a murder victim is less grieved by her death than he is concerned over the loss of a caregiver. He complacently allows his unmarried niece to take the responsibility for his well-being.

This is not to say that a natural affinity between fathers and daughters cannot be found in Rendell's fiction. But even then, the theme is often rendered not in terms of straightforward love, so much as in complicated or thwarted affection. In *Anna's Book* there are two fathers who, to one degree or another, reject the daughters whom they do not believe they have actually fathered. Swanny spends her later years obsessed with finding out who her real mother is, but the last link in the puzzle she strives to solve will be the revelation after her death of who her father was (see Chapter 5). Her adoptive father Rasmus clearly prefers her sister, whom he knows is his natural child. Another character in the same book repudiates the daughter he believes is not his biological offspring, whereas her natural father murders her mother and kidnaps her. The father-daughter relationship is a strong and reiterated sub-theme in *Anna's Book*, intertwined with the book's focus on mothers and daughters.

Fathers who become pathological because of intense love for their children or obsessive concern for their own role can be found throughout Rendell's fiction. In *A Fatal Inversion*, Adam is so protective of his baby daughter that his increasingly exasperated wife thinks he needs a psychiatrist. She, of course, does not know about a crime that had taken place ten years before, the murder of a woman and the death of a baby girl, nor of her husband's involvement in the crimes. That Adam loses both his wife and his beloved child constitutes a kind of justice in a novel in which the real killers are never tried for their deeds. But in other Rendell fiction, Adam's fate is held up as an example of extreme injustice. *Shake Hands Forever* is an example. Robert Hathall divorces his first wife to marry Angela. His mother and ex-wife are devoted to each other, and they influence his daughter Rosemary against him. He is bitterly aware that although he supports her, buys her presents, and arranges visits and outings with her, Rosemary despises him. Her antipathy signifies for him a life that has consistently cheated him.

For Michael, in the short story "Father's Day," the injustice is more abstract, involving what *could* happen to him, not what has actually occurred, and his growing obsession sends him over the edge into murder. Michael is convinced that he is going to lose his children, because, like all men, he is the potential victim of an unfortunate historical alteration in the rights of women. Until relatively recent times, children had remained in their fathers' custody should their wives be intrepid enough to leave them. Interestingly, Michael's obsessions reach their climax during a vacation in Greece, where some of the story's scenes take place in a café named the *Agamemnon*. The idea that overwhelms Michael is also a subject debated in the last play of the *Oresteia, The Eumenides (The Furies)*. When Orestes is tried for the murder of Clytemnestra, the jury must determine the greater crime: the failure to avenge a father's death or the slaying of a mother. To repeat an earlier discussion, in ancient Greece a woman was considered the mere repository of her husband's seed, and therefore killing Clytemnestra was finally decided to be the lesser crime. Orestes is thus acquitted of matricide. For his part, Michael perceives himself as redressing the wrong actually or potentially committed against countless fathers, who at one time were considered their children's only true parent but were now vulnerable to losing them. Such a father appears in *End of Tears*, in which a man who resentfully thinks he has lost everything in his divorce is reduced to baby-sitting his own children.

It is as a loving husband and father that Inspector Reginald Wexford has become endeared to so many of Ruth Rendell's readers. He is hardly unique among serial policemen. Their domestic life is a common enough motif in the genre of the police procedural (private detectives, in contrast, tend to be loners, often divorced and frequently childless). Nor is Rendell the first author to allow her readers into the homes of her investigators. But because of her depth of insight into her characters, and because her work almost always tends to be multi-dimensional, so too does her treatment of Wexford's domestic life become more complex than is usual in the genre. Since Wexford is, moreover, the father of daughters, it is not surprising that it is in the Wexford series that the most developed rendering of that relationship can be found (with perhaps the exception of *The Chimney Sweeper's Boy*). But because this was not so at the beginning of the Kingsmarkham books, this complexity emerges most clearly when Rendell's development of the Wexford family is looked at sequentially. To do so also requires a closer look at Dora Wexford, even if the focus of this chapter on fathers and daughters is somewhat blurred as she is brought into a discussion more fully developed in the next chapter.

At this writing, there are twenty-two books in the Wexford series, published over forty-five years (1964-2009). The most recent, *The Monster in the Box*, will be considered the last, even though others may yet appear. Not surprisingly, the series itself can be used to chart the development of Ruth Rendell's development as an author, as she proceeds from writing near-conventional *whodunits* to writing serious novels that are also mysteries. In general, they are far from being formulaic, narrative elements never plugged into a template, as is the case with many popular mystery series.

And increasingly they reflect the social changes taking place in England. So too do the Wexfords change from a family that the inspector can almost complacently contrast with the disturbed ones he meets every day in the course of his work, to one in which Wexford's and his wife Dora's peace of mind is eroded by the problems created by their daughters, Sheila and Sylvia. Wexford is no Agamemnon, and his daughters no Electras, yet the father-daughter relationship epitomized in the ancient stories supply an instructive backdrop as the series grows.

The earliest of the Kingsmarkham books are seemingly unremarkable *whodunits* except for the striking appearance of motives for murder that defy the usual ones, such as greed or heterosexual passion. Stronger emotions, often hatred, imbue the books with emotional intensity that foreshadows Rendell's later writing. In *From Dune With Death,* lesbianism drives the plot, as does brother-sister incest in *A Guilty Thing Surprised.* Throughout the series, human aberration lends the books their increasing depth, although Rendell does not immerse her readers in the truly horrific depths of human depravity, as do some other crime writers. In *Harm Done* a pedophile who has murdered a boy has been released from prison to the consternation of the community, many of whose citizens prove as sinister, primitive, and dangerous as he when they try to drive him out of the neighborhood. Still, Rendell does not take this theme (or others) to places that will twist her readers' insides because of the explicit detailing of atrocities visited upon child victims.

Early on, Rendell is less focused than she will later be on her investigating pair, her "Sherlock Holmes and Dr. Watson," Inspector Reginald Wexford and his next in command, Mike Burden. And in those first books, she seems to use Burden rather than Wexford to create comparisons and contrasts between the private lives of the police and those of the suspects they investigate. Other members of the Kingsmarkham force will appear and disappear from the series, and, later on, women officers will be added to the force as changes in society and laws make them both necessary (rape victims will more likely speak to women police) and deserving of their jobs. Karen Malahyde, trained in self-defense, proves in *Babes in the Wood* more able physically to overcome an abuser of women than Wexford himself. But Hannah Goldsmith is such an extreme feminist and is in other ways so politically correct that she exemplifies how absurd extremist views can be. And, in contrast to Malahyde's rescue of Sylvia in *Harm Done,* in *End in Tears,* Hannah must be rescued from extreme danger by a fellow policeman. The painful kick she delivers to her assailant's crotch, however, affirms her power and epitomizes some of the gender issues that make up her ideology. Political correctness and a heightened concern for an accused's rights have come to Kingsmarkham, and even though Wexford is sometimes scathing of the latter's potential for impeding his work and fostering a new kind of injustice, he is usually fair in his assessment of the changes in his personal and professional worlds.

Sometimes Wexford works almost as a lone private eye driven by private obsessions—for example, in *Shake Hands Forever.* At others, he heads an investigative team working on interrelated murders, as in *Kissing the Gunner's Daughter.* But in the early Wexford books, it was not clear that Rendell wanted to keep her series going. After the third, she wrote *The Secret House of Death,* which introduces for the first and last time another and rather uninteresting detective, a character who may, however, have found his inept counterparts in the investigating police in the non-Wexford novel, *The Rottweiler.* After *The Secret House of Death,* Rendell returned to Wexford, his community, his colleagues, and his family. About how she would use her serial characters she seemed undecided, ready to shift her points of view. In *Wolf to the Slaughter,* the third book, a large part of the story is devoted to a new member of the force, Mark Drayton, an ambitious young policeman who has Wexford's support but who destroys his own chances to advance in his career by becoming

sexually obsessed with a woman who proves deeply implicated in the crime being investigated. Drayton's affair with
her means that he must leave the Kingsmarkham police and
therefore exit the series.

After that, Rendell seems to have decided that it would
be Mike Burden who would supply the thematic parallels between the police department and the world outside it. The
first book in which Burden plays so important a role that
Wexford becomes a virtually background character, *No More
Dying Then,* is the one in which the widower Burden investigates the disappearance of a little boy and begins an affair
with the child's mother, Gemma Lawrence (see Chapter 8).
In *The Veiled One,* a later book, Burden once again takes a
leading part. Wexford is injured when a bomb exploding
in a car destroys much of his house. He must spend time
recuperating in the hospital. It is in this book that Burden
unwittingly assumes the role of Freudian therapist, ironically offering a suspect the promise of a talking cure when
what he is really trying to do is break him down during intensive interrogations (see Chapter 3). And in the previous
book, *An Unkindness of Ravens,* the pregnant Jenny Burden's
dismay at learning she will give birth to a daughter proves
to be thematically linked to the feminist ideas central to this
novel. Burden, in short, remains important to the developed
themes in these books, his role having come a long way from
A Guilty Thing Surprised, in which his own bickering son and
daughter, who seem genuinely to dislike each other, parallel the more intense antipathy of murder victim Elizabeth
Nightingale and her brother.

It is probably because, finally, Burden comes out of the tradition of the conservative, unimaginative Dr. Watson that he
cannot carry the consistent weight of narrative parallels as police and suspects interact in the Kingsmarkham community.
In *An Unkindness of Ravens,* Wexford muses on the irony that
his partner, who was such an "ordinary" and "salt-of-the earth
person" nevertheless experienced such upheavals in his life:
the death of his first beloved wife; his ill-fated love for Gemma

Lawrence; his second wife's rejection of him and her unborn child because the baby is predicted to be a girl. In Wexford's personal life, nothing like that has happened to unsettle him. And he gives thanks for this respite from the stresses of his job. Ironically, this personal tranquility will run out as Ruth Rendell turns the Wexford family into a foil to explore the problems faced in Kingsmarkham's social upheavals and the crimes that are caused by the resulting cataclysms.

In the first of the series, *From Doon With Death*, Wexford's family is not even mentioned. In the second, *The Sins of the Fathers*, Wexford is asked by a character seeking his help if he has any children and, if so, if they are married. It is here that Sheila and the married Sylvia make their first appearance, although unnamed. The man who has asked the question is worried that his son is about to marry the daughter of an executed murderer, for he is convinced of the importance of genetic inheritance (see Chapter 11). Since Wexford's older daughter married a man whose father is an architect, he insists, Wexford can expect to enjoy watching his two grandsons play with blocks and building structures, while he, when grandchildren appear, will anxiously look for signs of some bad seed.

This is the first of the comparisons and contrasts between Wexford's daughters and other characters. In *Wolf to the Slaughter*, only Sheila, the younger daughter is mentioned as Wexford thinks he may introduce her and her friends to the new policeman on his force, the ill-fated Drayton. Drayton, in turn, makes Wexford's seemingly ideal family a model for his own future. He will seek a wife as good looking and respectable as Dora and have pretty children like Wexford's. For he knows full well that the sluttish Linda Grover, whom he is powerfully drawn to, can have no permanent role in his life. When Drayton's mistakes come to light, it is with minor regret that Wexford lets the young man go, but also with major relief that, as Sheila's father, he had never followed through on his intention to offer Drayton some social life through an introduction to her.

There is another, in this instance slight, parallel created by Rendell in *Wolf to the Slaughter*, one that in later books will become more significant. Both the beautiful Linda Grover and Sheila Wexford look like their far less attractive fathers. Grover's smile is described as "oily and repulsive," but it is essentially the same smile that Linda employs to enthrall Drayton. This unhealthy father-daughter pair is typified both by the grubby shop Grover owns and that Linda works in, and also by the daughter's ruthless drive to get away from it. That Sheila, despite her radiant beauty, resembles her father, often described as ugly, rather than her handsome mother, establishes a strong bond between her and Wexford. Sheila basks in her father's protective adoration. The successes Sheila will enjoy and Linda does not are through Rendell's imagery associated with their fathers.

Once Ruth Rendell decided to use the Wexford family for thematic ends, another development could be discerned. While similarities and differences between the Wexfords and the families the inspector encounters can be found throughout the series, contrasts predominate in the earlier books, whereas similarities are notable in the later books. Most of the contrasts have to do with, first, the fact that Wexford loves children and not just his own. Crimes against children appall him and lead his thoughts protectively to his own family. In *No More Dying Then*, he is not only sickened by the brutal treatment children often encounter but also by the media that capitalizes on the public reaction to such crimes. In this novel, Wexford's devotion to his own children and grandchildren are contrasted with the indifference to the fate of missing Stella Rivers on the part of her mother, her father, and her stepfather (this family was discussed in Chapter 4). Here, however, another comparison/contrast serves to establish the Wexfords as a standard against which disturbed families can be measured. Stella was murdered, not by one of her uncaring relatives, but rather by someone who, like Wexford, deeply loves his own daughter, but with an intensity that, in the end, perverts that fatherly devotion.

The thematic connections between Wexford's family life and that of the victim and perpetrator is further complicated because *No More Dying Then* is also the novel in which the grieving and sexually frustrated widower Burden neglects his own children and is even jealous of Gemma's grief over her missing son, who she fears may be dead. Falling short in his role as father and father-substitute distances Burden from Wexford in this book.

Stella Rivers' family is not the only one that astounds Wexford, who despite his policeman's experience with human perversity, consistently finds himself measuring other families' reactions with his own. In *Some Lie and Some Die* and in *Road Rage*, Wexford encounters parents whose children have been murdered and finds he is unable to identify with them. In the earlier book, he understands that the death of a very difficult child may actually relieve the family of a former anxiety and need to present to the world a picture that was untrue. Still, Wexford has difficulty getting beyond his conviction that the "loss of a child is the one insupportable grief." When in *Road Rage* a father who loved and was proud of his daughter stoically identifies her body, Wexford thinks that if he had been the father, he would have made himself, that is a policeman, an object of his misery and rage, seizing hold of this representative of the law and demanding to have explained why his daughter's murder had not been prevented.

But even more astounding for him is the hatred that he often confronts between a father and daughter. In *The Best Man to Die* he feels sympathy for Nora Fanshawe, who despises her late father and feels only contempt for the mother who put up with his infidelities as long as he continued to bribe her with extravagant gifts. Wexford wonders what it would be like to have a daughter think of him that way, especially if he were dead. But the antipathy in the Fanshawe family pales before that of the Hathalls in *Shake Hands Forever*. They are a family, as Wexford puts it, so nourished by hatred that every family relationship has been poisoned. This includes a daughter who cannot stand the sight of her father any more than she can stand her mother or her grandmother, but who is particularly antipathetic to her male parent. Wexford thinks about his own daughters, who love him, and whom, because he loves them, he had reared and educated by using his own resources "freely and happily." He has difficulty imagining what the divorced Hathall went through, required by law to sustain a connection to a child he knows loathes him.

But when in *Death Notes*, a little more than halfway through the series, Wexford wonders what Natalie Comargue's part was in the murder of her father, and thinks of how happy he and his daughters had been with each other, he is describing the calm before a storm. He is not blatantly smug when he thinks of how there had never been any sort of "serious breach" between him and his daughters, congratulating himself on his good fortune compared to those whose disturbed family relationships have led to crimes. There is therefore a surprising turn in the entire series when similarities, not differences, emerge between the Wexfords and characters on the other side of the law. Some of the early parallels are weak and insignificant, almost as if Rendell herself, once she had changed the course of the Wexford family's role in the series, had not quite decided where to take it. For example, in *Speaker of Mandarin*, the beauty of a young woman Pandora Ingram is compared to that of Sheila Wexford, who is by then establishing herself as a TV star. Dora, whose role in the Wexford series is still evolving, wishes Sheila would make a film so that her beauty might be preserved. In later books, Dora would view Sheila's vanity and self-absorption with mild irony or exasperation. And Sheila and Sylvia would give their parents cause for significant concern, destabilizing this once secure family unit.

The real change for the Wexfords can perhaps be found most obviously described in *The Veiled One*. Sheila's marriage, which took place in *Death Notes*, has ended in divorce, and her love affair with a prosecuting attorney has resulted in a bomb placed in her car, almost killing her father and doing enough damage to the Wexford house for the inspector and Dora to need other lodgings while repair is made. Meanwhile, Sylvia, unhappy in her own marriage but nonetheless complacent about her life, quarrels with Sheila about the latter's radical politics. In subsequent novels, Sylvia would also rebel against her life as it was and be similarly divorced and similarly politicized. Meanwhile, the Wexfords are both sad and troubled at these changes in their family. They had optimistically assumed that with married daughters, a difficult period in their lives had been resolved, that now there "would be no more suitors brought home, the sight of whom aroused dismay or resignation or hope." The last sentence of *The Veiled One* is ambiguous, referring to the workers who arrive to "rebuild" the bombed house, but also symbolically describing the emotional cracks in the therefore weakening family.

The security of Wexford's home rests, of course, on Dora Wexford, a woman who earlier in the series appears far more commonplace than the more elegant and discerning wife and mother of the later novels, especially *Road Rage*. The series are essentially father-daughter books, ordinarily focusing on the inspector's relationship with his daughters rather than on his wife. Dora's bond with Sheila and Sylvia remains a relatively unexplored one, so that Dora will not be discussed in the next chapter, on Rendell's mothers and daughters. Still, it is Dora who holds the family together as Sheila and Sylvia become increasingly difficult. As her husband and daughters enter into troubled waters, it is her stabilizing influence that keeps them all afloat. That is why her disappearance in *Road Rage* is doubly threatening. That is also why the following discussion of Wexford and his daughters will briefly give way to a closer look at Dora and a detailed reading of what can be thought of as Dora's book.

In the introduction to this study of Rendell's fiction, Dora was likened to Penelope, the archetypal good wife and mother, who kept Odysseus's home intact while the Greek

201

hero fought in the Trojan War and meandered back to Ithaca. In two early Wexford books, there are allusions to *The Odyssey*. In *A Guilty Thing Surprised,* Wexford finds himself physically attracted to a young au pair, the sexually irrepressible Katje, whom Wexford believes needs the counseling of an old Dutch uncle, that is, himself. Then, laughing to and at himself, the inspector decides to let the counseling go and to "stay securely tied to the mast while the siren sang for others." In *A Sleeping Life,* he muses on his home as a haven and thinks, "what know they of harbours that sail not on the sea?," glad he has married a woman who supplies a resting place.

In contrast to her wanderer husband (in reality and in his imagination), Dora remains the consummate housewife. She is even contrasted in *Speaker of Mandarin* with Jenny Burden. Dora is the patient policeman's wife who has accepted her place in the home, while Jenny is constantly involved in activities outside it—evening classes, drama groups, and musical trios. When first asked to journey to China, Dora is quick to ask if her husband will be going as well, because she was used herself to being without him for long hours and days, but "would never go off and leave *him* of her own accord." Ironically, in this book the drinking of tea almost poisons Wexford. Dora not only serves tea but throughout the Wexford series also sees to it that her husband is fed even when he returns home late at night. She also serves food for comfort when her daughter Sylvia and son-in-law Neil bemoan their unemployed status in *Simisola*. In *Babes in the Wood,* Dora makes Christmas dinner after shopping for presents and wrapping them with great care. And she is a consistently loving mother and grandmother, even when her daughters try her usual patience, rarely becoming more than "mildly exasperated" as she often is with Sheila. Only in *End in Tears,* when she believes Sylvia is about to destroy their family, does she behave uncharacteristically, her emotions oscillating between coldness and rage. In an early story, "Blood Lines," Dora could not imagine a "girl betraying her mother," but now what she perceives as Sylvia's betrayal makes her all the more bitter because Wexford does not side with her against their daughter.

There are, however, signs that appear about midway through the series, suggesting that although Dora may be accepting of and even enjoying her role as wife, mother, and grandmother, she is hardly untouched by the changing times that, affecting her community, will also affect her. In *A Sleeping Life*, Sylvia's feminism, which in later books plays so important a part, leads to a confrontation with her mother concerning the limitations of Dora's life. An irked Dora retorts that in having a good home, two wonderful sons, and a good husband, Sylvia may in fact have a more fortunate life than she deserves. Later, she complains to Wexford that it is unpleasant "to have your own daughter tell you a woman without a career is a useless encumbrance when she gets past fifty, when her looks have gone." She is very upset that Sylvia thinks that a housewife such as Dora keeps her husband only because of his sense of duty and "because someone's got to support her." Later, in *Babes in the Wood*, Wexford will wonder if Dora is truly content with her life. But by then, his consciousness has been raised by his daughters' less than secure lives.

Road Rage can, again, be thought of as Dora's book. A proposed by-pass road threatens the still bucolic Kingsmarkham, its rural nature and its wildlife. Protestors, members of the community, and many outsiders who are conservationists or rebels seeking a cause, resist the construction of the road, and Dora belongs to one of the more peaceful and conservative of the groups hoping to avert, rather than subvert, completion of the project. In the midst of this turmoil, Sheila Wexford gives birth to her first child, and Dora, bearing gifts for the baby and new mother, prepares to visit her youngest grandchild. She gets into a taxi headed for the train station, but she never arrives in London. She is among several people kidnapped, the cessation of the by-pass construction demanded as ransom. For a long time, an agonized Wexford first wonders where Dora has disappeared to and then whether she will, as the kidnappers claim, be killed if their demands are not met. When Dora does return home, her strategic memorization of as many details as she can store in her memory, her discernment concerning human behavior, and her intelligence help solve the crimes, including the death of one of the hostages. Still, Dora's social activism and her role in the crime investigation do not significantly detract from her basic role in Wexford's life as his steadfast wife. Strikingly, however, in *Road Rage*, the inspiration behind how Dora is perceived comes not from the story of Penelope, but that of her counterpart, Clytemnestra.

In each of the three Electra plays, Agamemnon's children must devise some strategy to lure their mother to her death. It is in Euripides that we find a striking parallel to *Road Rage*. Electra sends false news to Clytemnestra that she has given birth to a child and needs her mother's help. Clytemnestra thus falls into her childrens' fatal trap. In *Road Rage*, of course, Sheila intends her mother no harm and appears not even to need Dora's help. A nursemaid and cook will help her while she comfortably nurses her infant daughter, rendering Dora's presence superfluous, except for the emotional support she can offer the new mother and the joy that she can anticipate for herself upon seeing a new grandchild, her first granddaughter. But like Clytemnestra, Dora discovers that, instead of this happiness and the satisfaction that comes from helpfulness, what she encounters is danger, a possibly mortal danger. While Sylvia and Sheila rally to support their father, living in Wexford's house and preparing meals he does not want to eat, the inspector finds for the first time in the series that his daughters are an unwelcome presence in the midst of his mounting concern for his wife.

Dora is, of course, never Clytemnestra. Nor are Sheila or Sylvia Electras except for being decidedly their father's, rather than their mother's, daughters. Many of the issues that surround the Agamemnon-Electra relationship nonetheless adhere to them, particularly as the series begins to respond to the social changes that affect Kingsmarkham. And Sylvia, in particular, may be said to be experiencing an unresolved Electra complex in that her life seems adversely affected by the fact that she knows, despite Wexford's efforts to conceal it, that her sister Sheila is by far her father's favorite child. That his guilt causes him to strive harder to show Sylvia affection only exacerbates Sylvia's feelings of being largely distanced from a father's love. Ironically, however, Sylvia will prove to be the more interesting daughter in the series. For it is she and not Sheila who raises the most significant and varied issues concerning how the father-daughter relationship can impact on a woman's life.

Again, Sheila Wexford appears early in the series when she is still an ambitious drama student. In subsequent books, she is the celebrity star of a TV series and eventually a lead actress in a prestigious English theater company. The degree of Wexford's favoritism toward this lovely and successful child reaches its most extreme point in *Road Rage* when the inspector, concerned over the fate of hostages, among them his own wife, who are threatened with death if construction of the by-pass is not halted, dreams that Sheila has been kidnapped. To his waking shame and consternation, Wexford, in his dream, offers Sylvia in exchange for Sheila—indeed begs the kidnappers to take Sylvia and let Sheila go. (This substitution of one daughter for another involves the sacrifice theme discussed in Chapter 4 and faintly echoes Agamemnon's willingness to sacrifice Iphigenia.) Wexford's favoritism is so blatant that it perhaps serves to alert readers to the possibility that at least on an unconscious level, Wexford's love for Sheila may cross a line into forbidden feelings.

Incest is a theme Rendell treats throughout her fiction and, more specifically, throughout the Wexford series. It should be made clear, however, that the following discussion will in no way imply that Wexford harbors consciously inappropriate feelings toward Sheila, whose beauty, charm, and affectionately ingratiating manner toward him are sources of delight that Sylvia never inspires. And even if he were to acknowledge desire for his beloved daughter, Wexford would never act on it. But an interesting slip of the tongue occurs in *An Unkindness of Ravens,* the novel in which Sara Williams accuses her father of sexual abuse and in which incest becomes a reiterated theme. Father-daughter incest, Wexford tells Burden, is hardly unknown. In fact, it had become a frequently treated subject in popular psychology. During his investigation of Rodney Williams' murder, the inspector and Dora attend a performance of Shelley's play *The Cenci,* in which Sheila has the lead role as Beatrice Cenci. Historically, Beatrice and her protective mother were executed for acting together to slay Beatrice's sexually abusive father. At first Dora does not understand what is alluded to in the play or why Beatrice is so emotionally distraught. Her father has raped her, Wexford explains, hastily amending his statement to a less generalized, more specific articulation: Count Cenci has raped Beatrice. This confusion, this blurred line between what has happened on stage, what happens in real life, and what fathers do with feelings they may not act upon will prove especially significant in *Kissing the Gunner's Daughter.*

It will be useful to briefly consider some basic ideas about the legal and literary treatment of incest, particularly in England, in order to discern how Rendell has treated the subject in the Wexford series. Incest is said to occur between persons if they engage in sexual intercourse when either consanguinity or affinity would legally prohibit their marrying. *Consanguinity,* as the word indicates, involves a biological relationship such as that between father and daughter. *Affinity* defines ties among family members united through marriage, such as stepfather and stepdaughter. Different cultures have different parameters concerning what constitutes incest. Writers, particularly feminists, have described how women have traditionally been objects of exchange. There are many societies in which a father receives a bride price when his daughter marries outside her group (the practice known as exogamy). Psychologically, women are also objects of exchange if within the family they are also seen as sexually available to the men to be used for the men's advantage. A woman's abuse might satisfy a male relative's lust or might in some other way regulate the tensions within the household. A mother who turned a blind eye to her husband's molesting their daughter, for instance, might be *exchanging* her child's well-being for the father's continued presence in the house and for his economic support. Typical would be Joy Williams' fury at being informed by her daughter Sara that her father Rodney had been coming to her room to rape her. Sara's charge would threaten to subvert the family's stability (such that it was). That Joy's fury is turned on Sara rather than Rodney is not at all unusual in the annals of incest case histories.

There is also the psychoanalyatic view in which terms such as *displacement* and *substitution* are often employed. These words are applicable, as was already discussed in Chapter 7, to Melville's novel *Pierre*, a probable influence on Rendell's *No Night is Too Long*. By having an affair with the same person, brother and sister have exercised both displacement and substitution, their incestuous feelings thereby indirectly and safely acted out, a more forbidden relationship substituted for by one less prohibited. If the Oedipus complex is universal, however, then all so-called normal sexuality involves incest and sacrifice, an approved love object always a substitute for the object of forbidden desire (the mother). And finally, there is—to refer back to Jung's employment of anthropology to explain a psychological theory—psychological incest. If, as Jung argues, children in a family must disentangle themselves from the web of intensely emotional relationships with parents and other siblings in order to be free to start their own families (in this case exogamy is narrowed down to individual families rather than larger societies), then any disturbed or seemingly unbreakable bond that obstructs this process can be thought of as psychological incest.

The idea of displacement, or the transferring of pro-scribed desires from a forbidden to an acceptable object can be found in *A Guilty Thing Surprised*, a book in which incest is the key to solving a homicide. Both Quentin Nightingale, whose wife was the murder victim, and Wexford are drawn to the young, irrepressible, sexually active and uninhibited Katje, an au pair employed in the Nightingale home. For Quentin, Katje supplies what his wife does not, sex, warmth, and companionship. For Wexford, Katje arouses a "passion-ate longing, bitter and savage," for his own youth and youth-ful desires. These passions are suppressed when Wexford catches a glimpse of himself in the same mirror that reflects the young woman provocatively clad in only a nightdress. Quite possibly an implied incest taboo asserts its inhibitory force, for what Wexford wryly recognizes is not only a young girl alongside a father figure but, because of the age dif-ference, a possible grandfather. He accepts the forbidden nature of his longings and these inhibit his acting on them with a young woman who seems happily and freely available to any man who desires her. The widower Nightingale, how-ever, plans to marry Katje, and he explains to Wexford that formerly he had tried to remember that he was in *loco par-entis* to the young au pair, insisting, however, that he had deluded himself when thinking of her as only a daughter. Wexford, at this point, is beyond self-deception. When he contemplates and rejects the idea of talking to Katje about this marriage as a mere Dutch Uncle, a disinterested adviser, he is distancing himself from the symbolic father-daughter dyad that transforms his own attraction to Katje into a genu-ine prohibition.

In a later book, *Death Notes*, Sheila Wexford is associated with a comparable situation. The murder of Sir Manuel Camargue is all that prevents his marrying Dinah, a woman young enough to be his granddaughter. Their bans are read in church at the same time as Sheila's, when she is going to wed Andrew, a wealthy businessman. These impending wed-dings involve Sir Manuel and Wexford moving in parallel, although opposite, directions. Here, displacement involves transferring from one character (Wexford) to another (Sir Manuel) feelings that are nonetheless applicable to the inspector and his relationship with Sheila. Dinah herself believes that in marrying her, Camargue is seeking to replace his real lost daughter, but because she is in love with him, she is ready to accept the celibate role of daughter/wife. Consciously, Sir Manuel does not recognize that Dinah is a substitute for Natalie, but unconscious wishes and desires strive toward consciousness as he contemplates married life with Dinah. For incest must be assiduously guarded against. She will be his daughter, but more than just a daughter, she will be his beloved companion. He sexually desires her, yes, as passionately as he had ever desired anyone in his youth. But he does not intend the marriage be consummated, for he "would never touch her." The idea of doing so makes him recoil as forcefully as Wexford would recoil at the idea of inappropriate sexual yearning toward Sheila—and recoil even more at the idea of acting on such desires as had Count Cenci when he raped his daughter Beatrice.

Still, Sheila's impending marriage arouses jealousy and resentment in Wexford. His now successful actress daughter moves in social circles that render inadequate the wedding reception her father can afford. Sheila is moving out of Wexford's world as her sister Sylvia has never done, and this in itself is for Wexford a cause for sorrow. But his emotional reaction to Sheila's marriage suggests less the dismay of a father who must adjust to the loss of his little girl than the resentment of a rejected suitor who has had to relinquish a precious love object. If, in *A Guilty Thing Surprised*, Wexford laments the loss of his own youth, neatly sidestepping the danger of even symbolic incest with a young woman who could be his daughter, in *Death Notes*, strong feelings for an actual daughter cause forbidden feelings to emerge more perilously close to the surface and in a potentially more threatening form.

It is in *Kissing the Gunner's Daughter* that the emotional collision course traveled by Wexford and Sheila reaches a crisis. The inspector, who in an earlier book congratulates himself on never having seriously quarreled with his daughters, now argues with his favorite in what Sheila suggests is more a lover's rift than a conflict between father and daughter. Sheila, now divorced from Andrew, has taken a lover, the insufferable Augustine Casey, whose esoteric novel had been a finalist for the prestigious Booker Prize. Not only does Wexford experience the minor jealousy always aroused in him by Sheila's lovers, but also the fury of a proud man patronized by one of these men in an extremely insulting fashion. Sheila, immensely flattered by the attention of Casey, whose intellect awes her, and fancying herself truly in love for the first time, does not want to hear what her father has to say about Casey. That Wexford is intemperate in expressing dislike only provides Sheila with ammunition to use against him. And she is not entirely wrong when she accuses her father of jealousy, of being unable to bear the idea that there might be a man in her life that she prefers to him. Almost in retaliation, Wexford turns his own affections to another young girl, Daisy, the only survivor of a massacre in which her mother, her grandmother, and her step-grandfather are killed. It will take but a short time for Wexford to realize that Daisy is but a temporary substitute for the alienated Sheila. In the meantime, *Kissing the Gunner's Daughter* introduces once again the themes of actual as well as fantasized incest as Wexford investigates a crime and endeavors at the same time to heal the wound caused by his break with his beloved Sheila.

Wexford and Daisy are in complementary positions. His quarrel with Sheila has deprived Wexford of his daughter, if only temporarily. And Daisy has permanently lost the father who left her mother when Daisy was only six months old. Her closest male parental figure is her grandmother's second husband, Harvey, a man much younger than his wife Davina. How Daisy feels about Wexford readers cannot know because the narrative excludes her point of view except for what she says or is reported to have said. But for Wexford, Daisy might be a reincarnation of Katje, and he believes himself to be foolishly in love. But just as reality took over when he caught sight of himself and Katje in a mirror, so does he come to his senses when he fantasizes making love to Daisy. It is a "grotesque" idea that causes him "positive revulsion." In his rational state, eighteen-year old Daisy reminds him of his daughters and he recognizes this. The possibility of Daisy marrying a dull young man who courts her also brings to his mind Sylvia's unwise early marriage. But Daisy's physical resemblance to Sheila carries him into more perilously dark psychological waters. Although Daisy is dark and Sheila fair, they are not only both beautiful but also alike in their features. The resemblance only points up his predicament. If Sheila persists in her relationship with Augustine Casey, Wexford will lose her. He thinks "she will cease to be [his] daughter," not daring to recognize that it is not just the father-daughter bond that torments him. Sheila comes closer than he to assessing the situation: her lover will always be for her father the other man in her life, Wexford's rival.

Although Wexford recoils even from indirect incestuous fantasies, Daisy effectively displacing Sheila as an object of desire, overt incest supplies some of the motives for murder in *Kissing the Gunner's Daughter*. For it is her grandmother's intention that Daisy ritually lose her virginity to her step-grandfather Harvey. Here it will be interesting to digress briefly into English legal history. In the early 1960s, an article on the need for reforming incest laws was published in England, much of the reform having to do with defining the relationships that placed sexual intercourse between two people out of legal bounds. The existing laws covered most consanguineous relationships but, according to the article, needed to be extended to those based on affinity, such as "stepdaughter, adopted daughter, or ward." Step-granddaughters are not explicity mentioned but are nonetheless covered by this category.

In *Kissing the Gunner's Daughter*, Harvey's age as Davina Porter's significantly younger husband makes him appear more like Daisy's stepfather than step-grandfather. Moreover, Davina had, throughout Daisy's life, exercised the control and influence ordinarily given to a mother, not grandmother. But Naomi, Daisy's mother, who remains a minor character, is another of Rendell's fey girls, not quite attached to the real world and unable and unwilling to be an active parent in her daughter's life. Clearly, she would never oppose Davina's astonishing idea that her husband Harvey should initiate Daisy into the pleasures of sex. Davina's ostensible reasons are many. Harvey is, according to her, a proficient lover and Daisy will from the outset experience sex as Davina thinks it should be. Her granddaughter would thereby be spared Davina's own unhappy sex life with her first husband. Also, Davina is a widely traveled anthropologist, and the idea of sex as initiation would be familiar to her.

Naomi's friend, who tells Wexford about Davina's plans for Daisy, reveals another motive, one more insidiously practical than Davina's theories would suggest. Davina believes herself too old for Harvey, unable to awaken his desire and satisfy his sexual needs. Daisy would substitute for Davina and thereby ensure Harvey's remaining within the family he has married into. It would be difficult for Rendell's readers to decide who was the most blameworthy, Daisy's grandmother, who concocts such a scheme, her mother Naomi, who would not have interfered, or her biological father, who is apprised of Davina's plan but, separated from his daughter since she was six months old, is indifferent to whether or not the incest takes place. Both Davina and Harvey are massacred before Daisy herself has to take a strong stand against her step-grandfather. Investigating the murders, Wexford has in the meantime displaced a myriad of feelings from Sheila onto Daisy. Only after honestly sifting through his emotions and his own motives and realistically adjusting his responses to both young women will Wexford arrive at a solution to the family massacre.

After *Kissing the Gunner's Daughter*, Sheila Wexford takes a less active role in the Kingsmarkham series. She seems happy with her new, live-in actor-lover, whom in *Not in the Flesh* she plans to marry, symbolically restoring some of the familial equilibrium threatened with extinction in the previous book, *End in Tears*. Her husband-to-be is the father of her two daughters and a man whom Wexford does not seem to view as a rival. In *Road Rage*, Sheila's giving birth to the first baby had been the occasion of her mother's kidnapping. In that novel, Sheila and Sylvia are about equal in importance and in their concern for their father. In the next three books, however, *Simisola, Harm Done,* and *Babes in the Wood,* Sylvia dominates as the Wexford daughter whose situation parallels what is happening in the main action. Perhaps Rendell had wrung from the Wexford-Sheila relationship all it could provide her fiction. But it is also possible that the author, who has always had her finger on the pulse of her times, became sensitive to the daughter whose relationship with Wexford was more problematic than her sister's. In recent years, the woman's movement has spotlighted the father-daughter bond. Because opportunities have opened for women, disturbed or less than satisfactory relationships with their fathers take on increasing significance. As argued at the beginning of this chapter, contrary to Freud's argument that an unresolved female Oedipus complex is not too serious because a woman's husband assumes the father's earlier role, the female Oedipus or Electra complex has assumed great importance. Marriage is no longer a woman's only option for her life and, even within marriage, the wife's role is no longer thought to be restricted to that of a submissive woman who has been trained for her role by being a submissive daughter.

In the later Kingsmarkham books, Sylvia has become a political and social activist whose commitments are very personal. In being the product of a life that has made her unhappy, they can be differentiated from the causes embraced by Sheila. Sheila's social causes seem almost random, as fashionable as the clothing she wears, causes that are essentially abstract and purely ideological. In *Speaker of Mandarin*, Sheila is described as an animal rights advocate who would not want her parents to bring her a souvenir made of ivory from the Far East. In *The Veiled One*, Sheila engages in antinuclear demonstrations and is actually arrested, ready to go to jail if necessary. In this rare instance in a series that can be thought of as consisting of Sheila books or Sylvia books, the sisters significantly interact, and Sylvia expresses a conservative disapproval of her sister's intentions. In *Simisola*, Sheila's involvement in Slavery International proves helpful to Wexford's investigations into a murder, but Sheila's participation in this cause seems once again arbitrarily chosen. This is also true in *Not in the Flesh*, where Sheila's concern for African women forced to submit to clitorodectomies seems but a ploy to introduce the theme into Rendell's novel. Sheila is also fickle about her commitments, as Dora Wexford will wryly observe. This is exemplified in *Road Rage*, where she causes Wexford consternation by insisting on giving birth at home instead of in a hospital. It had become the thing to do, partly because of another ideology: hospitals as institutions replete with male obstetricians and pediatricians embody patriarchy's control over women through control of their bodies (Rendell's novel does not spell out this often-used argument). Still, Sheila is not really a feminist: men, including her father, have usually been quick to court and pamper her, and she is unlikely to risk the loss of their devotion.

Why Sylvia takes up causes proves to be another matter. Her feminism results in part from her dissatisfaction with her marriage to a kind but dull husband, who at best treats her well but bores her, and at worse resists her when she decides to go to college and train herself for work and hence achieve independence. But when Sylvia takes on a volunteer job answering hotline phone calls at a woman's shelter, she reveals ambiguous motives, acting from the "pressures of her social conscience and her commitment to women's causes," but also needing to get out of her house and away from the tedium of her everyday life. She and Neil strive to remain together for their sons' sake, but in *Simisola* each has lost a job to England's economic recession and money problems strain their already tenuous bond. Now Dora's Penelope-like nurturing of her family, and her protectiveness of the hearth always available to Sylvia and her family, contrast sharply with Sylvia's strident feminism, her reproach of her husband, and her resentments over thwarted ambitions.

It was, again, against Neil's protests that Sylvia had managed to earn a college degree. Her growing knowledge of sociology and psychology prove useful to Wexford as an investigator. Still, while her helpfulness in the later Kingsmarkham books wins for Sylvia her father's growing respect, it does not win her more love in the unspoken rivalry with her sister. Even in *End in Tears*, where Wexford shows this daughter a special tenderness, it seems based on pity as much as love. Dora is infuriated at her daughter for being pregnant with a baby conceived for the sole purpose of supplying her ex-husband and his new girlfriend with the child they cannot have, and Wexford tries to compensate for his wife's uncharacteristic anger toward Sylvia. He appears less concerned with the family as a whole than the unhappiness he believes Sylvia is about to bring down on herself.

In the earlier *Harm Done*, many of Sylvia's concerns come together: her failing marriage; her equally failed life insofar as it falls short of her aspirations; her awareness that she lacks the obvious charm of her sister, as well as Sheila's facile ability to win people to her; and, most important, her status as Wexford's less favored daughter. Indeed, it is Wexford's concerted effort to act as if he loved Sylvia as much as Sheila that evokes her resentment. For she sees through his efforts, even if she does not understand why he loves her less: after all, she does not favor one of her sons over the other—or so she contends. What becomes clear in the later books in the series is that Wexford underestimates Sylvia. In *Simisola*, he at one point wants to escape Sylvia's company in order to telephone Sheila, politely asking Sylvia theoretical questions about areas she knows well to compensate for his lack of pleasure in her presence. Expecting the tedious disquisition on a subject that Sylvia is prone to, Wexford is surprised by the thoughtful and intelligent response that actually helps him break the case he is working on. And when, in *Babes in the Wood,* a now-divorced Sylvia is actually physically beaten by a live-in lover and turns to her father for help, he affords her the same frantic concern and help Sheila would have received.

Even here, however, Wexford does not emotionally re-act quite as intensely as he probably would have had Sheila been the victim. Again, Sylvia's life as a divorced woman and single mother makes Wexford's family life part of wide-spread and growing social ills. And, as the series develops, Sylvia has become the interesting daughter whose future life is in question, the one who causes the Wexfords persistent worry and upsets their previously complacent assumption that their lives as concerned parents might be behind them. It is also Sylvia's self-conscious contemplation of her role in the family that raises a myriad of questions about a daughter's place in the traditional nuclear family and about the parental relationships that shape her life. That Sylvia's in-ability to form a satisfactory love relationship might be the result of being too little loved by her father is a possibility the series leaves with its readers.

At the end of *Babes in the Wood,* Sylvia and Wexford are drawing closer together, but they still have far to go. Once again, Rendell supplies parallelism at the same time that she establishes a contrast. A seriously damaged relationship ex-ists between the missing Sophie Dade and her father, his bullying of her the cause of her antipathy toward him. At the novel's conclusion, her rebellion bodes ill for her future life, for it is a rebellion turned psychopathological, based as it is on cunning and hatred. In contrast, an abused Sylvia turns to her father for help and receives it. Yet both Sophie and Sylvia have been betrayed by their fathers, Sophie by Dade's failure to temper his strictness with love, Sylvia by Wexford's failure to love her as much as Sheila. But if Sylvia has failed to win as much of her father's affection as she wants and needs, she comes into her own as a Rendell character. For in *Harm Done*, the book in which she plays so significant a role in the action, Sylvia is also given long sections in which she becomes Rendell's narrative point of view. Rendell readers therefore come to know Sylvia as they never do Sheila. They are given access to Sylvia's thoughts as she works at the women's shelter, as she reveals ambivalence about her kind but dull husband, and bitterly experiences resentment at her place in Wexford's affections. In a particularly telling passage, father and daughter exchange sharp words. Then, as Sylvia lies in bed awake, contemplating her life, readers can witness her dismay as she wonders what is wrong with her that she could not get along well with her husband, her father, and even her mother. "She was marvelous with the disadvantaged, the poor, the socially excluded. Everyone said so. Why not with her kind, forbearing father?"

Wexford's kindness to Sylvia is significantly like the consistent kindness she had received from her husband. It is important but it is not enough. Wexford's attempts to be loving only drive home to Sylvia the realization that he must try, that his love does not flow freely toward her. Her husband she can and does divorce. But her father will persist as a problem for her, and that she contemplates their need to talk things through speaks to the problem but not necessarily the solution. Who knows? Rendell may have some surprises in still another Kingsmarkham book. Meanwhile, Sylvia is caught in a less than satisfying father-daughter relationship. To repeat, Rendell's fiction challenges Freudian ideas. The psychologist may have neglected the father-daughter bond because of a conviction that an unresolved female Oedipus complex caused a woman little damage as she moved from her father's to her husband's house. But in modern times, when marriage is but one choice among many that a woman may make, and when a marriage can be easily dissolved (at least, legally) if it proves unsatisfactory, the trajectory from mother to father to husband is more fraught with potential conflicts.

Contemporary feminists have encouraged women to cease being daddy's girls and to unite with their mothers. In *End in Tears,* the major conflict is between Dora and Sylvia as Dora dreads the loss of her grandchild after Sylvia gives up her baby. For her this loss of a family member will be the first step toward the essential disintegration of their family. Ironically, Dora's and Sylvia's alienation is caused by the potential rupture of the very bonds that draw mothers and daughters together, the daughter eventually becoming a mother herseslf. Were this not the case, Euripides' Electra could not have lured Clytemnestra to her death. Still, it is Sylvia's father who is most sensitive to the pain Sylvia is about to cause herself, because he does not believe she is strong enough to bear a child and calmly turn it over to others to raise. Mother-daughter and father-daughter relationships are intertwined in a very complex fashion, one that transcends stereotypical gender distinctions.

As noted in an earlier chapter, Sylvia Wexford contemplates the error of modeling oneself on the opposite-sex parent. The feminist defense of Clytemnestra is consistent with this encouragement toward female bonding. The internalization of patriarchy is viewed as destructive of female identity, and a firm female identity is argued to be absolutely essential to women. It is significant that, at the conclusion of *End in Tears,* Sylvia is relieved and happy to keep her new baby, significantly a daughter (and to judge by the most recent Wexford novel, *The Monster in the Box,* Sylvia may now join her sister Sheila as an only marginal character in the series). Paradoxically, however, women may need their fathers' support to alter the course begun with their early relationships. Instead of moving away from their mothers toward the fathers who will occupy the place eventually assumed by husbands, women may need their fathers' support to move toward their mothers, to their own secure self-image. Again, what this has meant is that an unresolved female Oedipus complex—an Electra complex—has become more, not less, important to resolve.

Psychological theory has yet fully to catch up with this realization. The failure to receive from a supportive, deeply loving father the emotional resources needed to separate from him may prove almost as much an obstacle to women's achievements and happiness as a restrictive patriarchy ever had. At the same time, of course, mothers must serve as new models for their daughters' development. There are many studies of fathers and daughters and of mothers and daughters, and in each set, the corresponding relationship will inevitably be raised. But no single study has focused on the multiple and criss-crossing ramifications of the parents and daughter triad.

The following chapter will consider whether indeed Clytemnestra can be rehabilitated, can serve as the symbolic mother that daughters need. Of all the parent-child relationships that Ruth Rendell has depicted in her fiction, the one between mother and daughter is perhaps the most fraught with conflict.

CHAPTER 10

MOTHERS, DAUGHTERS, AND SISTERS

The Electra complex centers on the father-daughter relationship; yet, as has been argued in previous chapters,
Electra seems driven less by love of her father than hatred
of her mother. Agamemnon is, of course, already dead in
the Greek tragedies, whereas a living mother exacerbates
Electra's fury. In Aeschylus, her anger reflects her current
plight as an outcast in the palace where she should enjoy
the honors of a princess. Her mother's power is for Electra
a bitter reminder of her own powerlessness, which finds no
remedy until Orestes reappears in her life. But in Aeschylus
there is no direct confrontation between mother and daughter. It would be Sophocles who exploited the dramatic possibilities of such a scene. In his *Electra*, Clytemnestra's rebuke
of her daughter and excuse for her own behavior combines
the personal resentment of one who thinks herself abused
and vilified by a disobedient child, and the plaint of one ap-
pealing to abstract justice, seeking redress for her inability to
prevent Agamemnon's sacrifice of their daughter Iphigenia.
As Clytemnestra mocks Electra with "Your father, yes, always
your father," she also seems engaged in a rivalry with her
dead husband over Electra's respect if not affection. In response, Electra is portrayed as an angry child whose retorts
can be heard as strikingly contemporary as she shifts the
lines of argument away from herself. Clytemnestra, she insists, killed Agamemnon to be free to indulge her lust with
Aegisthus.

Before continuing this discussion of how the Electra complex specifically impacts on mother-daughter relationships, an important aside is in order. In a portrait gallery of female fiends, beginning in ancient times, certain women have become renowned prototypes of feminine evil. Clytemnestra is one of them. The view of such women, according H. R. Hays in *The Dangerous Sex: The Myth of Feminine Evil,* has been modified by Wolfgang Lederer, a psychoanalyst who, in his book *The Fear of Woman,* concedes that the so-called inherent evil of women is a male projection of anxiety and other psychological difficulties men attach to women—their wives, their lovers, especially their mothers. In the Judaeo-Christian tradition, the ultimate evil was perpetrated by Eve when she ate the apple and brought death into the world. The sin of Adam and Eve may have evolved into a universal, original sin inherited by both women and men; but women in particular were depicted as the daughters of Eve. Ironically, Electra, who might be a sympathetic character as a victim of male domination if she were not so obsessive in her hatred of Clytemnestra, remains among the ranks of bad women because of a particular feminist perspective. It is *because* she is a daddy's girl and *because* she hates her mother and participates in Orestes' crime that she appears as a traitor to her sex. In this chapter on mothers and daughters, other traditions of feminine evil besides the ancient Greek one will serve as the context for analyzing Rendell's fiction. In particular, the biblical Eve will serve to illuminate the mother-daughter relationship in *The Crocodile Bird*—in which a woman also named Eve has murdered three men and has thereby created an identity crisis for her daughter Liza.

Meanwhile, Electra's insistence that Clytemnestra was motivated by lust for Aegisthus when she participated in Agamemnon's murder can supply a backdrop for one of Rendell's short stories, "An Unwanted Woman," which brings this source of conflict into the modern age. As the divorce rate climbs, more mothers enter into relationships with other men, frequently to their daughters' consternation.

That the younger woman may have difficulty with her mother's sexuality and that she may feel herself pushed aside in a relationship that makes her seem virtually extraneous, supplies the tension in this Rendell story, which even includes an Orestes-like character, a young and beloved half-brother. When Sophie Grant's father leaves her mother, the young girl feels abandoned, thinking of him as having deserted "us," whereas her mother defines his abandonment solely in terms of his having left her. When the ex-husband and father remarries and a son is born, Sophie becomes attached to the boy. But soon, her father moves his new family to America and makes no effort to see his daughter. Sophie's situation closely parallels Electra's. Both have twice lost their fathers. In both instances, foreign lands claim the men. Electra's father dies, a literal rendering of the abandonment Sophie experiences when her father leaves not just her mother but also her. And in both the ancient play and Rendell's story, the brother who goes abroad is virtually lost to his adoring sister.

When her mother meets the man she will marry, Sophie is at first content with the prospect of a new father. But the fourteen-year-old girl is still innocent of the sexual relation that the new couple is careful to hide from her until after the wedding. Then blatant demonstrations of their desire for each other repel Sophie, and she leaves, refusing to come back home until her mother rids herself of her new husband. But her mother rejects such an irrational demand, inspiring in Sophie feelings similar to Sophocles' Electra when she complains that Clytemnestra has driven away her lawful children to indulge her passion for Aegisthus.

The very title of *An Unwanted Woman* evokes Freud's argument in the essay on "Femininity," that women want to bear sons through whom they experience satisfactions otherwise denied them. Freud's argument and Rendell's use of it has been explored in detail in previous chapters. But some repetition here will help explain the alienated mothers and daughters found throughout Rendell's fiction.

The mother's low status, inherited as a cultural phenomenon, may infuriate the daughter. At the same time, the older
woman forced to raise her daughter to accept what she herself deplores may project her general resentment onto her
female child. Also, to follow Freud's argument, the birth of
a daughter effectively deprives a woman of the vicarious satisfaction she would experience through a son. A subtext of
that argument is that a woman turns away from her mother
to her father for the same reason. Freud's essay may be less
useful for achieving insight into the Agamemnon-Electra relationship than into the antagonism between Clytemnestra
and her daughter.

Although Rendell alludes to "Femininity" in her portrayal
of mother-son relationships, Freud's essay can only indirectly
supply a theoretical context for her treatment of mothers
and daughters. In the short story, "Divided We Stand," two
sisters unloved by their mother perpetuate with each other
the mother-daughter antagonism that has shaped both
their lives. Marjorie, a married woman with children, and
Pauline, a middle-aged spinster of forty-two, must provide
constant care for a querulous old woman who has suffered
several strokes. Despite some pangs of guilt, Marjorie, who
is terrified she will be expected to take this mother she does
not love into her house, takes refuge in the conventional
assumption that an unmarried sister would and should take
on the burden of an elderly and sick parent. Marjorie is also
thankful that Pauline had not been born Paul, a man with
a life of his own, who would not be expected to assume the
responsibility of an ailing mother. She is therefore dismayed
by rumors that her plain sister is going to marry and establish her own home. This will once again immerse Marjorie
in the problem of their mother. Meanwhile, Pauline meekly
continues her miserable existence.

The emotional distance that marks these sisters can be
traced back to their mother's rejection of her infant daughters. That Pauline was not a Paul had in fact been the source
of her mother's life-long unhappiness. Not pleased when

her first child was a girl, her mother was dismayed by the birth of a second daughter, taking out her disappointment on the child. Marjorie recalls that her young sister had been either neglected or treated cruelly. Pauline's ambitions to be a doctor were met with scathing resistance; and when she failed to marry, she was made to feel her mother's contempt. Both a man's world and that of a conventional woman were closed to Pauline, whereas Marjorie's marriage both protected and distanced her from their cold mother. Pauline's only escape from her misery had been a mental breakdown from which, as the story begins, she is recovering, a relapse virtually inevitable because no one can or will come to her aid. The form Pauline's final revenge takes allows speculation about what might have happened had Orestes not returned from abroad, or, like the putative Paul, had never existed. Would Electra, pushed deeper and deeper into her rage and despair, have killed Clytemnestra on her own?

Sometimes, of course, mothers are just not maternal, and it is their children and not just daughters they reject. In the short story, "The Vinegar Mother," this seems to be the case, although the rejected child is once again a girl, and therefore it is the mother-daughter relationship that is destructively played out. The title finds Rendell playing with words, actually highlighting what is a common subject in her novels, the virulent dislike that sets mothers and daughters against each other. The bacterial culture that is used to transform wine into vinegar is known as a "mother," and in this story, the slimy substance elicits disgust in young Alicia. Vinegar, of course, is unpalatable if drunk, and this story is another example of how Rendell uses food and eating disorders as metaphors for disturbed interpersonal relationships. In "The Vinegar Mother," Alicia's female parent has a "ferocious dislike" of children. When she speaks her daughter's name, she utters it as if a snake were issuing from her mouth. Both the vinegar and venom are the opposite of the tasty, nourishing foods that represent maternal nurturance.

Alicia's mother avoids her daughter, addressing her as little as possible—and then only to scold, never to praise. No wonder the child, starved for love, grows up given to rages or sulks. Nor that she develops a particularly obsessive aversion to the bacterial substance that in her house supplies a constant source of vinegar. On this "mother" she can vent the real hatred she dare not turn on a human parent. And when Alicia in a seemingly inadvertent moment of forgetfulness precipitates the story's fatal catastrophe, Rendell's readers may conclude that she has finally but perhaps unconsciously arrived at a way to revenge herself against the mother whose treatment of her was as sickening as a glass of vinegar would have been had she been forced to drink it.

Vinegar mothers can be found throughout Rendell's fiction, varying only in degrees of acridity. *The Tree of Hands* almost epitomizes Rendell's pathological, fictional mother-daughter relationships. This one interweaves three episodes concerning mothers and their children, but at the center is the conflict between Benet and Mopsa. The novel begins with Benet's memory—startling to the book's readers—that when she was fourteen, alone with her mother in the carriage of a train, Mopsa had threatened to stab her with the carving knife she had brought on board in a large handbag. Brandishing the knife, Mopsa had shouted and laughed wildly, uttering strange words, and had then returned the knife to her bag. But not before her daughter had pulled the emergency handle. Now, years later, Benet is herself the mother of a two-year-old (significantly) son. A successful fiction writer, neither married nor interested in living with her lover, she had chosen to have this child. Mopsa has, meanwhile, spent years in and out of psychiatric hospitals, diagnosed as a paranoid schizophrenic. Her husband, Benet's father, bears her with resignation, but Benet must constantly struggle with dislike for her totally self-absorbed mother, frequently repeating as if a self-protective mantra, "I must not hate my mother!" At some point, Benet's parents had moved to Spain and, as the book opens, Benet is waiting with trepidation at Heathrow Airport for Mopsa's return to England for medical tests.

During the visit, Mopsa evidences only slight interest in her grandson James, expressing surprise that Benet should prove to be such a devoted mother, that she should manifest such strong maternal instincts. Benet, who had decided to give a child what she had never had, a secure and happy childhood, has also been surprised by her absolute commitment to little James. Therefore, when the toddler contracts a respiratory infection, is hospitalized, and—against all odds—dies, Benet's world falls apart. Her mother's solution to her daughter's misery is an insane one; but then her mother is insane. When she sees a little boy of James's age and appearance, who had been left alone by his caretakers, Mopsa steals the child for her daughter. Benet, of course, intends to return Jason, whom the newspapers report missing, but Mopsa is terrified that if Benet does this, she will be returned to a mental hospital. Torn between her mother's terror and her intention to do what is right, Benet delays long enough, first, to discover in bathing Jason that he has been physically abused, and, second, to become attached to the little boy, not as a substitute for the dead James, but for himself. She determines to keep him and on this resolve the remaining plot rests.

There are many subplots in this novel, one of them involving Jason's real mother, Carol. She has three children, two with her husband, who is dead, and Jason with one of several lovers—she does not know which one. When the first two children prove to be more than she can be bothered with, she places them in care, having them home for visits. When Jason himself threatens to interfere with Carol's pursuit of her own pleasures, she considers placing him in care as well. The injuries Benet discovers on his little body indicate that Carol is a physically abusive as well as emotionally absent mother. When Carol holds the book's focus of interest, she is seen to hurt her daughter Tanya with a series of strong, repeated blows. Carol is a total narcissist as she pursues her own gratifications. Her greatest source of self-esteem involves her pleased contemplation in a mirror of her beautiful face and exquisite body (miraculously unaltered by three childbirths). Other subplots have to do with one of Carol's former lovers, a con man who lives off women, and Benet's former lover, the scheming father of James. As is frequently the case in a Rendell novel, the author sets the characters in these initially separate stories on a collision course that reaches a climax in the book's final episodes.

The Tree of Hands involves mother-son as well as mother-daughter relationships. Mopsa threatens Benet with a carving knife when Benet is only fourteen; Carol beats her daughter Tanya rather seriously. But Carol also has a son, and Jason's injuries indicate that his mother does not restrict her abusiveness to her daughter. Nor does the novel supply any reason to think that Benet would have been less devoted to a daughter than to the dead James. Still, in the context of themes found throughout Rendell's fiction, the birth of a son may avert the possibility of passing on, as if a defective gene, an inherent mother-daughter conflict. In short, it is possible to wonder if despite her success and status, Benet's love for James and then for Jason sustains at least part of Freud's premise about the ideal nature of the mother-son bond.

A year after *The Tree of Hands* was published, another Wexford book appeared, *An Unkindness of Ravens* (see Chapter 3). In it, the loathing of Joy Williams and her daughter Sara is mutual, whereas Joy dotes on her son. In the same novel, the pregnant Jenny Burden shrinks from the idea of giving birth to a daughter (see Chapter 5). To read back from *An Unkindness of Ravens* to *The Tree of Hands,* following narrative motifs from novel to novel, it is, once again, possible to wonder how Benet would have nurtured a daughter so long as her own mantra was, "I must not hate my mother." One of Rendell's most extraordinary novels, *The Crocodile Bird,* portrays how such a withdrawal from a mother affects a daughter's attempt to achieve a secure female identity of her own.

In *The Crocodile Bird,* Liza, a modern-day Scheherazade, relates to her lover Sean over an extended period of time the story of her life at Shrove House with her mother Eve, and how it happened that Eve had murdered three men. Liza is not yet seventeen when her mother presses some money into her hands, gives her instructions about how to make her way to a friend's house in London, where she would be looked after while Eve faced murder charges for deliberately shooting a man to death. What Eve does not know, however, is that her daughter has entered into a secret relationship with Sean, the handsome young man employed to work on the Shrove estate. Instead of going to London, Liza finds Sean's trailer home and moves into it. The couple, at first blissfully happy with their freedom, travel around the countryside, picking up temporary jobs to sustain themselves. During the ensuing months, Liza learns for the first time about the world outside Shrove. She also glimpses the possibilities of a more expansive life than she had with her mother on the virtually sequestered Shrove estate, or was likely to have with Sean if she followed him as his wife to Scotland, where he would be entering a management-training course that would guarantee their comfortable entry into middle-class life. When Sean discerns that Liza is growing away from him and increasingly attempts to control her, Liza realizes she must free herself of the relationship and be rid of Sean.

When her mother had found herself in a comparable situation, her solution had been to kill the interfering man. And Eve is the only sustained female model Liza has ever had. The book moves to the climactic outcome of Liza's plan to do away with Sean as her mother had done away with her victims, those who stood between her and a way of life she was determined to defend. The novel, however, proves more than a fascinating story of mother and daughter, or a book in which telling stories is comparable to journal keeping in other Rendell novels—allowing the narrator to come to know herself. For although Rendell is no radical feminist and in her books tends to speak of the woman's movement with some detachment and even irony (particularly in the late Wexford novels), it is clear in *The Crocodile Bird* that patriarchy itself has supplied the significant barrier to mother-daughter bonding. And one of the astonishing features of this Rendell novel is that as she explores this theme, Rendell effectively rewrites the story of Genesis. Her Eve has been the victim of men, and only because of this original victimization, she becomes their murderer. This reversal of Genesis' portrayal of Eve's sin, which doomed all human beings, is also reflected in an *Unkindness of Ravens,* in the name given to the radical feminist Eve Freeborn.

Like Genesis, *The Crocodile Bird* is about a fall and its opening sentence announces its central theme: "The world began to *fall* apart at nine in the evening" (italics added). As such, the book is modeled on what for Western tradition is *the* fall, the expulsion of Adam and Eve from the Garden of Eden after Eve ate the forbidden fruit and Adam shared in her sin by taking his own bite. The time before the expulsion can be characterized by Blake's word *innocence* (see Chapter 8), and the time afterwards as a period of *experience,* of the confrontation with harsh physical reality, with social ills, and with evil. In Blake and in other romantic writers, innocence is also associated with childhood; experience with adulthood. In that sense, every young person whose childhood is a happy one (as, notably, few Rendell childhoods are) is expelled into adulthood, a less happy state but a necessary one. The two realms were for centuries viewed as antithetical, just as childhood and adulthood represented contrary states. The supposedly necessary movement from innocence to experience could be characterized by St. Paul's assertion that when he was a child, he thought and acted as a child, but now, an adult, he has put aside childish things.

For Liza's mother, Shrove had been a veritable Eden, a beautiful country estate owned by the Tobias family, surrounded by forests and remote from the life of even the nearest village. Eve had grown up there, a bright young woman who had earned a place at Oxford, although she never takes her degree. Instead, traumatized by a gang rape on the road that connected Oxford to Shrove, now unmarried with a daughter of her own, she retreats to Shrove to take on the duties of its housekeeper, living with Liza in the gatehouse, determined to preserve the state of innocence for her daughter. As Liza grows up, Eve educates her at home, discourages almost all contact with the outside world, and tries to keep her daughter isolated from the world of experience as they dwell within the boundaries of their earthly paradise. The novel is narrated through the voice of Liza, so it is not clear what Eve thought would ultimately happen to her daughter, what Liza's life would be when she was an adult. It would seem as if Eve had never thought that far, and Rendell readers will be quick to pick up the contradictions in Eve's plans. But living at Shrove and keeping her daughter innocent of the world beyond it had become Eve's obsession.

Like her namesake's, Eve's life could be defined by a fall—indeed, a series of falls. And so she resists any idea that secluding Liza in paradise is a form of imprisonment. Eve has merged her identity with her daughter's so completely that she seems to have lost all sense of their being separate people; she therefore does not understand that her self-chosen imprisonment is Liza's enforced isolation. This disparity is made clear in an early episode in the book. When Liza is very young and Eve must leave her alone as she cleans the main house, she secures Liza in a locked room where she cannot endanger herself—although Liza can glimpse activities outside. When Liza eventually protests, Eve desists from locking her in the gatehouse. That their whole way of life, however, duplicates that shutting up of her daughter is not an idea Eve will consider, nor the possibility that in warding off experience, she threatens Liza's very survival in the world. For the world is precisely what Eve means to exclude.

The Shrove estate is not, of course, the earthly paradise. Its very name evokes the irrevocable loss of innocence. For *shrove* is the past tense of the verb *to shrive*, which has to do with the absolving of a penitent who has confessed to sin.

Shrove Tuesday is the holiday that precedes Lent and signifies this ritual confession and determination to cleanse one's
soul. In addition, in a nature-culture continuum, the Shrove
estate exemplifies a traditional idea associated with the expulsion from Eden, that nature as well as human beings fell
after Eve ate the apple. In addition, Shrove displays the negative signs of civilization. The grand house needs care, neces-
sitating caretakers who do not partake of its privileges—that
is, its existence speaks to a sharply defined class system. Eve,
who is devoted to the place, lives in a gatehouse that lacks
an in-house bathroom. She is not mistress of Shrove but
a servant who resides there in exchange for the labor she
performs, and also, perhaps, because she is the sometime
sexual partner of its owner, Jonathan Tobias. As youngsters,
they had been friends, even sweethearts. But adulthood
and social differences have divided them. Nor are Shrove's
grounds, which need tending and cultivation, cared for by
the owners, who are away more than in residence. Rather,
their upkeep requires hired help, and, ironically, this necessity leads to Eve's final downfall. Finally, the Shrove estate
may be beautiful, but nature is not always benign. In the
aftermath of a devastating hurricane, Eve surveys the damage to the grounds and muses, "Paradise destroyed"—for
Rendell's readers a strong clue to the literary influence that
so much of the book rests on.

For Eve, however, Shrove represents a refuge from the
world in which three men had raped her, one of whom is
Liza's biological father, although Eve does not know which
one. Secluding herself from the outside world, Eve views the
estate as not only the world's most beautiful, but also its saf-
est place. And when the years begin to erode her ability to
labor indefatigably, she fears for the decay of her self-created
paradise, but without perceiving the irony that her labor-
induced fatigue represents one of the curses of the original
fall, the injunction that humans must now earn their bread
by the sweat of their brow. Doggedly, she determines that innocence can be preserved and means to keep her daughter

Liza in the garden for reasons that she articulates twice in the book. One time she tells the lover who will become her second murder victim that she is determined her daughter will grow up to be herself, that is Eve, "but without the pain and the damage. She will be me as I might have been, happy and innocent and good, if I had been allowed to stay here." Later, she repeats these words to Liza herself, telling her to "be me as I might have been if I stayed here, happy and innocent and good."

In teaching Liza her lessons, Eve introduces the child to Genesis and the myth (not religious story) of Adam and Eve. Some Rendell readers may at this point discern how Milton's *Paradise Lost* impacts on Rendell's book, creating yet another irony. For Liza does not yet understand her mother and hence her own situation. Responding to this biblical lesson, Liza imagines "it was Eve and herself who hand-in-hand through Eden took their solitary way." She does not realize that in unknowingly invoking the ending to Milton's epic, she refers not to dwelling in paradise but rather to being expelled from it. Milton's expulsion motif and his final image of Adam and Eve are evoked at another point in the book in a more ominous context. This time it is a flight back to paradise rather than a departure from it that is being described. After Eve and Liza survey the damage caused by the hurricane, Eve fears that the uprooting of trees will expose the murder victim she has buried. "Hand in hand, they stumbled toward the gateway of Shrove."

Their fleeing back to the earthly paradise may echo yet another literary work, William Blake's *The Book of Thel*. Blake is a poet who makes his presence felt throughout Rendell fiction, in quotations (sometimes without attribution) and allusions. Blake, in turn, was greatly influenced by Milton, and one way of reading *Thel* is to consider it Blake's variation on the ambiguous ending of *Paradise Lost*, where Adam and Eve sadly exit Eden, but as adults prepared to take on the challenge of the world rather than living as perpetual children in paradise. One reason for taking a brief digression to look at *Thel* is that its portrayal of the confrontation between innocence and experience involves a unique, real, as well as symbolic mother-daughter relationship. Mme. Seraphin has many daughters and she is willing to allow them to leave the mythical Har and be born into the world (Thel and her sisters can be read as unborn souls on the threshold of bodily existence). She will let them go even though she knows her children will face the sufferings of the world and, inevitably, death. One of these daughters is Thel, a solitary being who, unlike her sisters, broods on what awaits her, finally deciding she will not cross the divide between her secluded innocence and worldly experience. The final two lines of the poem describe how "with a shriek," Thel turns away from life and "Fled back unhindred till she came into the vales of Har." If Ruth Rendell drew on this Blake poem to depict Eve and Liza escaping the ravages of the hurricane, it would be another instance of how she turned her literary sources upside down. In *The Crocodile Bird* it is the mother, Eve, who tries to keep her daughter in paradise, and the daughter, Liza, who finally breaks away. Strikingly, picking apples for a living (and also eating them) is an activity that helps symbolically to characterize Liza's existence *after* she leaves Shrove.

But in order to break away, Liza must also separate from her mother, for what Eve represents is a female identity defined by humankind's original mother, the Eve of Genesis. For that Eve was for centuries held responsible for the first cataclysmic fall, so that her subjection by man was perceived as both a just retribution and a necessity. Fallen man, it was generally believed, could only subdue his now-sinful nature by subduing—that is, controlling—the woman who had brought it about. It should be clear by now that it is no accident that the mother in *The Crocodile Bird* is named Eve. But just to say this is not in itself going to make clear what Rendell is doing in this novel by virtually rewriting the story in Genesis and reformulating an ages-old tradition. It is one that has characterized the usual relationship between men and women. *The Crocodile Bird* extends this paradigm to consider something that would not have interested past centuries, how Eve's history impacted on the ties between mothers and daughters.

For centuries it was contended—and depicted in the English literature Rendell would be familiar with—that when Eve ate the apple, she brought death into the world, effectively murdering not only her husband Adam, but also all of humankind, significantly known as mankind. The poet John Donne describes the event and its aftermath succinctly in a poem that purports to be a eulogy for the death of an innocent girl but nonetheless sustains a deeply ingrained antifeminist tradition. For all girls and women were assumed to be the daughters of Eve, and in writing of Adam and his wife, Donne proclaims:

> That first marriage was our funeral:
> One woman at one blow, then kill'd us all,
> And singly, one by one, they kill us now.

What Donne is alluding to is the belief in his time that ejaculation during sexual intercourse deprived a man of vital bodily fluids essential to his longevity. The blame, however, is attributed to the woman: in short, it is a corrupted and corrupting female sexuality that perpetuates Eve's sin through generations. But whereas the biblical Eve symbolically kills men, Rendell's Eve literally does so.

Ironically, Rendell's Eve bears out the traditional premise invoked by poets such as Donne. With the exception of the rapist who comes to Shrove to attack her, her murder victims are also her lovers. In one instance, her lust, rather than love, allows entry of the symbolic serpent into her prized garden. In another, sex and control over a man come together as she tries to secure Shrove for her own. But this is not Rendell's entire story. For Rendell's Eve, unlike her biblical namesake, is not someone who can be held up to justify male dominance so much as she is the victim of that dominance—as had been Eve's mother before her, and as Eve is determined her own daughter Liza will never be.

Eve's own mother Gracie had also been the housekeeper at Shrove. The widower Tobias had been so dependent upon her, especially as he underwent treatment for cancer, that he promised if she would agree to remain on the estate to care for him, he would bequeath Shrove to her. Her daughter, Eve, thus grows up on the estate in happy expectation that it will one day be hers. But Gracie herself is diagnosed with a uniquely woman's form of the disease, uterine cancer, and during her own treatment, she fails on one important occasion to be available for the elder Tobias. Despite his own suffering, he is completely indifferent to Gracie's, not caring that it is out of necessity and not carelessness that she cannot tend him. Selfishly, Tobias believes she has forfeited her right to Shrove and when his will is read, Gracie learns that she has been denied the promised inheritance. Her daughter Eve also loses what she believes to be a birthright. Both women are in that sense the victims of male ownership of property. In effect, Rendell's Eden/Shrove was never a woman's to forfeit, and the expulsion from paradise in *The Crocodile Bird* is laid at the feet of a selfish man and not a disobedient woman.

After Eve's youthful companion Jonathan Tobias inherits Shrove, Eve realizes that only marriage to him will result in paradise regained. But a series of disappointments that continue almost to the end of the novel depict a woman's weakness in the face of a man's exercising traditional prerogatives—to love and to leave a woman at his will rather than hers, and to dispose of his property as he chooses. The situation is complicated by Eve's determination never to live anywhere but at Shrove, so that she must finally and ironically choose between the estate and its owner, Jonathan. But her intransigence, again, reflects the injuries done to her by men so that Jonathan's forcing this choice on her is itself another blow she must endure at the hands of one of them. It is at the point when Eve almost wins Jonathan and her possession of Shrove is tantalizingly near at hand that Jonathan exercises the one, final right she cannot deny him—to sell the estate to recover losses from other failed investments. The series of events that ensue eventually imprison her in a cell that both is and is *not* of her own choosing.

Rendell's Eve has killed three men, but she has also been raped by three men, and that initial outrage fosters her continuing helplessness. In protecting her daughter from the world, Eve hopes to protect her from men, their sexual and their economic power over women. Liza grows up fatherless, her mother her only parent and her only model. But because her mother's legacy to her is derived from her own mother's powerlessness, Liza's inheritance is ultimately a mixed one. Almost intuitively she understands that it is wrong to allow a man unfettered power over her, and almost like the taboo in a fairy tale, she imposes a condition for their relationship on Sean: he must never force sex on her when she is unwilling. On the other side, when he violates that and other, implied, prohibitions, Liza knows only one way to extricate herself from her lover—and that way is deadly. The suspense in Rendell's novel comes from the idea that if Liza is to evade the trap her mother fell into, it will be because both literally and symbolically, she will refuse to be a daughter of Eve.

In *The Crocodile Bird*, Liza is without a psychological road map as she embarks on her literal and symbolic journey away from Shrove. Her mother, Eve, has at best supplied her with a confusing road to follow. As a generality, a young man described by Freud's Oedipus complex, who gives up his claim to his mother and takes his same-sex parent, his father, as his model, thereby takes his place in the world. In contrast, a young woman must turn away from her same-sex parent so long as woman's role is defined by her relationship with, first, her father, and, second, her husband, to whose authority she is expected to submit. Who will be Liza's female model? The book, in fact, supplies her with one, but it is not Eve. At the same time, Eve cannot merely be sloughed off if Liza is to become an independent woman. *The Crocodile Bird* dramatizes the way in which mothers and daughters confront each other across a divide that is difficult to bridge.

Above, Rendell's short story, appropriately titled "Divided We Stand," illustrates how the absence of a secure and loving relationship with their mother, who does not supply an adequate model for them, affects the bonds between sisters. The theme is worked out in an even more complex fashion in the novel *A Dark-Adapted Eye*, in which the sister who has assumed the role of her younger sibling's mother goes on to destroy this symbolic daughter. The relationship is spelled out early in the book: "It is a truism to say of a mother and daughter who are close that they are like sisters. Vera Hillyard and Eden Longley, who *were* sisters, were—in contrast—like mother and daughter." It is only later, when, ironically, motherhood itself divides them, that they became as sisters deadly rivals for the custody and love of (significantly) a little boy.

Opening the book, the narrator Faith describes the mood of her household on the morning that her Aunt Vera was scheduled to be hanged for the murder of Eden. This is one of those Rendell novels in which the murderer is known at the outset but the victim's identity is not revealed until close to the end. But not much is lost by revealing that identity here: perceptive readers will probably guess correctly long before the novel's conclusion; and a more tantalizing mystery remains unresolved even after they close the book.

Although virtually all of Rendell's novels rest on the interrelationships among members of a disturbed family, secrets revealed often pointing back to earlier generations, *A Dark-Adapted Eye* comes close to being a genuine family saga (*Anna's Book* and *The Blood Doctor* are other examples). While the relationship between sisters and what becomes a pseudo-mother-daughter pair are central to the narrative, this is also a book in which virtually all the parent and child pairings have gone seriously wrong. Arthur Longley, Vera's father, had had two wives in his lifetime, and the resulting family tree and disturbed relationships defy any attempt to briefly summarize them. To simplify, one of Arthur Longley's children by his second wife is his daughter Vera; fifteen years later, after the couple thought they were safely past childbearing, Edith, known as Eden, was born. Vera enjoyed pretending Eden was her daughter, and after their parents died, perpetuated a relationship that resembled a mother-daughter bond, doting on Eden while neglecting her own son, Francis. It is into this extremely contentious family that the novel's narrator Faith is born, and it is as historian of the disturbed Longley family that she succeeds in settling her own life. Interestingly, she does this with the emotional support of one of those substitute mothers one finds in Rendell's fiction—in this case her mother-in-law.

When World War II takes place, Eden joins a division of the woman's armed forces and is gone from home for a long period. During this time Vera gives birth—or apparently gives birth—to Jamie. Her husband had been home on military leave, but even so, Jamie would have had to be a ten-month old newborn. Vera's husband is suspicious and eventually sues for divorce. So an additional mystery arises: if Jamie is indeed Vera's, who was the man with whom she was having an extra-marital affair? A more profound and therefore more important mystery concerns why Vera's attachment to Jamie is so extreme. Was it to compensate for her virtual abandonment of Francis, who never misses an opportunity to hurt his mother if he can? Another, unspecified possibility, for those who enjoy following Rendell's psychological clues, is that if Vera thought of Eden as a daughter, and if Jamie were in fact Eden's child (it was not unusual for families to spare themselves disgrace by passing off the illegitimate child of one member as the legitimate child of another), then Jamie would be Vera's virtual grandchild. Women often dote on grandchildren more than on their children, and in many Rendell books, a loving grandmother takes the place of a weak or abandoning mother. But these grandmothers are not only loving but also sensible. Whether as his mother, his aunt, or his symbolic grandmother, Vera forms a bond with Jamie that is pathological in its degree of attachment.

A Dark-Adapted Eye is replete with compelling incidents that easily translate into filmable scenes. In one, Vera blissfully breast feeds Jamie in a virtual Madonna-child tableau. Another depicts Eden's miscarriage, blood dripping down her legs while she hosts a party, an event that foreshadows the coming rift with her half-sister/pseudo-mother Vera. For Eden had married a very wealthy man who wanted a family. Eden's infertility, whatever its source, threatened this advantageous union. When Eden eventually takes Jamie away from Vera, Vera is frantic. The female sibling relationship that had been problematic precisely because the closeness mimicked a tense mother-daughter bond becomes fraught with conflict, mutual pain, and murderous impulse. At the end of the book, evidence is supplied to support each sister's counterclaim to be Jamie's mother, but the rightful claimant is never definitively identified.

The complicated bond that ties Vera and Eden can be found in a poem Rendell quotes from in her book but does not identify—another instance of a literary allusion that highlights the major themes in a Rendell novel. The poem is "Goblin Market" by Christina Rossetti; the line is, "There is no friend like a sister." Rossetti's work is particularly fraught with irony and ambiguity. It tells of two sisters who are tempted by goblin men to buy forbidden fruit whose taste leads to instant addiction. But, sadistically, the goblins will sell it only once, and the addict thereafter pines away, dying for want of her fruit. And only more of the fruit—now unavailable—can provide an antidote. One of Rossetti's sisters is on the verge of death when the other saves her by tricking the fruit out of the goblins without partaking of its pleasure herself. There are two elements in this narrative that may apply to *A Dark-Adapted Eye*. The fruit sold by the goblins is in essence a kind of poison, and mushroom poisoning is part of Rendell's plot. More significant, the saving by a moral, upright sister of a more pleasure-seeking, wayward one points to Vera and

Eden. The analogy also indicates that Vera would indeed have tried to save Eden from the reputation she would have incurred if Eden had given birth to an illegitimate baby. Passing the child off as her own and raising it would be tantamount to procuring the goblin's fruit without tasting it and then vicariously enjoying pleasure through the child. In Rendell's novel, however, it is the rescuing sister who eventually becomes the addict, frantic to keep Jamie whether or not he were her biological child. Rendell may also have been familiar with another Rossetti poem on the same subject, "Sister Helen," in which a morally upright sister—that is, a surrogate for a mother—saves her more wayward sibling from herself by preventing her sister from eloping with an unsuitable man. In both Christina Rossetti poems, the roles of sister and mother have become blurred.

This merging of identities between mothers and sisters is a feature of one of Rendell's most recent novels, *The Water's Lovely.* Two sets of sisters, separated by a generation, inhabit the same house. Pamela has moved in to look after her sister Beatrix, who has suffered a permanent psychotic breakdown, probably brought on by the drowning death of her second husband Guy (see Chapter 11 for an analysis of this crime and ensuing punishment). By virtue of taking over Bea's care, Pamela spares Ismay and Heather the problem that their mother's illness would otherwise pose. In this sense, Pamela becomes a mother figure for her own sister and also for her nieces.

Meanwhile, Ismay and Heather are seemingly very close, although Ismay harbors some hostile feelings toward her sister. Heather is a problem to her for two reasons, one a pragmatic one, the other a more abstract, moral one. First, Ismay is passionately in love with a highly narcisstic man, Andrew, who resents Heather for preventing him from moving into Ismay's house. Ismay is therefore relieved when Heather becomes engaged to Edmund, for in marrying him, she will move out, making way for Andrew. The moral issue for Ismay is one that places her in the company of Rossetti's Maria, the character in Rossetti's poem who prevents her sister from eloping and thereby takes it on herself to decide what her sister's future life should be. For Ismay strongly suspects that Heather has murdered their stepfather and thinks that Edmund should be warned about her sister's propensity to kill. Her plan secretly to inform him about Heather supplies Rendell's plot with its central action.

It is not Rossetti's poetry, however, that provides the main literary sources of *The Water's Lovely*. Rather, Rendell makes clear that she has drawn heavily on Thomas Hardy's novel *Tess of the d'Urbervilles*, which is alluded to in this Rendell book as it had been earlier in *The Veiled One*. Both Rendell novels raise the issue of what happens to a relationship when an earlier, disapproved of union becomes known to one of the partners. How much in the way of true confessions does the supposedly erring member of the pair owe the other? In Hardy's work, Tess, on the eve of her wedding, informs her husband-to-be of what her society would consider past transgressions by slipping a letter under his door. Unfortunately, it slides under a rug and when they are married, Tess is under the mistaken impression that her husband knows all and has forgiven her. Similarly, Ismay makes an audiotape on which she tells Edmund what she suspects about Heather, and its getting lost is an element in Rendell's complex plot. The difference between Hardy's and Rendell's narratives is that in one case, the truth would have been revealed by the person who considers herself guilty of a transgression; in the other, it is a sister, Ismay, who holds herself to be morally superior to her sibling Heather, although she waffles between love for Heather and her own righteousness. Hardy's *Tess* will be discussed again in the next, concluding chapter of this study of Rendell's fiction, when Hardy's ironic treatment of human fate and humanly meted-out justice will be shown to involve some of Rendell's most compelling subjects. Meanwhile, the theme of sisterly conflict and the name *Ismay* suggests that, once again, Greek tragedy supplied Rendell with models for her fiction.

It is a notable feature of Greek dramatizations of the House of Atreus that Electra not only fails to grieve over her sister Iphigenia's death but also remains impervious to Clytemnestra's plea that she sorrowed over her slain child, whose death was her main motive for helping to kill Agamemnon. In Sophocles' *Electra,* another sister, Chrysothemis, is introduced, a character who serves as a foil to Electra. She claims she wants justice as much as Electra does, but fear holds her back from any complicity in the plot to avenge Agamemnon's murder. In scorn, Electra responds that Chrysothemis has become her mother's daughter while she, Electra, remains her father's. In this gender distinction lies the heart of the difference between the sisters, but it is a difference rendered paradoxical in ancient drama. When Chrysothemis argues that she must obey authority, she means male authority. But this acceptance of male domination is ironic, given her de facto siding with their mother against Electra. As a woman, she accepts her own powerlessness as a simple fact of her life, and she illustrates the Bachofen/ Freud thesis concerning the triumph of patriarchy in the *Oresteia* (see Chapter 3). Since for Freud the issue was not so much male power as it was the traditional contrast between masculine reason and feminine emotion, the timid Chrysothemis appears more rational than the sister driven by powerful, uncontrolled emotions.

These issues, dramatized through conflicts between sisters, are even more forcefully played out in another Sophocles play, *Antigone.* The antagonism of Antigone for her sister Ismene builds as Ismene declines to join her sister in defying Creon, who has forbidden the burial of their brother Polyneices (see Chapter 2). At the risk of her own life, Antigone is determined that he will receive ritual burial and she wants Ismene to take the same risk. But Ismene is more cautious, unwilling to defy the ruling powers of Thebes. She tells Antigone that they "must remember that [they] two are women / so not to fight with men." Sophocles' Ismene does not hold herself to be more moral than her sister, nor

243

would she actively oppose her sister's plans. But in this play that is fraught with moral ambiguity—it is one of the most thematically ambiguous of the Greek tragedies—there are strong ethical considerations attached to Ismene's effective decision to ally herself with Creon against Antigone. In contrast, Rendell's Ismay, whose nickname, Issy, could apply to Sophocles' character as well, if ancient Greek characters had nicknames, is a self-appointed moral arbiter, more like Antigone in her high-mindedness (although she is, again, also driven by self-interest). Ismay/Issie involves Rendell in another of her fascinating manipulations of her characters' names for thematic ends. She appears to have endowed Ismay with the attributes of both oppositional sisters in Sophocles' *Antigone*. At the same time, Rendell's sisters suggest an inherent, psychological tension that alienates sisters from each other, reinforcing the pattern in which sisters often act out against each other the conflicts that also separate mothers and daughters. For in both instances, it is their roles within a male-dominated society that helps promote discord between them.

Sophocles' *Antigone* is a specific reference point in one of Rendell's most chilling portraits of sisters, who face each other as both strongly bonded siblings and also deadly rivals. In Rendell's novella *Heartstones*, their opposition is derived from whether each one's primary attachment is to her mother or to her father, a possible working out of Electra's charge that while she remains Agamemnon's daughter, Chrysothemis belongs to Clytemnestra. Elvira is a daddy's girl who studies Greek and Latin with her classicist father, reading *Antigone* with him (among other plays). Spinny (Despina) is a mommy's girl whose mother unfortunately died when Spinny was too young to absorb the shock. Eventually, it is when Elvira chooses *not* to read *Antigone*, virtually repudiating her father's influence by putting aside the play, that she identifies herself not necessarily her own mother but at least with the concept of motherhood. At that point, she turns her concerns to her sister. But it may be too late, for Elvira cannot prevent Spinny's spiraling descent into madness. For both young women, domestic life has provided them with an unreal, illusory existence—possibly reflected in their names, which evoke characters from Mozart operas and thus signify the transcendent world of art rather than life. Escape for one of them into the real world finally seems within reach; but then Rendell suggests this possibility too is just an illusion.

Heartstones is an eerie piece of fiction in which a classical literary tradition is worked out in a gothic tale of mystery and terror—in the tradition of Edgar Allan Poe, to whom there are allusions in the novella. For Rendell is conducting her own excursion into the gothic in a story in which atmosphere, uncertainty surrounding events, and the confrontation between external reality and internal, psychological chaos leave readers with a sense of unresolved dread. Elvira and Spinny have already been introduced (see Chapter 4) as illustrating Rendell's interest in eating disorders. Here, Elvira's anorexia and Spinny's morbid obesity can be understood—again—according to Rendell's portrayal of one sister as her daddy's girl and the other as her mommy's.

Heartstones begins with the death of the girls' mother, Anne; later, their father, Luke, will commit suicide. From the beginning, the story emphasizes the differences between the sisters' primary attachment to one parent rather than the other. Elvira is so attached to Luke that she is convinced that the widower will need no one else but her, and when he plans to remarry, she becomes obsessed with the idea of killing her prospective stepmother, Mary. The latter does die in a seeming accident that may have been, however, precipitated by Spinny. Mary's fatal fall is one of those incidents around which hovers an unresolved mystery in which fantasy and dread conflict with material evidence. Elvira finds in her own pocket a frayed rope and a penknife that Spinny had received as a gift from their mother.

That Elvira is happy to study the classics with Luke appears to be the source of his interest in her. A clergyman as well as classicist, he lives in an abstract realm of literature and ideas, insisting his daughters learn Greek and Latin, only rarely descending to ordinary concerns. Rather inconsistently, however, it was Luke and not Elvira's mother who tended to Elvira's needs when she was an infant, even changing her diapers. Inconsistent as they may be, his early actions prepare for the way this father-daughter relationship develops to the exclusion of wife and mother. Wanting to inhabit her father's ideal world, Elvira comes to loathe the very idea that she ever needed diapers. Soon she tries to reject all bodily functions. Her hope would be to prick herself with a needle and fail to bleed. Disgusted by the idea of emerging from her mother's womb, her revulsion is also part of her tie to Luke—and a tie to one of the important motifs in the *Oresteia,* where as judge at the trial of Orestes, Athena is unmoved by arguments concerning the sanctity of motherhood. Elvira imagines herself Athena to Luke's Zeus, that is, a daughter who had bypassed the maternal womb in being born. Eventually, Elvira rejects food and is hospitalized when her anorexia almost kills her. Fortunately, a loving grandmother has moved into the household after Anne's death, and it is she, not the detached father, who becomes alarmed by Elvira's state of health and later aids in her recovery. Elvira, now well, hopes that similar help will save Spinny.

Their grandmother also understands that Spinny's overeating involves an incessant need for comfort. Deprived of her mother at a young age, shocked that her mother's illness proved fatal, Spinny devours food. She had from the beginning been her mother's special child, and Anne's death signals the onset of Spinny's derangement, as she begins to see ghosts and thinks herself haunted and persecuted by the nightly visits of a cat. The end of the novella finds her obese, consuming huge portions of food, and probably planning to poison Elvira. What, then, turns the sisters into antagonists, their antithetical eating disorders but a sign of what divides them? They had once been close and become even closer when Elvira begins the process of moving away from her obsession with their father. Recognizing Luke's self-absorption, Elvira is determined to make a healthy life for herself and for Spinny. Her concern, however, seems not to help Spinny at all. Daddy's girl and mommy's girl seem to face each other across a gulf that even love cannot finally bridge. In the end, sister cannot serve as mother. *Heartstones,* moreover, appears to argue that maternal deprivation may be even more damaging to a female child than paternal neglect. To use the vocabulary of British pediatrician and psychoanalyst, Donald Winnicott, neither girl has had good-enough mothering, but because Spinny was more dependent on her mother than Elvira, she was more damaged by what she lost.

An early sign of Elvira's insight into her father is her failure to appreciate a lecture he delivers on a speech Euripides assigned to Menelaus. Rendell does not say which one, but it may be the dialogue in *Iphigenia in Aulis,* in the course of which Menelaus tells Agamemnon that neither the Trojan War nor Helen is worth the sacrifice of a daughter (see Chapter 4). If so, then Agamemnon's murder of Iphigenia becomes a metaphor for a male parent's emotional detachment from his daughters. Eventually, Elvira will be hospitalized and will be cured of her obsession with her father and of her hatred of her body. She will start to associate her physical self with her mother (despite the mother's failings), a process aided by her nurturing grandmother, and she will resume eating normally. It is about this point in the story that she decides *not* to read *Antigone,* a play that continues the story of Oedipus's legacy to his family, one feature of which is the unshakable commitment of Antigone to a male sibling (Polyneices), leading to the unresolvable conflict with her sister Ismene.

Because Elvira is *Heartstones'* narrator, Rendell's readers can only chart the external course of Spinny's decline. All along, she has wanted to live a normal life, crying out at one point that she wishes her mother had not died, that she had a father whom she called by something other than his Christian name, that she didn't have to learn Latin and Greek, and that she could live in another house, one that wasn't haunted. Perhaps she recognizes that it is her sister who will eventually lead that normal life, cured of her anorexia while she, Spinny, gets fatter and fatter. Elvira attends a university and has met a fellow student with whom she is starting an appropriate romantic relationship, while what Spinny shares with her own boyfriend are mainly the sweets they gorge themselves on while watching television. Elvira relates that her father's death freed her; Spinny seems unable to recover from the death of her mother, who must have seemed to have abandoned her by dying.

Significantly, her mother had been named Anne, whereas Luke's intended second wife was named Mary. Elvira had contemptuously noted that her father was drawn to little women with little names. But, in fact, Anne and Mary are the names of a holy mother and daughter, a daughter who would go on to be even a holier mother (but to a son), and in that holiness is an ideal of the female bond that should exist between female parent and child—and hardly ever does in Rendell's fiction. *Medea* is one of the classical plays alluded to in *Heartstones,* and one finds more Medeas than Marys in Rendell. Spinny, of course, never comes to understand her mother as Elvira does her father. She does not know that Anne's refusal of surgery for her cancer, preferring death to mutilation, spoke to a vanity and self-absorption as thorough as her husband Luke's preoccupation with the classical past.

Losing maternal nurture at a vulnerable age, Spinny turns to food, largely nutritionally empty sweets that ultimately fail to supply more than momentary comfort. Spinny and her mother—or lack thereof—can be seen as epitomizing the destructive mother-daughter relationships found in so many of Rendell's books, in which good-enough mothering is only occasionally to be found. At the end of *Heartstones,* Elvira, with the help of her grandmother, has tried to assume some of the maternal role. She is planning to get on with her own life, but she is also filled with "pity and terror" for her sister. This Aristotelian formula for the catharsis produced by Greek tragedy returns the novella to the ancient dramas and to Aristotle's claim that disturbed families were their consistent subject. At the end of *Heartstones,* Elvira is intent on saving Spinny, on finding the stolen poison she fears Spinny will use to commit suicide, and on obtaining psychiatric help for her sister. The ending, however, hints at catastrophe, not a happy outcome.

Since this chapter will conclude discussions of how Rendell has treated parent and child relationships, which have been broken up into same- and opposite-gender pairings, and because it has been argued that the mother-daughter relationship seems to be the one most fraught with mutual antipathy in Rendell's fiction, it would be wrong to leave readers of this study with the idea that there are no good-enough mothers in her novels. Or no close mothers and daughters. In venturing into her treatment of this relationship, Rendell took up, often indirectly, the strong cultural reaction by contemporary feminists against forces that impede mothers from serving their daughters as positive role models (see discussion above of *The Crocadile Bird).* As earlier chapters have suggested, women may have reasons to wish for sons, but these reasons may not be the ones argued by Freud (see Chapter 6). Nor are women merely acceding to the male wish for heirs (however much fathers may experience Laius's fear of being replaced by a son). One result of a widespread reaction against patriarchy may involve the anger experienced by women at the burden that is placed on them when the son's (or daughter's) failures are traced back to poor mothering. The seeming compliment that was repeated throughout the nineteenth century in England, that behind every great man there was a good mother, has, of course, its corollary.

The idea of a good-enough mother would therefore be one that mothers would eagerly adapt, although Winnicott himself placed great stress on the early and primary maternal role. Descriptions of his good-enough mother may remain somewhat daunting and arouse concern in some mothers that "good-enough" is perhaps *not* good enough. Still, the popular understanding of that term can allow Rendell's readers to recognize that there are mothers in her novels whose parenting, if not necessarily perfect, serve their children well. Often, however, these good-enough maternal figures are loving grandmothers (as in *Heartstones* or *The Keys to the Street*) or psychological surrogates. It is interesting that in Sophocles' *Electra*, the Greek women chorus acts as a good mother attempting to turn Electra away from her self-destructive feelings and behavior.

> But only in good will to you I speak
> Like some loyal mother, entreating
> Not to breed sorrow from sorrow.

In *The Brimstone Wedding*, Genevieve has a good-enough mother, but in the greatest crisis of Genevieve's life, it is to another, older woman that she confides the problems of her affair with a married man. Stella, her confidant, reciprocates by narrating over a long period of time her own history of an adulterous relationship. Genevieve is a health aid and Stella, dying of cancer, is one of the patients she cares for. As they share their painful experiences, Stella's past affair helps Genevieve gain perspective on her present one, and they become very close. It is not that Genevieve's own mother is lacking in love for her child, for she appears in the novel as a sensible and concerned parent. But Genevieve realizes that while her mother would probably understand the extra-marital sex, she could not understand her daughter's emotional attachment to her lover. It is, therefore, Stella who, after her death, leaves Genevieve stronger and ready to assume an independent future. In the meantime, Stella has told Genevieve a story fraught with mystery and painful emotions, a story unlikely to be related by a mother to her daughter. For the story itself may alter for the worse a daughter's view of her parent.

Even Vranni, Faith's mother in *A Dark-Adapted Eye*, seems to be a good-enough mother, but she is made bitter by her husband's defense of the family that has rejected her, and in any event, she interacts very little with her daughter. In Rendell's fiction, seemingly good-enough mothers usually play minor roles; an example is Marie in *Anna's Book*. Joyce's mother in *Make Death Love Me* appears to have given her daughter the strength to persevere through her ordeal as kidnap victim (see Chapter 7). In the same novel, Oona is devastated by the death of the young daughter who burns to death on a visit to Oona's careless ex-husband. In *Simisola*, Laurette Akande is certainly a good-enough mother, despite the pressures to succeed she places on her daughter, and millions of mothers of teenage daughters can relate to her exasperation with Melanie. In *The Chimney Sweeper's Boy*, good mothering is treated in a very complex fashion. The sad and nurturing mother of Gerald Candless has rightly won her son's enduring love, but in effectively taking over a mother's role in his own daughters' lives, Gerald has made it impossible for Ursula to prove herself the good mother she would have been to Hope and Sarah.

Josie Cambus in *A Dark-Adapted Eye*, the novel in which almost all parent-child relationships go wrong, is, although a minor character, a stellar example of what mothers should be. She has two sons and eventually the narrator Faith will marry one of them. He is the lawyer Faith consults when she divorces her first husband. Readers have to infer from the description of Josie and her son Louis that if they experienced together the working through of his Oedipus complex, Josie's ability to love her child without possessiveness allowed him to go on to love a wife. A grown-up Jamie, who had been caught in a deadly tug-of-war between two of his "mothers," supplies a contrasting example. He was undoubtedly traumatized by his childhood experience, one "mother" murdered, the other executed for the crime; one "mother" willing to give him up if she could have other children, the other tying him to her so tightly that it is unlikely he could in any event have gone on to a happy relationship with another.

In this chapter, significant mother-daughter relationships in Rendell's fiction (and those of sisters who mimicked this pairing) frequently returned to discussions of mothers and sons. The maternal Josie has given birth only to sons, and it is over a son that Vera and Eden become enemies. Vera's definitively biological son hates her, and, again, the son who may or may not be biologically hers is seriously damaged by her obsessive attachment to him. Once more, Rendell's portrayal of satisfactory mother-daughter relationships rarely places them at the center of her narratives. To read her books is to come to the conclusion that despite her persistent challenge to Freud, Rendell does find the mother-son relationship the ultimate testing ground for a successful mother-child bond. The logic of *A Dark-Adapted Eye* in the context of Rendell's other writing is that the benefits of a loving mother-son relationship will fall to a daughter-in-law after the son moves unimpeded through his Oedipus complex. For that fortunate woman, a good-enough mother will be her unthreatening, loving mother-in-law. To date, Rendell has yet to write a novel in which the mother-daughter bond is both central to her complex narrative and also concludes with a strong and happy mother-daughter pairing. Significantly, the life of Liza in *The Crocodile Bird* takes a turn for the better when she experiences her epiphany, that although she need not reject her mother, she is *not* her mother and that she *need not be like her.*

CHAPTER II

CONCLUSION: JUSTICE, UTOPIA, AND FATE

After the brutal slaying of Eden and the execution of Vera, their niece Faith, the narrator of *A Dark-Adapted Eye,* describes how the Furies had gathered around Vera, unmoved by her suffering. When first introduced in the novel, these vengeful creatures are called by their Greek name, the Eumenides, the title of the third play in Aeschylus's *Oresteia* trilogy. Orestes is tried in a court of law for killing his mother and is acquitted. The Furies, representing an older, primitive form of justice that for generations tore apart the House of Atreus, must now be placated, the human thirst for retribution not so easily set aside. In Rendell's novel, the Furies would have been particularly antipathetic toward Vera because she murdered a blood relative, a particularly heinous crime in their eyes. But it is in a courtroom that she is condemned to death. Little of her trial is described and no serious defense is mounted on her behalf. If Orestes' trial by jury (as contrasted with personal vengeance) represents progress, Vera's, to the contrary, suggests a crime not only primitive in its motivation but also in its outcome.

A Dark-Adapted Eye may thus confirm an argument made by those opposed to capital punishment, that the Furies quest for retribution has been taken over by an institutionalized system that distances the individual citizen from the mechanics of revenge. Both advocates for and opponents of capital punishment could, moreover, find evidence in Rendell's novels for their arguments. Bell in *The House of Stairs* is found guilty of murder but is not executed because England had abolished capital punishment. She leaves prison after not too many years as predatory as she was when she entered it. Vera Hillyard, who would probably never again hurt anyone, hangs for her crime.

Aeschylus's *Eumedides* is a startlingly modern courtroom drama, raising issues that can be found in any number of the notorious trials making headlines today. The court is the provenance of Athena, who as the presiding judge casts the decisive vote when the jury of twelve men is split in their decision. The Furies act as a collective prosecuting attorney, concerned with the well-being of society rather than the individual, holding to the *law,* an older law than Athena is ready to sustain. As prosecutors, the Furies are deaf to mitigating circumstances, concerned that the acquittal of Orestes would unleash a wave of crimes committed by children against their parents. Athena challenges their inflexibility, insisting that "wrong must not win by technicalities." Her position can be recognized today as defense attorneys try to keep incriminating evidence out of court, and frustrated prosecutors find themselves unable to present crucial evidence to obtain convictions.

One of the Furies' complaints is that Orestes will not plead to the crime. Instead, he relies upon Apollo, who is at one and the same time defense attorney, adversary of the Furies, witness to the crimes committed against Agamemnon, and an accomplice in the slaying of Clytemnestra. It is Apollo who confronts the Furies with the atrocities committed in the name of their justice: horrific tortures, heads lopped off, eyes gouged out, young boys castrated. Apollo also tries to turn the Furies' principles back against them. Since they hold intra-familial murder to be particularly heinous, they should recall that Clytemnestra murdered her husband Agamemnon because he ordered their daughter Iphigenia killed. The Furies are not impressed, retorting that husband

and wife are not tied by blood as mother and son are. To this reply, Apollo evokes an argument that would eventually be seen as preposterous, that it is only the father who is a blood relation to his child, the mother only the vessel that receives his seed and nurtures the maturing infant until it is born.

Sophocles' Electra makes the same argument when she rebukes her sister Crysothemis for not taking part Clytemnestra's death, remarking, "It is strange indeed that you who were born of our father should forget him and heed your [not *our*] mother." A similar theme can be found in *Heartstones*, when Elvira, pathologically attached to her father, is repelled by the idea of issuing at birth from her mother's womb. As many commentators on *The Eumenides* point out, Athena, "judge" in the trial of Orestes, is a goddess who would have no soft spots for mothers nor a particular horror of matricide: she was born fully grown from her father's head, bypassing even the so-called vessel one might call a mother.

But perhaps the most important part played by Apollo in the trial of Orestes has to do with his complicity in the matricide, for in his role as Orestes' accomplice, he raises questions about Orestes' free will. The Furies include him in their indictment: "You are the one who did it; all the guilt is yours . . . you gave this outlander the word to kill his mother." Apollo admits the charge when he assures Orestes, "it was I who made you strike your mother down." Whether Orestes was thus acting as a free agent or was bound by divine decree becomes one of Aeschylus's themes, one of the persistent themes in ancient Greek drama. The Furies contradict themselves when, after charging Apollo with guilt by divine decree for the death of Clytemnestra, they also say of Orestes, "He murdered his mother by deliberate choice." Apollo does not accept this view. Because he is a divine being, Apollo's decree in effect becomes Orestes' fate. In killing his mother, he was responding to a powerful force outside himself, and not, as the Furies claim, making a "deliberate choice." Apollo therefore denies that Orestes can be held responsible for the murder of Clytemnestra. Centuries later, criminal defendants would argue that the devil, or some other external agent, perhaps an antidepressant drug, made them do it, altering the terms of the argument but not the argument itself.

In *A Dark-Adapted Eye* a competent defense attorney might have advanced arguments concerning Vera's victimization by Eden—to mitigate if not entirely justify the murder of one sister by the other. One of the several incidents recounted in the novel seems to suggest this possibility. The story is told of a possible serial killer of children, a man so badly hurt in the First World War that he had been subject to "crushing" migraine headaches. When experiencing his intolerable pain, he may have committed acts "for which he was in no way personally responsible," acts he may have forgotten when the pain subsided. Whether Vera could at least have avoided the death sentence if her lawyer had raised extenuating circumstances is not certain. The Furies were weakened but not entirely banished even in Aeschylus, for it is suggested in the novel that for reasons readers can only speculate about, Vera would have blocked such a defense, preferring to surrender to their vengeance.

As the last play in Aeschylus's trilogy, *The Eumenides* contains three major themes that are treated in Ruth Rendell's fiction. One of these, again, has to do with concepts of justice. About this, it is probably unnecessary to maintain that any author who writes novels in which a criminal action is the heart of the plot has an implicit or explicit idea of what constitutes justice and how it is likely to work itself out in society—sometimes in contrast to have it *ought* to work. Second, the trial of Orestes not only puts an end to the personal vendettas and outrages enacted by members of the House of Atreus against each other, but also signals an advance in the society that instituted courts of justice. The Athens that produced poets, philosophers, and the great Greek tragedians, was no utopia, although it gave western society Plato's *Republic*, a model for subsequent writings about ideal societies. The Hellenic world has, nevertheless, persisted in the educated mind as an utopic ideal. In theory, crime would not exist in the perfect society, but if it did, then how justice was dispensed would become a defining feature of that society. For Ruth Rendell, utopias seem only to supply a vantage point from which to depict social reality, including the way in which justice is implemented. Finally, the difficulty of exercising free will in the face of some countervailing determinism inevitably links ideas of human freedom to ideas of utopia and justice. It also leads to what is for Ruth Rendell the ultimate mystery: what motivates human behavior, what explains the enigmas that attach to criminal actions? And how do these enigmas affect the differentiation between excusable and justifiable crimes.

In traditional mysteries, murderers are almost always apprehended or die because of an event that leaves readers satisfied that law and order has been sustained. Many of Rendell's novels supply this satisfaction—for example when a rapist is injured by his victim and dies of an ensuing infection; or a multiple murderer is killed by a relation who hates her and effectively spares the community the cost and trouble of a trial. In *A Sight for Sore Eyes*, a murderer tumbles down stairs and joins the corpses of those he has hidden in a secret room. Some Rendell novels, however, will leave readers disconcertingly unsettled. Senta Pelham's madness overwhelms her, but Zosie in *A Fatal Inversion* and Liv in *Grasshopper* not only walk away from the crimes in which they have been involved, but also go on to live respectable married lives. In *Grasshopper,* Jonny, perhaps the most unrelievedly evil of Rendell's characters, seems to achieve all that is important to him, wealth and a hedonistic lifestyle. *Talking to Strange Men* depicts a young man who kills a pedophile and thus avoids becoming his victim. But whereas his nightmares reflect a persistent moral sense, his conscious thoughts suggest a weakening conscience. Because the boy knows he has gotten away with homicide, murder might in his future continue to be a solution to vexing problems.

The later Kingsmarkham books portray an underclass whose members are only too well versed in their rights under a system of due process so scrupulous about protecting the accused that the police are often unable to do their work. Today, Athena might be surprised by how often wrong prevails because of technicalities. In *Harm Done*, mob rule threatens Kingsmarkham when a pedophile is released from prison. During a riot, a policeman is horribly burned alive by a gasoline bomb, but the perpetrator remains undiscovered because those involved in the demonstrations close ranks against the helpless investigators. In these later books, Rendell deprives her readers of the complacent assurance, so dear to many mystery fans, that in literature if not always in life, murder will out, justice will be done. This is not to say that Rendell therefore advocates a more primitive form of justice in which the safeguards of due process are bypassed. To the contrary, in *Babes in the Wood*, a primitive rite allows members of a religious sect to confess their sins and to receive absolution if they agree to live by the stringent rules set down by the group's elders. In this novel, Kingsmarkham is besieged by rains, with homes threatened by rising waters in which those who cannot swim might actually drown. The scene evokes images of the biblical Noah and the floods that were God's judgment on sinful human beings. The narrowness of the sect proves not only atavistic in its beliefs (women are to be subservient to men and sexual urges to be repressed) but also malignant in its smugness and hypocrisy. Yet members are drawn to the cult because of a seemingly moral void that has opened up in society, which has difficulty sustaining its traditional values.

Paradoxically, one of the most primitive forms of justice—an eye for an eye—supplies the conclusion to Rendell's recent novel, *The Water's Lovely*. This work has already been discussed as an example of Rendell's treatment of sisters, centering on the belief by one sister, Ismay, that the other, Heather, has murdered their stepfather, and that Heather's fiancé should be apprised of this—at least—probability. In this earlier discussion (see Chapter 10), Rendell's allusion to Thomas Hardy's *Tess of the d'Urbervilles* was briefly taken up. Its similarity to Rendell's plot would be obvious to readers of Rendell and Hardy. How *Tess* influenced Rendell's treatment of justice might be less so.

Tess was the next-to-last of Hardy's novels, the author having become discouraged by the public response to his work—miscomprehension or outrage. What apparently most bothered Hardy's readers was less the content of *Tess*—illicit sex, adultery, the bearing of an illegitimate child, and a so-called fallen woman as heroine—than Hardy's final words on the tragic outcome. After Tess murders the man who had originally seduced her and continued to blight her life, she is condemned to death by a court of law and led to the gallows for execution. Alluding to a play by Aeschylus, *Promethus Bound*, Hardy wryly notes that with Tess's death, "Justice was done, and the President of the Immortals had ended his sport with Tess." But Hardy's angered readers read the Judaeo-Christian God for Zeus, president of the immortals, and concluded that Hardy was blasphemous.

Like Rendell's Vera, Tess has been tortured by circumstances, but in neither case had their torment headed off the verdict of guilty pronounced in court or their hanging. In the case of Heather in *The Water's Lovely*, her sister Ismay has effectively become her judge and jury, and Heather promises that after her honeymoon, she will surrender herself to the authorities for having drowned her stepfather. That honeymoon takes place in Southeast Asia, and the destructive 2004 Tsunami that claimed a quarter of a million lives along the shores of the Indian Ocean also takes Heather's. There are two aspects to how justice is reflected in this outcome. First, Rendell invokes a traditional idea of divine justice as she may have in *Babes in the Wood* when floods seem to indicate that another ark will be needed to rescue the citizens of Kingsmarkham—from a natural disaster and from their sins. (It is not being argued here that this is Rendell's view, but only that she has introduced it into her multi-layered,

complex view of crime and punishment.) In more enlightened societies, divine justice works through courts of law.
But what overtakes Heather is an atavistic manifestation of a
primitive eye-for-an-eye vengeance: Heather drowned a man,
and because of a natural disaster, she drowns—coincidence
or not. The archaic nature of justice in this novel is only
highlighted because it coexists in the book with a disturbing
element found in some of Rendell's novels and in general
new to the genre: two criminals in the book remain unpun-
ished, seeming, like Jonny in *Grasshopper,* to have achieved
their hearts' desires.

There is yet another level of complexity introduced in
The Water's Lovely. When Heather explains to the legalistic,
judgmental Ismay her reasons for murdering their stepfather (*whydunit* rather than *whodunit* prevails in this novel but
will not be revealed here), Ismay asks Heather whether she
thinks what she had done was "justifiable." The by-now overwhelmed Heather admits that she does not think so. Ismay,
being neither lawyer nor judge, nor a jury member receiving a judge's instructions on matters of law, is not likely to
understand that there existed in English law—at least as
far back as William Blackstone's still influential writings—a
very fine and not always easily definable line between "excusable" and "justifiable" homicide. Blackstone wrote that
"excusable" homicide could rest "upon a principle of self-
preservation." By the time Rendell wrote *The Water's Lovely, "*
self-preservation extended beyond the situation in which a
person might kill when attacked, under the conviction that
his or her life was in danger, whether or not it actually was.
Systematic abuse, such as Rendell describes in *Harm Done,*
poses threats to psychological as well as bodily self-preservation. The assault by a husband who cut his wife's hand with
a knife when she displeased him might provide her with an
excuse for murder if she felt driven to kill him (she didn't).
The crime might not, however, be viewed as "justifiable" because the law would then seem to give carte blanche to all
wives who were abused to murder their husbands. What has

come to be called the "abuse excuse" creates problems for prosecutors and even defense attorneys and makes the public wary of defendants averting a guilty verdict by too readily invoking an excuse that may thwart rather than aid justice. It also complicates the mystery writer's art, unless that writer has the ability to render these legal and philosophical fine lines coherent as well as dramatically effective.

The beginnings of such problems for the legal system can be glimpsed as far back as in Aeschylus's *Eumenides* as the Furies make their claims against the system of trial by jury. There even existed in Athens a separate court for those who pleaded justifiable homicide, known as the Delphinion, its name indicating its connection to Apollo, whose principle shrine was at Delphi, and whom the Furies perceived as their antagonist in the trial of Orestes. Trial by jury in ancient Athens is one feature of Hellenistic society that has traditionally lent it an aura of utopic idealism.

To repeat, in Rendell's novels, utopian ideals become the backdrop against which social reality can be measured. But she approaches this theme backwards, so to speak, creating not memorable fictional utopias but noteworthy *dystopias*. Previous chapters have discussed books in which communal living constitutes rebellions against conventionality: *Grasshopper, A Fatal Inversion,* and *The House of Stairs.* The communities do not foster mutual love and respect, but rather mutual exploitation and an hospitable breeding ground for evil. Ironically, in *A Fatal Inversion,* the character who most strongly clings to her utopic vision, and who acts most altruistically, precipitates the novel's murder.

Commentators on utopian ideals often point out that totalitarian forms of government are needed to control those members of the society whose individuality or dissent may subvert those supposed ideals. In the long story, "High Mysterious Union," Rendell illustrates this argument. At the same time, she undercuts her fictional utopia by describing it in terms of a male fantasy, laying bare the extent of illusion necessary to conceive of, much less perpetuate, the perfect society. The narrator, a young man, finds himself living in a strange and remote community in which his domestic needs are taken care of by extraordinarily beautiful housekeepers who are also content to sleep with him without any other requirement than that their lovemaking be mutually satisfying. Their fathers and fiancés seem totally agreeable to these arrangements, but at the same time rigidly defend and enforce their family structures. The narrator commits the unpardonable sin of falling in love with one of the women and attempting to interfere with her marriage to another. When he imposes his own moral and emotional values on the group, its members close ranks against him and he finds his very life threatened. Later, ruminating on his strange sojourn in a world that hardly seems to belong to this earth, he decides that he had been lured into this seeming paradise because its members recognized the dangers of inbreeding and required the addition of "new genes to their pool." Citizens of the hedonistic paradise in *High Mysterious Union* appear to be the antithesis of the sexually prudish, repressive cult members in *Babes in the Woods*, but in the end the two groups are the same: narrow, intolerant of dissent, and totally opposed to human individuality.

The themes of utopic and dystopic societies can be found throughout Rendell's fiction. In the early works, suburbia is contrasted with large urban centers, such as London. Inexorably, however, the problems of the cities encroach on the bucolic villages that cannot resist the erosion of their way of life. In *To Fear a Painted Devil*, one of Rendell's earliest books, the motive for murder involves the erecting of contemporary mock-Tudor dwellings on the grounds of an old manor house and park. In *Some Lie and Some Die*, one of the Wexford series, a folk/rock concert takes place on the Sunday estate, a once vast property that has shrunk to a house, garden, and but a few acres of parkland as pieces of it are sold off and developed. The concert brings to peaceful Kingsmarkham thousands of young people, hippies, and other youth who do not value what Kingsmarkham still holds important. Their unconventional clothing and un-restrained sexual behavior, their disregard for the natural setting as they set up their temporary camps, their prefer-ence for loud music that interferes with the peace of the neighborhood—all spell the destruction of some ideal that Kingsmarkham represents in the earlier books in the series. These visitors or invaders (depending on whether Burden's or Wexford's view prevails) even seem to worship different gods, their idolized rock singers.

Mike Burden disapproves of what he perceives to be an invading horde of barbarians. In an earlier novel, *Sins of the Fathers,* he is described as contentedly driving around Kingsmarkham, hopeful that, despite the appearance of new homes, a supermarket that would threaten small coun-try stores, and a spate of road signs that suggested increased access to the town and therefore inroads into their peace-ful life, "things had not changed much in sixteen years." Wexford, despite his greater tolerance of the young people who attend the concert on the Sunday estate, essentially shares Burden's hope that their town can be preserved. He has no illusion of an unrealistic utopia, or any kind of ideal society, for after all, crimes are committed in Kingsmarkham, which requires a police force. Still he thinks of it as a place that supplies its residents with a peaceful and secure life.

At one time, however, Kingsmarkham *had been* Wexford's earthly paradise. In *Murder Being Once Done,* references abound to Thomas More's *Utopia.* Wexford had suffered a minor stroke and with Dora had gone to London to recu-perate in the home of a nephew and his wife. While in the city, the inspector helps to investigate a crime. But in con-trast to Dora, who is enjoying what London offers, Wexford is homesick for green Sussex meadows, pine forests, streets inhabited by people he knows and who know him, his house with its warming fire, and proper (read plain and whole-some) bread and food in his own refrigerator. *Shake Hands Forever* finds him back in London, working with his nephew, a member of the Metropolitan Police, but once again longing for the "unspoilt" Sussex countryside. His romantic recollections of its harvest time perhaps owe something to romantic poetry, in particular Keats's *To Autumn.* In Kingsmarkham the "wheat had been cut, the fields were a pale blond, shining like sheets of silver gilt in the sun."

It is in a nonfiction book that Rendell's pastoral vision is most obvious. The text of *Ruth Rendell's Suffolk* accompanies stunning photographs. Even here, the near perfection of the rural landscape is posed against a countervailing reality. The contrast is sustained, once again, by Rendell's literary allusions. Rendell describes her then home in Polstead, "a deep pastoral countryside" only sixty-five miles from London. Implicitly, the larger city represents some culture and energy beyond whose reach she would not wish to place herself. That Polstead was the site of a famous murder, moreover, reveals its potential fascination for a crime writer, while at the same time subverting ideas of perfection. Perhaps Rendell is unintentionally ambiguous as she describes the pretty villages in which it is impossible to find "a mean village street." The word *mean* denotes insignificance or inferiority: there is in Polstead no street that is low or commonplace. But the words might also conjure up for crime fiction aficionados Raymond Chandler's famous image of the private investigator, who walks alone and unaided on the urban *mean streets* on which crimes are routinely committed.

Once again, a literary allusion may speak metaphoric volumes. Rendell notes that "probably Suffolk's most distinguished literary figure" was the writer George Crabbe, who had, in Rendell's words, "set himself in revolt against an eighteenth century convention of the innate nobility of the peasant and the enviable delights of the pastoral life." Crabbe's quarrel in verse with the writer Oliver Goldsmith is a notable episode in the literary history of England's eighteenth century with its debates about the country versus the city.

Oliver Goldsmith's *The Deserted Village* was written as an attack on the Enclosure Acts that forced off the land families who had never owned pieces of it but who had dwelled on and worked it for generations in expectation of remaining there. Instead, they were forced to migrate to the city where, for example, young women whose lives would have been respectable if not easy in the country were forced into prostitution, while their brothers became criminals. Goldsmith's image of village life is so idealized that it is difficult to believe he ever intended it to be more than symbolic. Village men, for example, only gathered in taverns for fellowship's sake and none of them ever drank away the family's income or returned home to abuse wives or children (much less throw fire bombs at policemen). And the village pastor was so purely Christian that his like could not be found in English literature since Chaucer's country parson. A realistic Crabbe matched Goldsmith point by point. Crabbe's villagers are as corrupt as Goldsmith's are idealized.

If Kingsmarkham had been almost Wordsworthian in Rendell's depiction of village life, it had about midway through the Wexford series changed, its alteration, however, only gradually apparent from book to book. By the time *The Veiled One* was written, not just a supermarket but also a large shopping mall have replaced the disappearing natural landscape. The shops have become trendy, what they sell an indication of the disappearing distinction between urban and suburban life. Burden, for example, who had once dressed not only impeccably but also conservatively, is still impeccable in his designer jeans. But much of Kingsmarkham stylishness has become ominous because not all who live there can avail themselves of it. In *Simisola*, the unemployment office, where much of the action takes place, reveals only too clearly that hopelessness breeds violence. A growing underclass in the town becomes an increasingly troublesome force to deal with. In the short story, "Blood Lines," Kingsmarkham citizens are afraid to venture out of their homes at night. In B*abes in the Wood*, the town must not only contend with the rising flood waters, but also with the looting of stores unprotected during the storms. Things have changed so radically that by

265

Road Rage, Wexford does an about face and contemplates living in London, not for the excitement offered by the city, but so that he does not have to watch the destruction of what he had held so dear. And in the most recent Wexford novel, *The Monster in the Box*, the inspector persistently ruminates on Kingsmarkham past and present.

Clearly in the struggle between nature and civilization, nature is losing. In *Road Rage*, a proposed highway by-pass threatens not only the beauty of the surrounding country-side but living species such as a kind of butterfly that may become extinct. The by-pass construction is halted, but Rendell makes it clear that her book depicts a skirmish in a war unlikely to be won. Where nature does appear to be triumphant in her fiction, however, the triumph may prove equally threatening to human well-being. From her earliest writing, Rendell had taken as a theme the conflict between heredity and environment, today expressed as the opposition between nature and nurture. In *The Sins of the Fathers*, she manages to evade an absolute commitment to environment as the most powerful shaper of human character and personality, but also declines to endorse the idea that inherited traits are passed down from generation to generation and can thereby fully explain criminal behavior.

By Rendell's more recent books, however, the contemporary pendulum swing from nurture (environment) to nature (genes) had a significant impact on her writing. Original sin has raised its secular and symbolic, but no less ominous, head, as genetic inheritance becomes the new fate, intruding into human lives and influencing concepts of law and justice. The ancient writers understood that unless human beings were granted at least some portion of free will, they could not be held responsible for their acts. Ruth Rendell's later books raises analogous issues about whether people can be held responsible for the many possible kinds of bad seeds they carry within them.

In the early *Sins of the Fathers*, Rendell introduces the Anglican Priest Henry Archery, who cannot sanction his son's marriage to Tess Kershaw, daughter of a murderer hanged for his crime. Although Tess is a fine girl, an Oxford student, Archery fears that she can and probably will nonetheless pass on to his grandchildren an inherited predisposition to violence. As a priest, he is undoubtedly influenced by theological ideas as well as scientific and quasi-scientific ideas about inherited character traits. He wants Inspector Wexford to reopen the case of Tess's father, hoping that justice had miscarried. Opposing Archery is Tess's stepfather, Tom Kershaw, an engineer and practical man whose ideas rest squarely on the side of a nurturing environment as the key to good character development. He is therefore impatient with Archery's qualms. "A personality isn't made by heredity . . . but by environment." It had been his avowed purpose to raise his stepdaughter Tess in a home where she would thrive, as indeed she has. The [step]father and prospective father-in-law stand at opposite poles of the heredity-environment controversy. And today, the controversial issue of whether violent crime can be traced to one or more genes or some abnormality in the criminal's brain, or whether crime is mainly a socially constructed phenomenon, continues to generate arguments. Two mothers in the novel will also become actors in the debate.

Uncertainty concerning heredity and environment are found in the contrast between Tess and her childhood companion Liz Crilling. At first glance, Liz is the privileged one and Tess the girl whose early unhappy home life and family history should have predicted a life as bleak as that lived by her parents. But Rendell seems to have deliberately tangled the threads of character traceable to nature and nurture. Liz becomes the wild one, addicted to drugs and drink, who kills a young man with her car while recklessly driving. Tess, the murderer's daughter, is the one who goes to Oxford and becomes the fine young woman Archery would have been pleased to have as a daughter-in-law were it not that he feared she would pass on to her children some gene that would express itself in a propensity to commit criminal acts.

As Archery contemplates the paths actually traveled by the two girls, he thinks of how "God moved in a mysterious way," of how Liz, the privileged daughter became a delinquent, while Tess remained a paragon.

It turns out, however, that Liz's environment did not add up to bright prospects for a happy life. When very young, she had discovered the bloody body of the woman Tess's father had murdered. Requiring repeated psychiatric intervention, Liz is still given to nightmares when the book opens. But even this childhood trauma is not a sufficient explanation for her later behavior, and heredity may play as large a part in her future as, theoretically, it might in Tess's. Liz's mother is frequently a patient in mental hospitals, which suggests some inherited psychological trait she may have passed on to her daughter. In direct opposition, Tess's mother seems almost purely the product of her environment. Her overwhelming need for respectability takes precedence over all other considerations, including her daughter's happiness. It will turn out that all along, she could have resolved Archery's predicament and could have eliminated the impediments to Tess's marriage. But then she would have had to expose herself to the critical, probably disapproving, eyes of others. In the case of Mrs. Crilling, it is difficult to separate heredity from environment as influences on Liz; in the case of Mrs. Kershaw, her fanatical obedience to the social environment of her day is itself a negative environmental factor. Both Mrs. Crilling and Mrs. Kershaw prove less than good-enough mothers.

In later books, Rendell will make it even more obvious that human behavior constitutes a mystery that defies the traditional conventions of the crime fiction genre. Historically, the *whydunit* replaced the *whodunit* as a central mystery in crime fiction that aspires to the status of serious literature. But it will turn out that whereas it is possible to discover who committed a crime, why he or she did it will remain elusive. Interestingly, in *The Sins of the Fathers* the murder victim's surname is Primero, which can translate as "first," evoking a chain of events and stages of inheritance that reach back to Genesis and the first sin. In one of the Wexford books, *The Best Man to Die*, the inspector ruminates on what makes a murderer commit crimes. With resignation, Wexford wonders whether to answer that question he would have to begin with the criminal's parents or with Adam and Eve. But to answer *what* about them? To an original sin that became a legacy for all future generations? Or to a chain of events that broadly influenced the environment? In *A Dark-Adapted Eye*, the narrator Faith remarks on how "Murder reaches out through a family, stamping transfers of the Mark of Cain on a dozen foreheads, and though these grow pale in proportion to the distance of the kinship, they are there and they burn into the brain."

A microcosm of the broader human family can be found in *A Sight for Sore Eyes*. Agnes is a cold mother, softening only slightly to reach out to her grandson, Teddy. Her own daughter, Eileen, is so emotionally absent a mother that she can barely muster enough interest in her baby to give him a name. Ignoring Teddy's infant cries, she remains indifferent to just about everything as her son grows up. It may appear little wonder that Teddy develops into a psychopath and a murderer. But Rendell does not allow her readers to comfortably attribute the person he becomes solely to his dreadful environment. During her pregnancy, Eileen had no prenatal care and her lack of concern for health crosses the line into self-abuse. Teddy is like a child born with fetal alcohol syndrome: physical factors harm the developing fetus, and after birth, the environment characterized by an alcoholic parent perpetuates the damage. Of course, even prenatal abuse may be categorized as belonging to the category of environment; nonetheless, children damaged before birth can be said to come into the world with *biological* if not necessarily *genetic* "bad blood." Again, Rendell is very aware of the inseparability of the factors that go into the formation of an individual's character.

The analogy to fetal alcohol syndrome is particularly applicable to the character of Jonny in *Grasshopper*. His mother died of a heroin overdose when he was two years old, and it is reasonable to infer that she was an addict during her pregnancy. Then, when he was still a young child, his father handed him about for the pleasure of his pedophile acquaintances. Unlike Teddy, who possesses a strong appreciation of beauty and produces beautiful artifacts, Jonny displays no redeeming qualities. As Clodagh says about him, until she had met Jonny, she had clung to the belief that there is some good in everybody; but he "was bad, evil through and through." But what makes Teddy and Jonny different? Is there a gene for a keen aesthetic sensibility that Teddy inherited along with his good looks? Does such a gene allow him to adapt to and survive as an artist both nature *and* nurture? Or is it that the indifference of Teddy's mother was not quite as malignant a factor in his development as the overt brutality of Jonny's father? And is there something on Jonny's chromosomes or on some site in the brain as yet undiscovered that would render his father's abuse and his mother's addiction insufficient to explain his warped personality? In the end, do all attempts to account for human—and particularly criminal—behavior break down? In *The Blood Doctor* Rendell suggests that it may.

After Clodagh and her boyfriend had climbed the electric pylons and he is electrocuted, her own parents view her as if she were well on the way to a deviant existence. She imagines them wondering if she had been tainted by some congenital damage, while at the same time they protested that they could not imagine where the taint came from. With impatience bordering on contempt, she thinks of how her parents assume that "every action you performed and every mistake had been made by a string of ancestors before you and passed on in a gene of thoughtlessness or daring—or evil." This is, of course, another variation on the family curse that pervades Greek tragedy. When in Sophocles' *Electra*, Orestes is about to kill Aegisthus, the latter realizes that his death is but another episode in a string of events stretching back to Tantalus's butchering of his own son,

Pelops (see Chapter 2). Aegisthus wonders if the carnage in which he took so active a part would ever end, or whether the House of Atreus "by absolute necessity" must "see the evils of the Pelopidae, now and to come?" Similarly, in *The Libation Bearers,* the second play in the *Oresteia,* Orestes concludes that only private vengeance can "staunch the wound that bleeds our race." The Chorus also traces the "house of suffering" to the murders that marked the royal line. These reiterated themes concerning a cursed family also evoke the image of a house in ruin, its "fall" signifying the end of its line (as in Poe's "The Fall of the House of Usher").

The disintegration of houses is a theme found throughout Ruth Rendell's fiction, and it may explain the hold on her imagination of Dickens' *Bleak House,* in which litigation over an inheritance destroys those family members caught up in a fight from which only lawyers will benefit. Dickens' novel is specifically cited in Rendell's *A Judgment in Stone.* After most of a family is massacred by its servant and an accomplice, the few surviving relatives engage in ongoing suits because each Coverdale parent brought into the family children from a previous marriage, so that the order of death will significantly affect the inheritance of money and property. But the matter of why the Coverdales were murdered in the first place makes this novel another of Rendell's works of fiction having to do with other kinds of inheritances. Was it an inherited genetic flaw that eventually revealed itself in the violent behavior of a murderer, or was it her being raised in a house that not only failed to nurture her but instead succeeded in blighting her future?

Eunice Parchman kills her employers and most of their children because, the book says, she could not read. Her illiteracy seems the result of her environment: the schools did not do their job; her mother did not seem to care; and social workers were too busy to address the problem. That Eunice lacks a skill most others possess at least on a basic level has the effect of isolating her, her personality becoming void of any, paradoxically, "natural" sources of warmth toward others. "Illiteracy had dried up her sympathy and atrophied her imagination. That, along with what psychologists call *affect*, the ability to care about the feelings of others, had no place in her make-up." Rendell has created ambiguity through her use of the word *natural*. The story leaves open whether Eunice suffers from some congenital absence of a basic human trait or whether her upbringing has warped in her something that in other circumstances might have flourished. Her surname is almost a homonym of the word *parchment*, suggesting a page of writing that might as well be blank since Eunice cannot decipher the marks upon it, but also the blank slate (*tabula rasa*) used to describe the theory associated with John Locke, that a baby is born into the world neither completely innocent nor flawed by original sin, and that the environment produces the character and personality the baby will take with it into adulthood.

This ambiguity concerning Eunice fades, however, before the puzzle concerning why her accomplice, Joan Smith, whose maiden name is significantly Skinner, appears to defy an attempt to explain her behavior. Any psychologist who predicted behavior based on environment would have thought that Joan would become a "well-adjusted, worthy, and responsible member of society." Never neglected, abused, or deserted, she was lovingly nurtured by her parents. And when, during World War II, she was sent for safety's sake away from the city that endured nightly bombings to foster parents, they were equally nurturing. But, as the story unfolds, one day Joan, "out of the blue," walks into a police station and falsely accuses her foster father of beating and sexually abusing her. Being sent away from home was undoubtedly a trauma for Joan as it was for large numbers of young people who must have worried on a daily basis whether their homes and families would survive the German attacks on Great Britain. Still, this does not supply a sufficient explanation for Joan's extreme alteration in personality and growing madness. For the book leaves no doubt that, at the time of the Coverdale killings, Joan would have passed the test for the insanity defense, unable to distinguish between the rightness or wrongness of her crime. Joan is not only mad but also evil by the time the massacre occurs, but Rendell never resolves the question of why Joan spiraled downward from her promising youth. Was some natural predisposition, inactive so long as her environment was a good one, later activated under stress during and after the war? Was her name, Skinner, a reference to the psychologist who thought the environment was *the* formative influence on a child's development? In which case, did a too-controlled or a too-protected environment frustrate Joan's ability to cope with the crises of adult life? *A Judgement in Stone,* moreover, raises another perplexing question implicated in the nature-nurture debate: what is the relationship of evil to psychopathology? Not all insane people are evil. But are all evil people insane?

Again, where in the nature-nurture antithesis can free will be located? When Reverend Archery fears his son might marry a young woman bringing bad blood into the family, he sympathizes with the young woman who is hardly to blame for her murderous father. Comparing her to the sinners who come to him for confession, he likens Tess to a leper, both "condemned" by a disease visited upon them. Rendell readers should pause over Archery's disease metaphor. Leprosy is a contagious but not an inherited illness as are Huntington's disease and hemophilia, the literal and metaphoric sicknesses that inform two other Rendell novels, *The House of Stairs* and *The Blood Doctor.* The disease metaphor is significant for a reading of these novels because it evokes a theme Rendell shares with ancient Greek drama, the family curse passed on from generation to generation. The illness may constitute a metaphor for psychological disturbance, but the disturbance itself can also be a consequence of the disease or of fears of affliction. Moreover, the nature-nurture dichotomy is thematically highlighted when the novel's subject is an inherited disease. In *The House of Stairs.* Elizabeth, the narrator and one of the main characters, learns that she has a fifty-percent chance of contracting Huntington's, the degenerative neurological disease that killed her mother. As a result of her knowledge, or more accurately, lack of knowledge, she spends her life making choices based on the danger she faces but not attributable solely to her danger. In *The House of Stairs*, the question of free will emerges as a dominant subject.

Elizabeth is told of the threat she faces when she is only fourteen. Later she will wonder if a few more years would have made a difference. Or whether knowing for certain one way or another whether she was destined to have the disease would have changed her life. Still, she resents being told when she was so young, psychological damage added to a possible genetic blight. Her mother, she also realizes, chose to have her child even though she had reason to do otherwise (shades of the Oedipus story). In her treatment of the doomed house or family curse, Rendell has ingeniously merged these themes with those concerning fatality and free will.

There is, certainly, no family curse more obvious than the passing on of an inheritable and deadly disease, nor any doom as inexorable as acquiring the illness. Setting *The House of Stairs* in a time when there was no test for Huntington's disease allows Rendell to balance almost equally the roles of fate and free will in human behavior. A fifty-fifty chance of becoming ill involves a virtual toss of a coin, for there is an equal chance that one will not be afflicted as that one will. Responsibility for choices then rests on the person who chooses between two equally possible outcomes. Any other statistical probability would be highly significant. More than a fifty-percent chance of becoming terminally ill, for example, could have justified the *carpe diem* philosophy Elizabeth lives by (eat, drink, and be merry, for tomorrow we die). But perhaps just not knowing serves the same justification. For as she describes her situation, Elizabeth has lived in the shadow of paralysis and death. And so it is the hedonistic life that Elizabeth elects, wanting to remain alive, but acting with the recklessness anyone might who was living with the fear that the disease might suddenly strike. (Today, those who prove positive for Huntington's can also learn when they can expect it to manifest itself, a psychological complication in itself.)

Elizabeth also wonders whether, if she had grown up in the era of the support groups that later existed for virtually all human ills, some counselor might have influenced her to live her life differently, and she ruefully notes later in her life that if Huntington's had come, she would have found unequivocal justification for the life she decided to live. But would she have? Reference is made in the novel of two women in Elizabeth's position who choose not to have children but who finally prove free of the disease. The outcome, however, does not call into question the soundness or ethical implications of their choices (although it might have had they decided to abort a fetus with a fifty-percent chance of being healthy). Human life should involve more than a toss of the dice. Perhaps a better gambling metaphor is one Rendell creates when one of her characters in this novel is given to playing Russian roulette. It turns out that this game is not quite as risky as might be thought. The single bullet in the gun's chamber weights it in such a way that it is unlikely to be discharged. But then again, Russian roulette is a gamble one chooses to take. Huntington's disease involves a chance thrust upon a child at birth, like some kind of original sin.

Uncertainty in *The House of Stairs* is compounded by Ruth Rendell's choice of a first-person narrator. Throughout the novel, Elizabeth is often curious about what goes on inside someone else's head, but of course she can never know. Readers can only know what Elizabeth is thinking or feeling, but this knowledge is only partial because Elizabeth hardly understands herself. The book is replete with speculation, uncertainty, guesses about past behavior, and doubts about future ones. Still less can one be sure about a reading of another person's motivation. At one point, Elizabeth speculates about Cosette's first exposure to Bell (see Chapter 8) and the language of this speculation characterizes the entire novel: Elizabeth *imagines* Cosette would find it worth almost anything to be young and beautiful, as Bell is. Elizabeth admits that she can, however, only *guess* what is in Cosette's mind from the retrospective vantage point of later events. In *The House of Stairs* most of the characters appear to live on the edge of solipsism.

Huntington's disease, and the fifty-percent chance of contracting it if one parent has had it, becomes in *The House of Stairs* a metphor for unknowingness. Being right about something is itself often a matter of chance. *Halves* supply recurrent images throughout the book (none of the italicizations of the word *half* below are in the book). Even when Elizabeth speculates on her life and choices, she knows she is being only *half* truthful with herself. When she thinks of the kinds of books she has actually written instead of the ones she might have, books guaranteed to sell and make money rather than the serious literature she is capable of, Elizabeth says that if she had contracted Huntington's, she would have been proven right for not *half* starving alone in a rented room to write. She *half* expects lovemaking with another woman will not feel like the "real thing." She describes Cosette, the woman she chooses as a maternal substitute for the biological mother who first blighted her physical life and then her emotional well-being, as fighting a battle with weight that she loses about *half* the time. Bell tells Elizabeth that *half* her trouble is that she reads too many books, which will ironically prove prophetic in the case of James's *The Wings of the Dove*. And when Bell assesses her plan to reproduce the plot of James's novel in order to take possession of Cosette's fortune, she *half* guesses something had gone wrong with her scheme. At the end, Elizabeth, who cannot seem to extricate herself from Bell (for reasons neither she nor readers can fully comprehend), thinks of a larger house in which she and Bell will each live in *half*, minimizing daily contact with each other.

Elizabeth infers that she is also *half* mad by reference to another diseased state when she asks herself if she is crazy to want to look after Bell when the latter is released from prison and once again insinuates herself into Elizabeth's life. But she fears invoking madness as an explanation, for madness also permeates her family, whose inheritance is made up of "*schizoid* delusions." An informal use of *schizoid* often refers to the coexistence of disparate, even warring elements within an entity, such as Elizabeth reveals when she admits the extent to which she has always ignored that part of her that might be emotionally and physically sound, using the danger that faces her as if it were an inexorable fate she could not evade. As a literary metaphor, Huntington's disease, as it was understood when Rendell wrote her novel, allowed her to hold fate and free will equally poised as factors in human life. By the time a reliable test for Huntington's existed, it was too late for Elizabeth to take it. But this does not put aside other questions that the book only implicitly raises. What if the test had been available and Elizabeth had chosen not to take it? What if she were pregnant but could only know her unborn fetus had the same fifty-percent chance? Should she abort a child who might be born completely healthy or live many years before becoming symptomatic? The legal and ethical issues surrounding abortion itself would be compounded. Today, preimplantation, the segregating of embryos without the gene for Huntington's and the implanting of these through in vitro fertilization, has become a possibility. But because of the expense of the genetic testing and of the in vitro procedures, only the very affluent could avail themselves of these options. (See Sources.)

The practical and ethically charged problems of money, who has it and who does not, raise Rendell's treatment of her themes to another level in *The Blood Doctor*. The novel takes up the subject of expense and joins it to an account of existing reproductive technology that seems to belong more to science fiction than reality. Putting *The House of Stairs* together with *The Blood Doctor* raises the question of what would happen to the fate versus free will debate if it were possible to "design" babies (to evoke here Rendell's use of the term "designer babies" in *The Blood Doctor*). Preimplantation to eliminate Huntington's disease or even the novel's subject, hemophilia, is not raised as a possibility, but preimplantation involves the technology employed to allow the narrator's wife to carry a baby to term after she has suffered several miscarriages. By inference, however, preimplantation becomes a future possibility for many conditions caused by genetic inheritance. What ethical problems would accrue to these possibilities? Who could or would benefit from the new science? The matter may not be as critical as decisions concerning who receives an organ for transplanting. But for parents who are desperate to have children, as many are in *End in Tears*, modern technology seems to offer the difference between psychological life or death. But technology, it appears, may only complicate the role of fate and free choice in human affairs.

The Blood Doctor is among the most thematically dense of Rendell's novels, covering four generations and a myriad of family secrets associated with the family's hereditary disease, hemophilia. Between the time of Henry Nanther, in this fictitious work Queen Victoria's specialist on blood diseases, and Martin Nanther, who sets out to write his great-grandfather's biography, science had made great strides in many medical areas. But with these advances had come ethical concerns that form explicit and—again—only implied themes in the novel. And as if bioethics were not a rich enough subject in Rendell's novel, there also exists in *The Blood Doctor* a multiplication of elements involved in the dichotomy between fate and free will. Fate itself breaks down into *inevitability, probability, chance,* and *coincidence*—and a divine *providence,* as inexorable as the Greek concept of fate. Henry Nanther, an agnostic, had struggled against the yoke of inevitability, only to learn the hard way that to reject it outright might involve the age-old sin of pride.

At the end of his investigations into his great-grandfather's life, Martin Nanther concludes that circumstances are always bigger than the individual, so powerful that the seemingly free will can only "cower" before them. And if the central *mystery* of *The Blood Doctor*—that is, the secret at the heart of its narrative as well as its depiction of human actions that defy explanation—could be described succinctly, it has to do with one man's perversion of free will because he renders human freedom a self-sufficiency it does not possess. And this error, no less than Laius's crime against Chryssipus, unleashes the family curse that will pursue so many of Nanther's descendents. The precise details of this mystery will not be disclosed in the following discussion, although perceptive and experienced Rendell readers may guess it long before finishing the novel.

The narrative structure of *The Blood Doctor* is divided between the recounting of events in Henry Nanther's life and events that take place as his great-grandson endeavors to write his biography. Martin's insistent use of the present tense throughout allows Rendell to achieve several ends. It focuses on Martin's life and his generation of Nanther kin. And it elicits from readers an awareness of how the events of the past have come to rest on the present. In short, it serves the theme of the family curse. Several mysteries surround Henry's life. Why was he so fascinated by blood? Why, ambitious as he was, did he bypass the chance to marry a beautiful and wealthy heiress with whom he seemed to be as much in love as he was capable of being, in order to marry a rather ordinarily pretty and certainly not rich girl? And why, when she was murdered, did he marry her sister? Did Henry have a hand in that murder? Why, when children were born, did Henry seem so indifferent to his four daughters and older son but dote on his last child, another son who died young? What made one of these daughters angry enough at her father to write the letter that draws Martin Nanther into the family mystery three generations later? What role did Henry's long-time mistress and apparent mother of his illegitimate daughter play in his final choice of a wife? And, a question not to be answered until the last pages of the novel, what had Henry done that had virtually cursed his descendents and caused him such remorse?

As Martin Nanther pours over letters and diaries and both discovers and tries to explain the mysteries that each decade of Henry's life reveals, he faces his own problems. Because Queen Victoria had made Henry a lord, Martin is an hereditary peer in the House of Lords during a time when England has decided that blood (another meaning of *blood* in the novel) is not sufficient reason for an individual to occupy a seat in the House. Martin must accommodate the possible loss of his prestigious position, decide how it affects his self-identity (see Chapter 5), and, if he is not one of those elected to keep his position, lose the salary that comes with his seat. And this diminution of income comes at a time when money takes on a new importance for him. For his wife Jude is desperate to have a baby, suffering one miscarriage after another. Each time Martin wakes to blood-soaked sheets or finds his wife sobbing amidst her stained garments, he knows that once again she has been overcome with grief over the child who would not be. Eventually, doctors will discover the source of their fertility problem, and present them with the extremely costly opportunity for Jude to carry a pregnancy to term.

Blood as substance and as metaphor is what links the two parts of Rendell's narrative, and the opening of *The Blood Doctor*, like a Greek epic, announces that *blood* will be its theme. Or at least that it will be Martin's theme in his proposed biography as he runs through all the possible meanings and uses of the word. One of these has to do with how earlier times used the word *blood* where, today, the reference would be to genes. Significantly, these meanings as well as the significance of hemophilia in the book allow Rendell to pursue the questions surrounding fate and free will in human lives. For unlike Huntington's disease, hemophilia involves not one statistical possibility about inheriting the disease but several possibilities. The daughters of men with hemophilia will inevitably be carriers of the disease. But their sons have only a fifty-percent chance of being hemophiliacs. The daughters of female carriers have the same fifty-percent chance of being carriers themselves. So, for example, if a woman's brother is a hemophiliac, she may be a carrier and will have to make decisions concerning marriage and parenthood. Again, these figures have to do with possibility (a fifty-fifty split wipes out probability). A discouraging reality is that hemophilia itself may begin with a mutation in a gene, so that a seeming chance event can set the whole cycle in motion again. Attempts to trace the genesis of the illness Queen Victoria is supposed through her children to have spread throughout the royal houses of Europe suggest such a chance mutation. On the more positive side, whereas a diagnosis of Huntington's disease brings with it no promising treatment, there has been progress in treating hemophilia.

Chance plays a frequent role in *The Blood Doctor*. When a friend of Henry Nanther's sets out on a train journey on which Henry was to have accompanied him, a telegram arrives informing Henry that his mother is dying. He has to choose between going to her bedside, even though she would not know him, and joining Richard. This is perhaps one of the most obvious interactions of chance and free will in the novel. Duty wins: otherwise, Henry would have died on the train and Martin would not exist to puzzle out the life of his great-grandfather. Chance shows up in other minor and major episodes and commentaries throughout the book, the point being made that it is unlikely that two people carrying the same recessive gene will meet, marry, and have children who suffer the results and/or continue to perpetuate the genetic situation. But two people often do and some forms of genetic testing are today almost pro forma (such as the test for Tay Sachs disease when two Jews plan to marry). Lady Henry Nanther would call it providence when this improbability occurred, but her great-grandson Martin does not share this view, influenced as he is by a more agnostic and scientific age. Yet he will come to recognize that chance can be as implacable a force in human life as a determined fate.

An hereditary seat in the House of Lords is also a matter of chance in that occupying it reflects no achievement of one's own. The bill intended to rectify this elitist situation and the decision to elect the hereditary peers who would remain in the House after the others had been removed takes much of the element of chance out of the composition of the House. Electioneering itself, or the framing of a position that may influence another to vote for one, involves an act of conscious will. Finally, in *The Blood Doctor*, Martin will discover that what appeared to be remarkable coincidences in his great-grandfather's life were neither coincidences nor chance, but engineered events having to do with an individual trying to control outcomes. Like his wife, Henry Nanther believed that providence, which he must have invoked ironically, agnostic as he was, had deprived him of an opportunity to break fresh ground in his studies of blood diseases. And when Martin tries to fit together the pieces of Henry's life, chance plays a crucial role. The final piece of evidence Martin seeks is found in a museum in Switzerland, where he and Jude, pressed for time and having to decide where to spend their remaining hours, elect to visit a particular museum among the many others they might have chosen.

Martin's great-grandfather Henry believed that chance could be counteracted by an act of human will. His maiden speech in Parliament contained his credo: "Control circumstances and do not allow circumstances to control you." Not content with his successes in medicine and the rewards conferred on him by Queen Victoria, he was frustrated because he had not broken scientific fresh ground as had, for example, William Jenner. Jenner, one of Queen Victoria's physicians, claimed his place in medical history after developing a vaccine against smallpox. In *The Blood Doctor,* Jenner became the standard against which Nanther measured himself, hoping to make similar progress against hemophilia. His quest to discover effective treatments and perhaps even a cure was undertaken, however, not so much for humanitarian reasons but rather as self-validation. In his own time, it would still have been understood that Henry was guilty of the sin of pride. From his point of view, providence, fate, chance—whatever he would have called it—had not allowed him the opportunity to distinguish himself. And so he created his own opportunity.

Ironically, another of Henry's great-grandsons—an American cousin whom Martin meets for the first time in the course of his investigations into his family—is both a medical doctor and member of a successful research team. Genial enough, he shows only scant interest in Martin's project to write the life of their great-grandfather, for he places the truths of science above the history of science, even if one of his own ancestors had played a part in that history. In direct contrast to this cousin is another Nanther relative who virtually wills herself to believe something about disease that is scientifically untrue, resistant to being proven wrong. Either way, human will is a problematic entity in *The Blood Doctor.* Henry Nanther, who commited an act that was an extreme example of an attempt to control circumstances, came to experience remorse over what he had done. Yet there is no evidence that he arrived at Martin's conclusion, that circumstances, like the decrees of the gods, are often a kind of fate against which the human will has little effect.

But Martin himself makes a significant choice when he decides that, in the end, he will not write and publish the biography of Henry Nanther to which he has devoted so much time and energy. His decision encompasses two aspects of free choice. The first has to do with the probability rather than the absolute certainty that his solution to the mystery of Henry's life is the correct one. Henry's last written notebook, which might have proven the matter, had been destroyed, ironically in a chance occurrence. Second, again, is Martin's growing dislike of his great-grandfather and his reluctance to be associated with Henry. It was seen in Chapter 5 that Martin has to struggle against his own English snobbishness and prejudices. (In *A Dark-Adapted Eye,* the narrator's family is reluctant to have the story of Vera published and thereby to be inevitably associated with someone executed for murder.) This raises questions about the extent of Martin's freedom of choice in making the decision to abandon his project. In a book in which nature seems to prevail over nurture as a factor in human life, environmental factors consistently come into play. Blood is not a self-sufficient explanation for human behavior. Or, perhaps, blood and the environment almost inevitably interact. Blood and chance place one in the House of Lords, where aristocratic pretensions take precedence over democratic ideals. Such ideals, when they prevail, may be thought of as historical "mutations," which may or may not be historically inevitable.

Even what an author writes about is a matter of conscious choice and thus a will not entirely shaped by a powerful force the writer may not be able to resist. Interestingly, Henry could not write the magnum opus to which he devoted so much time and effort, and three generations later, Martin discards the biography of Henry. Each is governed by strong emotional and also very personal reasons, but the decision to abandon a project is freely chosen. But Martin Nanther cannot *will* the correct solution to the mystery that was his great-grandfather. For unlike Inspector Reginald Wexford and a legion of fictional detectives before him, Martin can never be sure that his was the correct solution. Here, one of Henry Nanther's memorable statements before Parliament, one that earned him some measure of scorn from his constituents, is worth citing. Henry had asked, "What is the answer, that is the question?" This conundrum can invoke the intriguing title of the book on crime fiction cited in the introduction to this study of Rendell, *The Mystery to a Solution.* In *The Blood Doctor,* Rendell refuses to supply the comforting certainty readers expect from mystery novels, just as in other recent writings she has withheld the assurance that, in the end, justice will be done.

For Rendell's readers, especially those who have delighted in her allusions, *The Blood Doctor* offers another instance of how what she has read has contributed to the complexity of what she has written. The Victorian age in which the fictional Henry Nanther lived and practiced medicine produced renowned works of literature. The close friendship between Henry and his deceased friend Richard Hamilton, whom Nanther may have loved as much as it was possible for him to love anyone until his younger son was born, and who died in the ill-fated train wreck, may resemble one of the most famous of similar Victorian friendships. This is the attachment between the poet Alfred Lord Tennyson and Arthur Hallam (at one point in the novel, Rendell refers to Tennyson, possibly as a clue to her readers). Both the Victorian poet and Henry Nanther were made lords by Queen Victoria. Like Tennyson, Henry Nanther met his close friend when he was at college. On vacation, Hallam contracted a fatal illness, leaving Tennyson distraught and depressed by his loss, just as Hamilton died after setting out on a pleasure trip that he was to have shared with Nanther. In each case, a sister's role complicates the emotions attached to the loss of a dear friend. Tennyson's sister was to marry Hallam; Henry Nanther was interested in Hamilton's sister, although no formal engagement ever took place. After Hamilton's death she married someone else.

But the most significant comparisons and—in an inversion typical of Rendell's use of literary sources—contrasts between Tennyson and Hallam on one side, and Henry Nanther and Richard Hamilton on the other, have to do with how the death of a friend affected the survivor's writing. Martin Nanther is very dependent on his great-grandfather's diary as a source for his biography, and he notes that after Hamilton's death, Henry not only stopped referring to his friend but, also significantly, changed the way he wrote his diary. Entries became rather matter-of-fact accounts of events, such as the birth of his children, which Henry recorded without emotion. To the contrary, Tennyson's grief resulted in one of the masterpieces of Victorian poetry, his book-length elegy for Arthur Hallam, *In Memoriam.* It is the work that Tennyson published the year that Queen Victoria appointed him Poet Laureate of England (a comparable event in Rendell's novel would be the queen's appointing Henry Nanther to a position on her personal medical staff). And, to cite one more significant comparison/contrast, whereas Martin Nanther realizes that Queen Victoria would never have read his great-grandfather's writing on hemophilia, because she would not have wanted to recognize herself as a carrier of the blood disease, she would certainly have read Tennyson.

Subjects Tennyson raises in *In Memoriam* bear a striking resemblance to themes in *The Blood Doctor.* In struggling with his grief and trying to imbue the life and death of his beloved Hallam with some transcendent meaning, Tennyson also grappled with questions of human autonomy and free will. The world he knew was virtually being transformed as he wrote, and he had to confront the science of evolution, which today has emerged in the highly controversial principles of evolutionary psychology—which, again, challenge ideas of free will. Tennyson was troubled by the possibility that human behavior could be reduced to the study of the physical world in a universe void of all spiritual meaning. Early on in the poem he says of nature,

> And shall I take a thing so blind,
> Embrace her as my natural good;
> Or crush her, like a vice of *blood,*
> Upon the threshold of the *mind?* (italics added)

It was not just that science was endeavoring to narrow the gap between humans and animals. Rather, in an almost prophetic fashion, Tennyson discerned the possibility that science would reduce—or try to reduce—all human behavior to the working of the *brain.* He may have been among the earliest writers to take up the mind-brain argument, the debate over whether humans possess a *mind* at all. For the mind, like the immortal soul, would never show up in an autopsy or reveal itself in the study of anatomy. Many scientists who today map the areas of the brain, thinking they will eventually account for all human behavior, out-and-out deny the existence of the mind. For their opponents, it is the mind that makes people uniquely human and that individuates them. Tennyson writes in his protest,

> I trust I have not wasted breath:
> I think *we are not wholly brain*
>
> . . . .
> Not only cunning casts in clay:
> Let Science prove we are, and then
> What matters science unto men...? (italics added)

Tennyson concludes the stanza by adding, "at least to me," an addition that emphasizes the individual choice he has made about what to believe. Read that way, the lines become a personal challenge to the seeming inevitability of a world ruled by scientific ideas that sweep away all human will and thereby become a new determinism. The analogy is not precise, of course, but Tennyson's protest against being reduced to his material body has a parallel in Martin Nanther's unwillingness during the time Jude is desperate to conceive and bear a child to be reduced from his wife's lover, friend, and companion to her sperm-provider. Tennyson and Rendell are affirming human values that can neither be validated nor denied by science.

Ruth Rendell does, however, recognize that in the face of changing scientific ideas, the conventions of novels that can be categorized by the genre of crime fiction will be transformed. The ultimate cause of, if not the immediate impetus to commit a crime, may at the present time exist beyond any self-sufficient explanations the writer has at hand. To recapitulate a point made in the introduction to this book,

287

the struggle of a serial killer in *The Rottweiler* to comprehend the reasons for his attacks on women, his discovery of an immediate stimulus that falls short of being a complete explanation, may reflect the mystery writer's own dilemma. The mystery to the solution, that is, may not in the end be resolved. Most of Rendell's latest books indicate her reluctance to create neat case histories to explain her characters. Her writing suggests that if scientists ever do make good on their promise (threat?) to account for all human action and emotion—including the emotion of love, which proved to be Henry Nanther's undoing—by reference to genes, sites in the brain, or evolutionary processes, crimes will continue to be committed. But the mystery genre might entirely disappear into its increasingly popular literary rival, science fiction.

AFTERWORD

$\mathbf{A}$s I finish this book, I am aware of how much more I could have said about the books I discussed and of how many books I have not covered. *King Solomon's Carpet, The Keys to the Street,* and *A Sight for Sore Eyes,* in particular, are among Ruth Rendell novels I did not include but would have liked to were space not a consideration. They—and others—were omitted not because they fail to provide compelling reading, but rather because what I would have talked about, such as alienated mothers and daughters, I had discussed elsewhere. It is not that Ruth Rendell keeps repeating herself; to the contrary, characters who resemble each other or who confront similar problems remain, nonetheless, strikingly unique. The family relationships she revisits in every book promise a wide variety of possibilities. But it was not possible to pursue every variation on a theme, and with reluctance, I let go all or parts of the analysis of a story or a novel that had fascinated me and that yielded many rereadings.

Because of my love for so much literature alluded to by Rendell, it was also very tempting to stray from my focus on how the family dynamics in ancient literature are paralleled in her fiction. In particular, I regretted not being able to pursue the motif of the "birthmark." Perhaps influenced by Nathaniel Hawthorne's famous story, Rendell seems to have found this theme of great interest. In Hawthorne's story, a man with a beautiful wife causes her death when he tries to excise her one physical imperfection, a birthmark. Similarly, in *The Keys to the Street,* a husband is infuriated rather than proud when his wife donates bone marrow to be used in the treatment of leukemia. The slight mark left by the surgical procedure, unseen by anyone but him, has the same effect on him as the birthmark has on the husband in Hawthorne's tale. Also, a birthmark in the form of a nevus is the source of Dolly's misery in *The Killing Doll.* And in *A Judgement in Stone,* a description of Eunice Parchman's illiteracy creates the image of a port wine stain: a flush "darkened her face to a deep wine colour." Just such a stain supplies an important motif in *The Monster in the Box.*

My readers will have their own favorite authors who might be echoed in Rendell's fiction and will find pleasure in discovering these literary connections. I hope that I have provided Ruth Rendell admirers with a guide to the complexities of her books, so that they might experience for themselves the pleasurable rereading associated with literary art.

ACKNOWLEDGEMENTS

First, I would like to acknowledge the contribution of my late mother, Marion Widom, to this book. Throughout her life, she was an avid reader of crime fiction, a genre she introduced me to when I was still in elementary school. We talked about my study of Ruth Rendell the night before my mother died, how her influence had earned her the dedication if the book were published, and she joked with me about the suitability of a mother introducing her daughter to a literary world of crime and evil.

My friend and colleague David H. Richter was responsible for my excursions into a serious study of crime fiction. He scheduled courses for the English Department at Queens College where I was a professor, and he assigned me classes in the mystery genre. I taught courses in Women and Crime Fiction and Crime Fiction and Culture while steeping myself in the scholarship written about the genre, scholarship more voluminous than I would have expected. Professor Richter also read the Rendell novels I was working with and we had lively discussions about her work. It was he who pointed out to me that the names Despina and Elvira (*Heartstones*) were derived from a Mozart opera; and that the collapse in 1879 of the Tay Bridge, which Rendell describes in *The Blood Doctor,* was an actual event that inspired a narrative poem by the Scottish poet William McGonagall. I think Professor Richter would have picked up literary allusions in Rendell's fiction that I have missed.

I would also like to thank my fellow members of The Institute for the History of Psychiatry, Department of Psychiatry, Joan and Sanford I. Weill Medical College of Cornell University, where I hold an honorary faculty appointment. I have been privileged to present to the Institute papers on crime fiction; on the neglect of Jocasta in the literature on the Oedipus complex; on the controversy among Freudians concerning the Chryssipus story; and on the evolution of critical studies concerning Freud, Oedipus, Hamlet, and Orestes. I am particularly grateful to Dr. Doris Nagel Baker, who is a fan of Ruth Rendell and who has generally supported me in this project by sharing her enthusiasm and by reading sections of the work in progress. She brought back for me from abroad some Ruth Rendell novels that had not yet been released in the United States.

I also appreciated the constant encouragement of my niece, and published novelist, Celia Gittelson. She kept assuring me that my analysis of Rendell's fiction, parts of which she made time to read, was for her absorbing.

Last, but hardly least, I want to thank my husband, Peter B. Leavy, for his interest, his encouragement, and his loving willingness to sacrifice some of our time together so that this book could be written. He has consistently transferred my files onto those memory sticks that continue to baffle me and has in many other ways taken an active role in this book's publication.

SOURCES AND
ADDITIONAL COMMENTS

Not everything that I have read for this study is cited below. My choices had to do with establishing the bases for my ideas, with crediting other scholars and critics with concepts that I have drawn on by citing their work, and with guiding my readers should they wish to learn more about subjects that illuminate Ruth Rendell's fiction.

Sources and additional comments are arranged below according to the chapters in this book.

Chapter 1. Introduction

The persistently low status of mystery novels is epitomized in the August 10 & 17, 2009, issue of *Newsweek*, which features Walter Mosley's essay on America's obsession with true crime, a personal memoir by the son of a criminal, an update on the Manson murders, and more. Closer to the point is the piece on "Death Becomes Them: When Literary Superstars Turn to Pulp." The headline of the piece cites crime fiction as ordinarily located "at the bottom of the literary food chain," and begins with a reference to Edmund Wilson's "eye-rolling put-down of detective stories titled 'Who Cares Who Killed Roger Ackroyd?'" Although Malcolm Jones, author of this piece, notes that the popularity of the genre makes it obvious that many people care, and that

Wilson might make his pronouncements more gingerly today, he thinks Wilson would not essentially change his belief that "tripe is tripe." Nor does Jones rescue the genre from such scathing criticism by discussing contemporary authors whose writing itself elevates crime fiction. Form, not content, according to his piece, makes these authors worthy of attention.

This "put-down" of the genre remains an obstacle to writers of mysteries who wish to be taken seriously as literary artists and a barrier to literary critics who wish to treat their work with the deep analysis usually reserved for acknowledged major writers. John T. Irwin's study, *The Mystery to a Solution: Poe, Borges, and the Analytic Detective Story* (Baltimore: Johns Hopkins University Press, 1994), cited in my introduction and last chapter, goes a long way to raising the status of crime fiction. Irwin establishes the criteria for distinguishing crime fiction as ingeniously wrought puzzle from crime fiction as literary art.

The status of crime fiction may be the reason that probing studies of the literary art of Ruth Rendell can hardly be found. There are many interviews with her in newspapers and magazines, but these do not constitute literary criticism. There are, of course, reviews, and she is sometimes treated in single chapters in books on mystery writers, particularly books whose subjects are women practitioners of the genre. But the space she is allotted in such books discourages any deep analysis of her novels. For a general overview of Rendell's writings and a guide to secondary sources up to 1995, consult Robin Winks, *Mystery and Suspense Writers: the Literature of Crime, Detection, and Espionage* (Vol. 2, New York: Scribner's Sons, 1998).

My study of Rendell emphasizes that plot is not what makes her books capable of fruitful rereading. She herself admits that plotting is not her strong suit and cedes to Agatha Christie's superiority in this area. I have quoted Rendell on this comparison with Christie and on how Rendell's voracious reading has affected her plots: "A Folklore Plot in Ruth

Rendell's Wexford Series," published in a scholarly journal devoted to the mystery genres: *Clues* (20: Fall/Winter, 1999).

A probably significant point of interest is that recent Rendell subtitles omit the word "mystery" or "detective" as adjectives. *The Blood Doctor* is called "A Novel." *Not in the Flesh* is "A Wexford Novel." Unlike the praise by Patricia Cornwell, that Rendell is "unequivocally the most brilliant mystery writer of our time," Scott Turow says that she is "surely one of the greatest novelists presently at work in our language."

My book treats Rendell as a novelist not a writer of mysteries, as my title indicates, but in fact, my experience with presses and editors seems to come from assumptions established by Edmund Wilson. Despite the existence of book-length studies of individual writers such as Ross Macdonald, and despite my having published four unambiguously scholarly books, I found Rendell's persistent reputation for being perhaps the finest practitioner today of the mystery genre an obstacle to publication. Even worse is the corollary assumption that Rendell readers are not going to want to read *about* her fiction, a particular irony given Rendell's defense of literary criticism in *The Best Man to Die.*

The study of culture is today such a popular endeavor that it permeates many books written in many academic disciplines. On the nuclear family and its relation to culture, I have quoted Adam Kuper in *The Chosen Primate: Human Nature and Cultural Diversity* (Cambridge, Mass.: Harvard University Press, 1994).

Chapter 2. The Ancient Stories

The edition of the Greek tragedies I have used is the four-volume set of *The Complete Greek Tragedies,* eds. David Grene and Richard Lattimore (Chicago: University of Chicago Press, 1959). I also consulted many other translations as well as numerous commentaries on the plays based on the Greek texts. An important textual matter for my discussion (and for controversies among classicists) concerns Aeschylus's *Seven Against Thebes.* In most translated editions of this surviving play in Aeschylus's Oedipus trilogy, when Oedipus's son Eteocles realizes he is soon to die, he cries out that the gods have always looked on him with disfavor. But in commentaries, classicists point out that Eteocles realized he had incurred Apollo's enmity. This specific reference to Apollo is found in the literal translation found in the Loeb Classical Library series. There is a significant difference between the gods in general and Apollo in particular. It is Apollo who warns Laius that he will be killed by his own son (but, as one commentator has pointed out, one does not incur the anger of Apollo merely by failing to heed his Oracle). Whether or not the wrath of Apollo goes back then to Chryssipus is not, however, a settled issue, but it has been argued that Aeschylus's treatment of the House of Laius probably included the Chryssipus episode. H. Lloyd-Jones has taken up these speculations in *The Justice of Zeus* (see below).

Most scholars refer to Agamemnon's family as the House of Atreus. There is no such consistency where it comes to Oedipus. Those who push the story back to his grandfather designate the family as belonging to the House of Labdacus. But the myths can be pushed back still further, including the story of Pentheus, who was torn to pieces by his own mother and the Bacchic women. Because I began with the sins and fate of Laius and how these affected Oedipus, I use the designation, "House of Laius."

For studies related to this chapter, see Philip E. Slater, *The Glory of Hera: Greek Mythology and the Greek Family* (Princeton: Princeton University Press, 1968); psychoanalyst Bennett Simon, *Tragic Drama and the Family: Psychoanalytic Studies from Aeschylus to Beckett* (New Haven: Yale University Press, 1988), which, significantly, focuses on the House of Atreus and says almost nothing about the Oedipus story so central to psychoanalysis; "Commentary" by M. J. Cropp on Euripides' *Electra* (Wiltshire, England: Aris and Phillips, 1988); R. P. Winnington-Ingram, *Sophocles: An Interpretation* (London:

Cambridge University Press, 1980). Also see E. R. Dodds' classic essay, "On Misunderstanding the *Oedipus Rex*," reprinted in Harold Bloom, ed., *Sophocles' Oedipus Rex* (New York: Chelsea House, 1988).

Useful for an understanding of male homosexuality in ancient Greece is Eva C. Keuls, *The Reign of the Phallus: Sexual Politics in Ancient Athens* (2d edition, Berkeley: University of California Press, 1985). In a chapter entitled "The Boy Beautiful: Replacing a Woman or Replacing a Son?," a challenge is issued to "the widespread argument that ancient Greece condoned and even glorified sexual relations between adult males involved in a consentual relationship." It is not necessary to enter into such a controversy to recognize that the complex themes concerning fathers and sons (and son substitutes in young boys who become the love objects of older men) in ancient mythology and literature will be illuminated by Keuls' study. Interesting for the subject of ancient Greek pederasty, in general, and for Rendell's *No Night is Too Long* in particular, is Andrew Lear and Eva Cantarella, *Images of Ancient Greek Pederasty: Boys Were Their Gods* (London: Routledge, 2008).

There are two controversies concerning the stories of Laius and Oedipus. One of these has to do with Freud studies (see Chapter 3 sources below). The other exists among classicists, who still do not agree on the subject of Chrysippus, or the answer to the question of why Oedipus was fated to kill Laius, or what can be deduced from *Seven Against Thebes* about how Aeschylus's trilogy on the House of Laius might have altered how Oedipus has come to be seen or his place in Western psychology. See D. J. Conacher, *Aeschylus: The Earlier Plays and Related Studies* (Toronto: University of Toronto Press, 1996) and Hugh Lloyd-Jones, *The Justice of Zeus* (Berkeley: University of California Press, 1971).

The wry reference to "inappropriate eating" as characterizing the cannibalism of Tantalus and then of his grandson Atreus is that of Elizabeth Vandiver in her recorded lectures on *Classical Mythology* (Chantilly, Va.: The Teaching Company, 2 vols.).

The neglect of Jocasta as the subject of her own story is the basis for the study by Christiane Olivier, *Jocasta's Children: The Imprint of the Mother,* trans. George Craig (London: Routledge, 1989). I presented a talk entitled "What About Jocasta?" to members of the Institute for the History of Psychiatry, Department of Psychiatry, Joan and Sanford I. Weill Medical College of Cornell University, my presentation inspired by Rendell's *The Chimney Sweeper's Boy.*

Chapter 3. Freud, Jung, and Their Complexes

I have used *The Standard Edition of The Complete Psychololgical Works of Sigmund Freud,* trans. James Strachey (London: Hogarth Press, 1964). The last volume has an extremely detailed subject index in which it is possible to find the many entries for the Oedipus complex and the three on the Electra complex. The entry on the *Oresteia* will locate what Freud had to say on matriarchy and patriarchy in the Greek trilogy. The essay on "Femininity," which Rendell cites in two novels and seems to draw on in others is found in Vol. 22, Lecture 33 of the *New Introductory Lectures on Psycho-Analysis.*

For Carl Jung, I used the *Collected Works* (New York: Pantheon Books, 1953-79). The lectures on Freud's psychoanalyatic theories can be found in Vol. 4. For an understanding of Jungian terms (such as "shadow," used in Rendell's *The Veiled One*), see *The Essential Jung* (Princeton: Princeton University Press, 1983).

There are many studies of Freud, of Jung, and of the Freud-Jung relationship. See John Kerr, *A Most Dangerous Method: The Story of Jung, Freud, and Sabina Spielrein* (New York: Knopf, 1993); Duane P. Schultz, *Intimate Friends, Dangerous Rivals: The Turbulent Relationship Between Freud and Jung* (Los Angeles: J. P. Tarcher, 1990); and Robert S. Steele, *Freud and Jung: Conflicts of Interpretation* (London: Routledge and Kegan Paul, 1982). Often quoted in Freud and Jung studies is Jung's letter to Freud of February 25, 1912, the year, significantly, that Jung introduced the Electra complex. Jung announces quite clearly in this letter that he does not wish to be Freud's (or perhaps anyone's) disciple. See *The Freud/Jung Letters: The Correspondence Between Sigmund Freud and C. J. Jung* (Princeton: Princeton University Press, 1974).

Essay studies of the Oedipus complex have been collected by George H. Pollock and John Munder Ross in *The Oedipus Papers* (Madison, Conn.: International Universities Press, 1988). This collection includes discussions of many areas fruitful for looking at how Rendell has used the story of Oedipus in her fiction, and its essays generally shed light on family relations. Of particular interest is an essay on Jocasta, usually neglected (see sources for Chapter 2 above). Useful for readers interested in Chryssipus is the inclusion of the 1953 essay by George Devereux, "Why Oedipus Killed Laius," which appears to have spearheaded many controversies over Chryssipus and Freud.

The significance of Chryssipus for Freud studies is the subject of books by Marie Balmary, *Psychoanalyzing Psychoanalysis: Freud and the Hidden Fault of the Father* (Baltimore: Johns Hopkins University Press, 1982); and Marianne Krüll, *Freud and his Father* (New York: Norton, 1986). In *Freud and Oedipus* (New York: Columbia University Press, 1987), Peter Rudnytsky rejects the arguments of Balmary and Krüll, who contend that Freud's own relationship with his father as well as his commitment to a universal Oedipus complex caused him deliberately to omit Chryssipus from his considerations.

As Orestes is treated by psychoanalysts, the matricide symbolizes the rejection of the mother as an erotic object. For psychoanalytic treatments of Orestes and Oedipus, see H. A. Bunker, "Mother-Murder in Myth and Legend," *Psychoanalytic Quarterly,* (Vol. 17, 1948); J. Friedman, "Orestes," *Psychoanalytic Quarterly* (Vol. 13, 1944 and Vol. 20, 1951); Melanie Klein, *Our Adult World* (Basic Books, 1963); D. M. Rein, "Orestes and Electra," *American Imago* (Vol. 11, 1942 and Vol. 18, 1949); H. Fingarette, "Orestes," *Psychoanalytic*

Review (Vol. 50, 1963); L. H. Rubinstein, "The Theme of Electra and Orestes: a Contribution to the Psychopathology of Matricide," *The British Journal of Medical Psychology* (Vol. 42, 1969); and Lilla Veszy-Wagner, "Orestes the Delinquent: the Inevitability of Parricide," *American Imago* (Vol. 18, 1961). For discussions of matricide and of Orestes, also see Ernest Jones's classic study, *Hamlet and Oedipus* (Garden City, N.Y.: Doubleday, 1954); and Frederic Wertham, *Dark Legend: A Study in Murder* (New York: Book Find Club, 1945).

For the connections between the Oedipus and Electra complexes, see Patrick Mullahy, *Oedipus Myth and Complex* (New York: Hermitage Press, 1948). And of course, Jung's lectures on the Oedipus complex at Fordham University (*Collected Works,* Vol. 4.) In 1956, Jung returned briefly to the Electra complex in his discussion of schizophrenia in "The Psychogenesis of Mental Disease" (Vol. 3), and in a "Foreword" to Eleanor Bertine, "Human Relationships" (Vol. 18). A psychoanalytically-based argument in favor of an Electra complex is Hendrika C. Halberstadt-Freud, "Electra versus Oedipus: Femininity Reconsidered," *International Journal of Psychoanalysis* (Vol. 79, 1998).

For discussions of Freud's reasons for giving up the seduction theory in favor of the Oedipus complex, see Paul Robinson's critique of Jeffrey Masson's attack on Freud in *Freud and his Critics* (Berkeley: University of California Press, 1993); also see John E. Toews, "Having and Being: The Evolution of Freud's Oedipus Theory as a Moral Fable," in *Freud: Conflict and Culture,* ed. Michael S. Roth (New York: Alfred A. Knopf, 1998).

Chapter 4. Selected Ancient Motifs in Ruth Rendell's Fiction

For an important study of sacrifice, which explores its significance for the way justice is perceived, see René Girard, *Violence and the Sacred,* trans. Patrick Gregory (Baltimore: Johns Hopkins University Press, 1977).

Martin S. Bergmann discusses the Chryssipus story in the context of child sacrifice *In the Shadow of Moloch: The Sacrifice of Children and its Impact on Western Religion* (New York: Columbia University Press, 1992).

The idea of sacrifice runs through the psychoanalytic literature. Theoretically, it is the child who does the sacrificing, giving up his erotic attachment to his mother in order to work through his Oedipus complex. Jung takes up the theme of "sacrifice," its significance for the child who "sacrifices," that is gives up, infantile wishes, and in so doing Jung links several themes Rendell would treat in her novels.

Chapter 5. Oedipus and the Search for Identity

The subject of the "self" involves complicated questions that I addressed in my book *To Blight with Plague: Studies in a Literary Theme* (New York: New York University Press, 1992). A good place to begin to think about the "self" is Theodore Mischel, ed., *The Self: Psychological and Philosophical Issues* (Totowa, N.J.: Rowman and Littlefield, 1977). A particularly useful essay in this collection for a study of the theme of selfhood in Rendell's fiction is Stephen E. Toulmin, "Self-Knowledge and Knowledge of the Self."

Chapter 6. Fathers and Sons

Since Chapters 6, 7, and 9 will take up the subject of incest, all pertinent sources will be cited here. Incest is a subject widely studied by scholars of nineteenth-century English and American literature, and interested readers will have no difficulty finding material. The legal issues in England referred to in the discussion of *Kissing the Gunner's Daughter* (Chapter 9) can be found covered in Graham Hugh, "The Crime of Incest," *The Journal of Criminal Law, Criminology and Police Science* (September 1964). Also see Richard A. McCabe, *Incest, Drama, and Nature's Law, 1550-1700* (Cambridge, Eng.: Cambridge University Press, 1993). A classic study of father-daughter incest, one that has provoked controversy, is found in Judith Herman and Lisa Hirschman, *Father-Daughter Incest* (Cambridge, Mass.: Harvard University Press, 1981). While this is a useful book, its central premise, that a father who abuses his daughter is more interested in wielding patriarchal power than experiencing forbidden sex (a similar argument about power is frequently made about rape), no way applies to Rendell's Wexford and his perhaps guiltily repressed feelings about his daughter Sheila. To the contrary, Count Cenci seems to be used by Rendell in part as a contrast to Wexford, although, again, Rendell's very invoking of the Cenci family is an important clue to how she is handling the theme of incest in *Kissing the Gunner's Daughter* (see Chapter 9). In fact, Wexford's repression of any erotic thoughts about Sheila would win the approval of contemporary feminists who see the erotic elements in the father-daughter relationship as something a father must resolve for himself, thereby helping his daughter transfer her love to an eventual partner or spouse. See source notes to Chapters 9 and 10 below.

Incest between fathers and sons has been a subject about which there has been little written, although pedophilia is often in the news and the connection should be fairly readily arrived at. See Walter DeMilly III, *In My Father's Arms: A True Story of Incest* (Madison: University of Wisconsin Press, 1999).

Chapter 7. Mothers and Sons, Sisters and Brothers

For a study of the mother-son relationship aimed at a popular readership, see Dr. James J. Rue and Louise Shanahan, *Daddy's Girl, Mama's Boy* (Indianapolis: Bobbs-Merrill, 1978). Obviously, all four parent-child combinations will be treated in this book. But the Oedipus complex has generated so much discussion of mothers and sons that most of the sources I cite will deal in one way or another with the subject. Also see sources to Chapters 9 and 10 below, since studies of the parent-daughter relationships will inevitably contain implications for mothers and sons.

There is no lack of scholarship on Melville in general and *Pierre* in particular. A good overview is provided by Andrew Delbanco in "Melville's Fever," (*The New York Review of Books* April 4, 1996). John Updike's assessment of *Pierre* is quoted in this piece.

Chapter 8. Electra and Rendell's Fey Girls

Fey girls and fair/foul women in folklore and literature occupied the greatest part of my writing before my excursion into the crime fiction genre. Most of what I have drawn on here in Chapter 8 is included in my first book, *La Belle Dame sans Merci and the Aesthetics of Romanticism* (Detroit: Wayne State University Press, 1974). The themes are also explored in my co-authored study (with Per S. Jacobsen), *Ibsen's Forsaken Merman: Folklore in the Late Plays* (New York: New York University Press, 1988), whose title reveals that there are fair/foul men too, shapeshifters and demon lovers. Shapeshifting women fall into the fair/foul category, and I treat their appearance in the world's folk and fairy tales in *In Search of the Swan Maiden: A Narrative on Folklore and Gender* (New York: New York University Press, 1994). Even in my book on plague literature (see my sources for Chapter 4 above) I treat the fair/foul motif, the poison damsel, a seductress who kills her lovers, and who, in modern legend, is thought to be a spreader of sexually transmitted diseases, today, specifically AIDS.

The name *Senta* in *The Bridesmaid* suggests a possible and interesting Rendell source, Richard Wagner's opera, *The Flying Dutchman*. The Dutchman is thrall to the devil and can only be redeemed by the enduring, faithful love of a woman. Wagner's Senta abandons Eric, the man from her community who loves her, and sacrifices herself to save the stranger, the doomed man. In a typical Rendell twist, her Senta chooses an ordinary man, Philip, and tries to raise him to the level of the extraordinary. According to her insane thinking, his murdering someone will allow him to transcend the mundane and thereby to be saved from the commonplace. In this way, Senta, like her namesake in Wagner, thinks she will redeem her lover. I thank my friend, Elaine Hoffman Baruch, for leading me to this source.

For discussions of Electra, see sources cited above for Chapters 2 and 3, and sources for Chapters 9 and 10 below.

Chapter 9. Fathers and Daughters (and the Wexford Series)

This chapter is what I think of as the Wexford chapter, for I have treated the series as a unit of discussion. Although I also discuss other Rendell fiction in which the father-daughter theme is central to the plot, I have not emphasized some of the truly dreadful father-daughter relationships. Several are as awful as the terrible mother-daughter pairings found in her work, but there are not as many of them, and so across her many books, they seem as a group less obvious. In addition, there is a certain thematic consistency in my seeming to overlook the awful fathers and focusing on the mother-daughter relationship, as I do in Chapter 10. Women are now urged (contrary to Freud's teaching) to separate from their fathers and bond with their mothers, and good fathers are defined as those who make this possible and who do not withdraw their support during the process. In *Fathers and Daughters* (London: Routledge, 1994), Sue Sharpe appears to be reacting against the spate of studies that focus on mothers and daughters, and she has produced a kind of "how to" book for male parents, as has Victoria Secunda in *Women and Their Fathers* (New York: Delacorte Press, 1992). Maureen Murdock picks up from Secunda's book the idea of the "good-enough father," a concept obviously adapted from Winnicott's good-enough mother. In *The Hero's Daughter* (New York: Fawcett Columbine, 1994) Murdock also creates the rather ambiguous term "father's daughter" as perhaps a corrective to the seemingly denigrating popular term, "daddy's girl."

But the mother-daughter relationship gone wrong seems even more dangerous for a woman today than it did in the past—as I have argued in Chapter 10. The subject is a complex one. Both Sylvia in *Harm Done* and Sarah in *The Chimney Sweeper's Boy* ruminate on the psychological importance of modeling oneself on the same-sex parent. Not yet arriving at the insight that will lead to a closer bond with her mother Ursula, Sarah thinks of how she and her sister Hope had modeled themselves on their father and "couldn't undo it now, wouldn't want to undo it now."

Neither Sheila nor Sylvia in the Wexford novels models herself on her mother, Dora, perhaps because the Penelope-like figure, however important she may be to a family's stability, lacks the dynamic qualities evidenced by the tortured Clytemnestra and Electra. In an age of woman's liberation, Penelope is not to be despised, but she will find herself in the position of defending her role in the home, as Dora does in *A Sleeping Life*. Wexford will come to wonder if Dora is satisfied with her role in their family. His ruminations become particularly significant in *Road Rage*, where Dora's disappearance raises questions about her role as the loyal wife, the churchgoer who keeps her family together and, in general, defends family values. Actually, Rendell evokes in this novel the image of Caesar's wife, who must be above suspicion, as Dora cannot be so long as she is absent from home and it is not known why. But even here the allusion to Caesar's wife suggests the difficulty, at least in literature, of making Penelope a role model: it is Cleopatra whom readers and audiences of Shakespeare and Shaw are likely to find the most memorable character in Caesar's life.

Chapter 10. Mothers, Daughters, and Sisters

Since Jung introduced the idea of an Electra complex, one would expect Jungians who treat the importance of the mother-daughter relationship to address the conflicts between Clytemnestra and Electra. Instead, one finds a deafening silence on the subject. I spent hours in the hospitable Jung Institute Library in New York, poring over books on female development, finding virtually nothing on Electra. Ironically, Marion Woodman, a Jungian analyst who has written extensively on women's spiritual quest for a uniquely feminine identity, presents a case history in *The Owl Was a Baker's Daughter* (Toronto: Inner City Books, 1980), in which a woman is described as having "in Freudian terms" an "Electra complex." Surely Woodman knew that Freud rejected Jung's use of a contrary myth for female psychological development and, in so doing, rejected Electra as a significant figure. And, more important, that the idea of an Electra complex belongs to Jung.

Because Electra is, as I have argued in this book, the ultimate apostate, enemy of matriarchy and hence, implicitly, of the ability of mothers and daughters to bond, her crime is not only perceived as directed against her mother, but against the archetypal Great Mother. In her *Descent to the Goddess* (Toronto: Inner City Books, 1981), Sylvia Brinton Perera succinctly describes the necessary connection to this archetype: the "return to the goddess . . . is a vitally important aspect of modern woman's quest for wholeness . . . We need to return to and redeem what the patriarchy has often seen only as a dangerous threat and called terrible mother." According to this view, Clytemnestra can and should be rescued from her reputation as an evil woman. Kate Millett takes on this rescue in *Sexual Politics* (Garden City, N.Y.: Doubleday, 1970). Also see Kathleen L. Komar, *Reclaiming Klytemnestra: Revenge or Reconciliation* (Urbana: University of Illinois Press, 2003); and Craig S. Barnes, *In Search of the Lost Feminine: Decoding the Myths that Radically Reshaped Civilization* (Golden, Colorado: Fulcrum Publishing, 2006). Jill Scott has a far more difficult task in making a feminist hero out Clytemnestra's murderous daughter in *Electra after Freud: Myth and Culture* (Ithaca: Cornell University Press, 2005). Jungians, such as Woodman, would undoubtedly be pleased by Scott's rather misleading title since it detaches Electra from Jung. See my review of Scott's book, in the *Annual Report to the Friends of the Institute for the History of Psychiatry* (July 1, 2005 to June 30, 2006), Department of Psychiatry, Joan and Sanford I. Weill Medical College of Cornell University.

Chapter 11. Conclusion: Justice, Utopia, and Fate

The discovery of a test for Huntington's disease at first evoked celebration in the scientific and medical community, but this early elation quickly gave way to concerns over the psychological impact on a patient who learns that becoming symptomatic is only a matter of time, and over the bioethical problems surrounding the ability, for example, to test a foetus and even an embryo for the gene, allowing parents to abort the life of the unborn child. For a history of the test and its aftermath, see the chapter on "A New Social Contract" in Robert Cook-Deegan, *The Gene Wars: Science, Politics, and the Human Genome* (New York: W. W. Norton, 1994). For the psychological problems surrounding the test for Huntington's, see Amy Harmon, "Facing Life With a Lethal Gene," *The New York Times* (Sunday, March 18, 2007). In *The House of Stairs*, Elizabeth makes the point that there was no test when she first learned about her chances of having Huntington's disease and that now, as she writes, it is too late. This chronology makes it possible for Rendell to use the uncertainty that existed for Elizabeth as an important element in her book. Today, the pressure to make difficult choices has intensified. As for hemophilia, the inherited genetic disease in *The Blood Doctor*, the novel itself contains the scientific information and depiction of the psychological and bioethical concerns that Rendell's readers might wish to become familiar with.

RUTH RENDELL'S FICTION: A CHRONOLOGICAL LIST

Note: The original title of the book published in England is cited in parentheses.

Inspector Wexford Novels

From Doon with Death (1964)
The Sins of the Fathers (A New Lease of Death) (1967)
Wolf to the Slaughter (1967)
The Best Man to Die (1969)
A Guilty Thing Surprised (1970)
No More Dying Then (1971)
Murder Being Once Done (1972)
Some Lie and Some Die (1973)
Shake Hands Forever (1975)
A Sleeping Life (1978)
Death Notes (Put on by Cunning) (1981)
The Speaker of Mandarin (1983)
An Unkindness of Ravens (1985)
The Veiled One (1988)
Kissing the Gunner's Daughter (1992)
Simisola (1995)
Road Rage (1997)
Harm Done (1999)
The Babes in the Wood (2002)

End in Tears (2005)
Not in the Flesh (2007)
The Monster in the Box (2009)

Novels

To Fear a Painted Devil (1964)
In Sickness and in Health (Vanity Dies Hard) (1966)
The Secret House of Death (1968)
One Across, Two Down (1971)
The Face of Trespass (1974)
A Demon in My View (1976)
A Judgement in Stone (1977)
Make Death Love Me (1979)
The Lake of Darkness (1980)
Master of the Moor (1982)
The Killing Doll (1984)
The Tree of Hands (1984)
Live Flesh (1986)
Talking to Strange Men (1987)
The Bridesmaid (1989)
Going Wrong (1990)
The Crocodile Bird (1993)
The Keys to the Street (1996)
A Sight for Sore Eyes (1998)
Adam and Eve and Pinch Me (2002)
The Rottweiler (2003)
Thirteen Steps Down (2004)
The Water's Lovely (2007)

Novels Written as Barbara Vine

A Dark-Adapted Eye (1986)
A Fatal Inversion (1987)
The House of Stairs (1988)
Gallowglass (1990)
King Solomon's Carpet (1992)

Anna's Book (Asta's Book) (1989)
No Night Is Too Long (1994)
The Brimstone Wedding (1996)
The Chimney Sweeper's Boy (1998)
Grasshopper (2000)
The Blood Doctor (2002)
The Minotaur (2005)
The Birthday Present (2008)

Novellas

Heartstones (1987)
The Thief (2006)

Short Story Collections

The Fallen Curtain (1976)
Means of Evil (1979)
The Fever Tree (1983)
The New Girl Friend (1985)
The Copper Peacock (1991)
Blood Lines (1995)
Piranha to Scurfy (2000)

Made in the USA
Charleston, SC
28 May 2010